TREACHEROUS ESTATE

By the same author

ONE MAN AND HIS PLOT
YANKEE DOODLES
THE COMPANION GUIDE TO NEW YORK
BAREFACED CHEEK
TREACHERY?
THE LAST DAYS OF THE BEEB
KINNOCK
THE BOOK OF LONDON (general editor)
LONDON'S RIVER

TREACHEROUS ESTATE

The Press after Fleet Street

Michael Leapman

Hodder & Stoughton
LONDON SYDNEY AUCKLAND

Acknowledgment is due to the following for permission to quote from copyright material.

Macmillan, Inc. for *The Kemsley Manual of Journalism* by Viscount Kemsley; Weidenfeld and Nicolson for *Good Times, Bad Times* by Harold Evans, and for *Charles: A Biography* by Anthony Holden; Macdonald for *Fleet Street* edited by Vivian Brodsky; Faber & Faber for *Night and Day* by Tom Stoppard; Macmillan Press for *The Media and the Falklands Campaign* by Valerie Adams; Curtis Brown for *Takeovers* by Ivan Fallon and James Srodes.

All copies of newspaper pages within this book are reproduced by permission of the British Library.

British Library Cataloguing in Publication Data

Leapman, Michael
Treacherous Estate: Press After Fleet
Street
I. Title
338.47072

ISBN 0-340-57742-8

First published in Great Britain 1992

Published by Hodder and Stoughton,
a division of Hodder and Stoughton Ltd,
Mill Road, Dunton Green, Sevenoaks, Kent TN13 2YA.
Editorial Office: 47 Bedford Square, London WC1B 3DP.

Photoset by Rowland Phototypesetting Ltd,
Bury St Edmunds, Suffolk

Printed in Great Britain by St Edmundsbury Press Ltd,
Bury St Edmunds, Suffolk

Contents

Introduction and Acknowledgments

Francis Williams's *Dangerous Estate*, published in 1957 when I was nineteen, was the first book about the press that I read, and it remains among the best. The title of the present book is intended as a sidelong tribute to a work that, without glamorising the trade of journalism, drew me towards it. By adapting Williams's title I do not mean to suggest that my book is comparable to his in terms of its scope. Much of *Dangerous Estate* was a thrilling account of the early years of British newspapers: that ground has been well covered by now and I tread on it only lightly as a basis for my chief objective, to look back at the tremendous changes that have occurred in British journalism in the years since that book appeared, then forward to the beginning of the twenty-first century.

In 1950 Viscount Kemsley wrote in *The Kemsley Manual of Journalism*:

> Many newspapers seem to be at the parting of the ways. Are they to perform a responsible and useful public service of information and enlightenment? Or are they to make circulation the be-all and end-all of their existence, and use every device of sensationalism and every trick of triviality to serve that end? Perhaps the danger of that second course is less than it appears to be . . .
>
> I have always taken the view that, apart from other considerations, the dignity of a journalist is reduced when he is asked to intrude into the private affairs, and in particular the private grief, of others, or to twist his own honest view of a story to suit a political or any other angle.

That high-minded and complacent view of the national press, its functions and practices, was a dominant influence on Fleet Street for more than two decades after Kemsley enunciated it. The concept of journalism as something of a heroic enterprise, overwhelmingly a force for good, was reinforced by the flowering of investigative and campaigning journalism, notably on the *Sunday Times*, with its influential Insight pages. Even the tabloid *Daily Mirror*, the best-selling paper in the 1950s and 1960s, introduced a feature called Mirrorscope along the

7

same lines as Insight, although naturally aimed at its very different market. It seemed as though the question posed by Kemsley was being answered in the way he clearly advocated and anticipated. In 1972 Charles Wintour, then editor of the *Evening Standard*, was able to write in his book *Pressures on the Press*, on the subject of intrusions into privacy: 'Serious lapses are few, and getting fewer.' He argued against legislation protecting privacy because it could inhibit the work of investigative reporters.

Yet the optimistic characterisation of the press as a benign social service – slaying unworthy dragons, giving succour to the weak and enlightenment to the ignorant – had already begun to come under strain, like much else in British society, in the 1960s. A symptom was the failure of the *Sun* under Hugh Cudlipp and Cecil King, masters of the *Daily Mirror* group. The *Sun* had been created in 1963 from the ashes of the fading *Daily Herald* and was a botched attempt to lift the standards of popular journalism without sacrificing its popularity. The closure of the *News Chronicle* in 1960 had been a forewarning of how difficult a trick that is to pull off.

The *Sun* under Cudlipp and King never made money and in 1969 was effectively given away to Rupert Murdoch, an Australian who had just entered the ranks of British press proprietors by buying the mass-circulation Sunday paper, *News of the World*. With the *Sun* his editor Larry Lamb reversed the Cudlipp–King formula and sought to give the public what he perceived they wanted by going down-market of the *Mirror* and appealing brazenly to the popular appetite for sex, scandal and sensation, often extending truth up to and occasionally beyond its limit to give a story extra lift.

The *Mirror* was forced to move in the same direction but could not prevent the *Sun* overtaking its sales within five years. The *Express* group launched its own racy tabloid, the *Daily Star*, to exploit the market the *Sun* had created and in time the erstwhile more responsible papers in the middle market – the *Express* and the *Mail* – were obliged to take note of the new uninhibited approach of the down-market tabloids. They felt they had to move at least some way towards competing with stories of dubious veracity about the private lives of celebrities, especially television personalities and the royal family. Increasingly they were having to compete for readers and advertising with television, a more immediate medium, which could deliver the *real* news faster and often more vividly than the newspapers. The half-true, salacious scandals were a genre that the tabloids had to themselves, an area where television could not or would not compete. Newspaper proprietors and editors reasoned that they had to exploit such stories to maintain circulations and revenue.

Equivalent excesses in the quality press concerned the financial interests of the proprietors. Most notoriously 'Tiny' Rowland, chief executive of Lonrho, gained control of the *Observer* and used it as a vehicle for conducting a feud against the al-Fayeds, a pair of Egyptian brothers who had bested him in a battle for control of the House of Fraser store group, which includes Harrods. And Rupert Murdoch's papers shamelessly promoted his Sky satellite television channels.

The cumulative effect of these self-interested and/or scandalous tendencies was to weaken overall respect for the press. When the victims of the tabloids sued for defamation, juries awarded higher and higher damages – culminating in the £1 million paid out of court by the *Sun* to the singer Elton John in 1988. Public opinion did not always make too fine a distinction between the tabloids and the responsible newspapers. The result was that there was very little sympathy for the press when the Government began to place restrictions on what the papers could report: by trying to suppress *Spycatcher*, the memoirs of a former member of the security service; by trying to prevent leaks from the civil service (the Clive Ponting and Sarah Tisdall prosecutions); by strengthening the Official Secrets Act. And there was a lot of support for MPs who sought to introduce private bills in Parliament to protect privacy by law and to give a statutory right to reply to people who felt they had been abused in the public prints.

If the unsavoury editorial developments of the 1970s and 1980s could at their root be attributed to Rupert Murdoch, his influence was also apparent in other directions. In 1981 he bought *The Times* and the *Sunday Times* from Thomson Newspapers, which had been unable to solve growing labour problems with trade unions who feared that the introduction of new technology would erode their long-established dominance in Fleet Street. The first Lord Thomson, a Canadian who had bought the *Sunday Times* in 1959 and *The Times* seven years later, was one of the last of the millionaire proprietors prepared to run papers at a loss for the privilege of owning them. After his death in 1976, his son Kenneth could not see the logic of weakening the Thomson group, an international conglomerate covering a variety of interests, by clinging on to holdings whose problems did not respond to conventional management solutions. Murdoch and the new proprietors of the 1980s – Lord Stevens, Conrad Black, Robert Maxwell and 'Tiny' Rowland – had their eyes more closely focused on the balance sheet, although in Maxwell's case there was also a whiff of the desire to influence great events.

These changes in proprietorship and management had their effect further down the line, on the editorial floor and in the production departments. The traditional camaraderie of Fleet Street – the drinking, the merry evenings at the Press Club – masked an increasingly untenable industrial situation. The labour-intensive techniques of hot-metal production, essentially unaltered for decades, could not be sustained, partly because the out-of-date machinery was no longer being manufactured. But the unions were determined to hang on to their privileges and 'old Spanish customs' for as long as they could. They were skilled at deploying their ultimate power to prevent papers from being printed, or to delay them so that full national delivery could not be achieved. Once lost, a day's newspaper production is irretrievable.

Murdoch saw that the problem could not be solved in the unalterably corrupt environment of Fleet Street. During the 1970s he had bought land in Wapping, part of the old London docks area, and built there a modern newspaper facility. In secret, he equipped it with machines that allowed direct input of copy by journalists and advertising personnel. He trained electricians to work the presses so that he would not need the print unions. At the beginning of 1986, faced with a strike at his plants at Gray's Inn Road and Bouverie Street, he moved production of all four of his titles to Wapping overnight. He attracted the hostility of the labour movement – the unions and their supporters mounted protests outside the plant for a year – but he was never prevented from producing or delivering his papers and he cut his costs dramatically, making the *Sun* and *News of the World* even more profitable than they were.

One pretext Murdoch used for the flit to Wapping was the imminent prospect of fresh competition from a new paper that would be printed away from Fleet Street without expensive union agreements. Eddy Shah, a publisher of weekly newspapers in Warrington, near Manchester, had hit the headlines in 1983 when he defied the print unions and produced his papers despite a hostile picket on his plant. On the strength of that reputation, he had managed to raise £20 million in the City to start a new daily paper printed at a series of locations around the country, by-passing the print unions. Eddy Shah's *Today* was never a success – and still struggled after Murdoch himself bought it in 1987 – but it did strike the first real blow against union domination of the national newspaper industry. Murdoch followed it up with the knockout punch.

Just before the Murdoch move to Wapping, three journalists from the *Daily Telegraph* announced plans to launch a quality broadsheet, the *Independent*. Like Shah, they found that City financiers were now ready to back newspaper ventures based on new low-cost production techniques. Then Robert Maxwell, the new owner of the *Mirror* group, said he was going to start a London evening paper and a group of left-wing organisations prepared a prospectus for a left-of-centre Sunday paper, based in Manchester but circulated nationally. Then came the *Sunday Sport*, an exercise in near-pornography. Many of these failed: only the *Independent* and *Sunday Sport* succeeded, for very different reasons. But the spate of launches reflected the fact that the days were over when artificially high labour costs made it impossible for anyone to start a newspaper from scratch.

Other proprietors of established newspapers followed Murdoch in quitting the congested Fleet Street area for offices and printing plants on the perimeter of the capital, using modern technology and with far fewer production staff. By 1992, only the *Mirror* group – dangling in a state of uncertainty following the mysterious death of its proprietor Robert Maxwell and the scandalous disclosures about his financial misdeeds that followed – was still in its 1960s headquarters at the north end of Fetter Lane. The romance of Fleet Street was over but the newspaper industry was on a sounder financial footing than for some thirty years, despite the prolonged recession. Yet the irony was that, under pressure from competition, from the law courts and from the Government, the papers were finding it harder to maintain decent professional standards.

Journalists are uncomfortable with abstractions, which is why most books written about the press by people who work in it are constructed around reportage of incidents and are often heavy with anecdotes, exuding the aroma of lunchtime gossip from the heyday of El Vino's. With that heyday past, my chief sources have been interviews with the leading participants in the incidents I describe. Most I spoke to specifically for this book but in some cases I have drawn on interviews I conducted in writing articles for other newspapers and magazines, particularly the *Independent*. My thanks to all of them, and to the many other journalists with whom I have informally discussed issues addressed in this book, and whose views have helped crystallise my own.

Those interviewed specifically for the book were: John Biffen, Conrad Black, Sir Gordon Brunton, Lord Cudlipp, Lord Deedes, Ivan Fallon, Joe Haines, Ron Hall, Lord Hartwell, Max Hastings, Bernard Ingham, Clive Irving, Terence Lancaster, Ann Leslie, Magnus Linklater, Andrew Neil, Jim Nicoll, Peter Preston, Sir Frank Rogers, Patrick Sergeant, Michael Shea, Bernard Shrimsley, Lord Stevens, Colin Webb and Andreas Whittam Smith.

Those interviewed in other contexts were: Louis Blom-Cooper, John Bryant, Peter Cole, Joe Cooke, Sir Zelman Cowen, Jeremy Deedes, Tony Elliott, Sir David English, Harold Evans, Stephen Grabiner, Roy Greenslade, Richard Hall, Anthony Howard, Sir John Junor, Andrew Knight, Nicholas Lloyd, Lord McGregor, David Montagu, David Montgomery, Robin Morgan, William O'Neill, Eve Pollard, Viscount Rothermere, Eddy Shah, Ron Spark, Richard Stott, Donald Trelford, Lloyd Turner, Charles Wintour and Peregrine Worsthorne.

The book owes an enormous amount to Michael Pountney, whose idea it was when he was editorial director to Unwin Hyman, and who made some valuable suggestions. He left the company on its acquisition by HarperCollins in July 1990, when the manuscript was incomplete. I am grateful to my agent, Felicity Bryan, for the speed and energy with which she placed it elsewhere, and to Ion Trewin and Alex Woolf at Hodder and Stoughton for nursing it through its final stages with such efficiency and enthusiasm.

1

A Voice from the Pulpit

The popular press has never been respectable: a bewhiskered American joke goes as follows. Some schoolchildren are asked by their teacher to tell the class what their fathers do for a living. After the expected doctors, bankers and train drivers, one boy says: 'My father plays the piccolo in a bordello.' He is sent outside and the shocked teacher summons his mother to report the incident. 'Yes, that's what we tell him,' she admits, 'because the truth is even worse. He works for Hearst newspapers.'

*　　*　　*

St Bride's church off Fleet Street, though virtually rebuilt after wartime bombing, is one of Christopher Wren's finest; but it is so hemmed in by tall office blocks that you could easily walk down the street and not notice it. Its unobtrusiveness well suits the spiritual home of London's ungodliest profession. Journalists, with their keen sense of tradition, like to know that the church is there, but not to be reminded of it too often. Since 1500, when William Caxton's apprentice Wynkyn de Worde established London's first commercial printing press by the Fleet River, the church on this site has been the institutional place of worship for what is now called the communications industry – and it remains so even though the newspaper offices have dispersed. It is the customary and fitting venue for memorial services for journalists. One such took place in November 1988.

A splendid array of some of the big names in popular journalism, as well as politicians of the left, had turned out at noon on a cold day to honour Sydney Jacobson, the first editor of the *Sun* and, before that, a respected political editor of the *Daily Mirror*. The interior of the church, well lit through Wren's massive arched windows despite its crowded location, is unusual in that the two long rows of superbly carved pews, in blonde oak, are ranged parallel with the central aisle, rather than facing the altar in the conventional manner. It has something of the feel of the House of Commons in terms of its layout, though not its architectural detail. Thus when Hugh Cudlipp, the former managing director of the *Mirror* group, moved to the lectern in front of the columned oak reredos to give the main address, it was as though he were taking position behind the dispatch box. Given the political nature of what he was about to say, that was quite appropriate.

The brass lectern is in the form of an eagle in flight. Cudlipp, now a member of the House of Lords, with stooped shoulders and his famous shock of hair gone quite white, placed his notes on the eagle's outstretched wings and straight away launched into a deeply felt attack on what he called the dark age of tabloid journalism. He described Jacobson as one of the last of the 'journalists who used to give tabloid newspapers a good name'. Today's proprietors and editors, by contrast, had 'decided that playing a continuing role in public enlightenment was no longer any business of the popular press'. Still speaking of the present (though using the past tense) and quite uninhibited by the venue, he went on:

> It was the age when investigative journalism in the public interest shed its integrity and became intrusive journalism for the prurient; when nothing, however personal, was any longer secret or sacred and the basic human right to privacy was banished in the interest of public profit; when Bingo became a new journalistic art form; when the daily nipple-count and the sleazy stories about bonking bimbos achieved a dominant influence in the circulation charts; when significant national and international events were nudged aside by a panting seven-day and seven-night news service for voyeurs on the one-night stands of pop stars with teenage delinquents . . . the homo and hetero peccadilloes of television stars and the ordained, the nocturnal Olympics of prominent gentlemen's outfitters, the exclusive definitive autobiographies of kiss-and-tell nymphets aged eighteen and a half and of course, though on a marginally higher plane, the latest inanities in the royal soap opera . . .
>
> Some of these foolish things are worthy of mention in the popular press. They have always been allotted a share of the newsprint and more than their fair share of the headlines: now it's overkill. If you have prayers to spare save one, just one, for the proprietors and editors of the tabloid press. At the birth of a new century they apparently live in fear of instant bankruptcy if they dare to mention in their newspapers the activities of the human race when not in bed.

Old men do not so much forget as subtly adjust their perceptions of what has gone before. Thirty years earlier, on 11 June 1958, Cudlipp had made another speech about the tabloid press, using equally colourful language to express an almost diametrically opposite view. Earlier that year *The Times* had opened its correspondence columns to scores of readers complaining about the callous excesses of reporters and photographers from the popular press covering two specific events: the murder of a young Dutch woman in Essex and the Munich air disaster that wiped out most of the Manchester United football team. The editor of *The Times*, Sir William Haley, had added his voice in a leading article that chastised the popular press in the paper's best thunderous tradition.

Cudlipp was scheduled to speak at a meeting of the Commonwealth Press Union held in the London home of Lord Astor, the principal proprietor of *The Times*. Careless of his host's sensibilities, Cudlipp took the opportunity to respond to *The Times* in the forthright manner he often assumed when writing editorials in the *Mirror*, effectively accusing *The Times* of disloyalty to the trade of which it was a part, even if a rather rarefied part. He spoke of 'an orgy of self-destructive propaganda' from the 'self-styled quality papers ... the fifth column of our own profession'. *The Times* had become 'the zealous and self-appointed leader of this movement for ritualistic suicide'. He went on: 'The ammunition is damp but it is eagerly passed from hand to hand among the traditional traducers of our profession' who appeared to believe that 'while they are busy every day bringing down ten more tablets from Mount Sinai, the popular press was solely occupied with the activities of Sodom and Gomorrah.'

The Times correspondence had begun in January when, following the murder of nineteen-year-old Mary Kriek near Colchester, Essex, a friend of hers had written to the paper complaining that reporters and photographers had, without permission, swarmed over the house where she had been staying and harassed her parents when they arrived at Harwich from Holland. For the next fortnight *The Times* published an average of three letters a day on the question, most of them severely critical of the press. The following month, the sensational reporting of the Munich air crash gave fresh impetus to the correspondence. Haley's leader was published between the two events. Its message about the dangers of intrusive reporting has become a familiar one down the years:

It is the press as a whole that will suffer – and with it the best interests of the nation – if public opinion and Parliament should react to the point of deciding that liberty had been so intensely abused by some newspapers that it must be curtailed for all ... Things are done in the name of the press that must make any decent-minded, let alone sensitive journalist feel ashamed. The fact that so many columns of so many popular papers are filled with the inanities of trivial and worthless people who clearly dote on publicity seems to have led a section of the press into one or other of two grave errors. Either they believe that all people want publicity and that reticence – no matter what the circumstances – is a tiresome pose. Or they believe they have an absolute right to intrude wherever they think there may be something to titillate their readers. They must be shown sharply how wrong they are on both counts. Arguments that they print what the public wants are irrelevant. The excuse that the methods of their wrongdoing are sometimes used for right-doing is no more than a charge against their own sense of proportion and judgment. A man who goes around maiming people with an axe is not allowed to keep it merely because it is also occasionally useful to him to cut firewood.

Nothing about bonking bimbos, but otherwise those are sentiments to which the Hugh Cudlipp of the late 1980s, and the other internal and external critics of the tabloids, would subscribe. They might even find a good word to say for Randolph Churchill, the scourge of the popular press of the early 1950s. In a speech at a literary luncheon in 1953, marking the publication of Cudlipp's book *Publish and Be Damned*, Churchill referred to 'the river of pornography and crime which streams today from Fleet Street'. A month later, in another speech, he said: 'The offence of such publications as the *Sunday Pictorial*, the *Daily Mirror*, the *Daily Sketch*, the *Sunday Dispatch*, the *Weekly Overseas Mail* and *Reveille* is that they masquerade as newspapers when in reality they get their sales from crime and sex and, of course, inaccurate impertinences about the Royal Family thrown in.'

As these examples suggest – chosen from countless similar attacks down the ages – the changes that have taken place in the British press over the last thirty years may in some respects have been less radical than is often assumed. The popular press has never lived up to the ideals that others would like to impose on it. There will always be Churchills, Haleys, Kemsleys and even, in the end, Cudlipps to declare that the 'rags' have finally gone too far beyond the bounds of decency; but despite that the bounds shift constantly outwards. By the time Rupert Murdoch qualifies for his memorial service at St Bride's – or more suitably St George's, Wapping – no doubt the present editors of his *Sun* and *News of the World*, as well as those of *The Times* and *Sunday Times*, will be on hand to look back fondly on the 1980s as the age of innocence, compared with the dreadful things going on under their successors in the early years of the twenty-first century.

2

'So insensibly rude . . .'

The press is a frail vessel for the hopes it is meant to bear. The best that it can do can never quite be good enough to illuminate what Walter Lippmann called the 'invisible environment', the complexity of forces and agencies we cannot monitor for ourselves, but which affect all our lives. A free, cultivated, diverse, resourceful and honest press can only try, and if we ever get one it will be interesting to see what it achieves.

Harold Evans, *Good Times, Bad Times*, p. 400

When in 1962 the entrepreneurial young publisher Michael Heseltine decided he would have to shut down *Topic*, an ailing news magazine he had acquired only a few months earlier, he cannot have guessed that he was starting a process that would change some of the rules of public life (which he would shortly enter) and alter the ambitions and perceptions of a generation of journalists. *Topic* had been launched a year earlier as a British version of *Time* and *Newsweek*, and its lack of commercial success served to confirm the received wisdom that, for a mixture of geographical and sociological reasons, there was no market for a weekly news magazine in Britain. (Nearly two decades later, the failure of James Goldsmith's *Now* was to reconfirm it.) *Topic*'s last editor was Clive Irving, an energetic young journalist with a penchant for design who had worked briefly on the *Sunday Times* and the *Observer*. He had been engaged by Nicholas Tomalin, who for a while edited both *Topic* and *Town*, Heseltine's longer-established magazine for men.

Based in a poky office above a supermarket in Edgware Road, West London, with minimal staff and resources, Irving could not hope to match the breadth of global coverage of the magazine's two American role models. For example, to cover the Cuban missile crisis, for which *Time* could call on scores of people in bureaux throughout the world, *Topic* had just one staff reporter, Irving himself. He flew to Washington and had less than two days to talk to people and dictate a long, cogent account of the unfolding melodrama. He calculated that if he and his small staff were to contribute anything fresh to British journalism, what they had to do was pull together the strands of the week's news and set them out in a more coherent and considered way than was being done by the piecemeal daily coverage in newspapers and on television. And he was developing the technique of pinpointing exactly the time and place of significant developments in the story, emphasising the local colour. One section of his missile coverage began: 'On October 13 Kennedy was conducting his party's election campaign with typically breathless energy. A whistle-stop tour – of the new variety, by jet – had taken him to Indianapolis . . .'

This new approach failed to attract readers or advertisers quickly enough to forestall Heseltine's axe. It had, however, been noticed by news professionals. Within hours of the announcement that the magazine was to close, Irving received calls from three editors asking him to discuss with them how the approach could be adapted for their purposes. They were Denis Hamilton of the *Sunday Times*, Michael Berry (later Lord Hartwell) of the recently launched *Sunday Telegraph* and, most unexpectedly, Geoffrey Cox of Independent Television News, just beginning to explore new ways of presenting news on the small screen.

The spontaneous and separate interest of these three men in what Irving and his colleagues had been doing reflected a growing feeling that the press, in 1962, was falling down on its job. The generation born just before or during World War Two were leaving universities and reaching adulthood with the conviction that they were the victims of a conspiracy to prevent them from finding out what was really going on – and that the press was part of that conspiracy. Protest, satire and anger became fashionable, as evidenced by BBC Television's *That Was the Week That Was*, the launch of the fortnightly *Private Eye* and a string of anti-establishment plays at the Royal Court Theatre.

Until the start of the 1960s, press reporting had been conducted according to a fairly rigid formula that was essentially reactive rather than proactive. Partly because of the newsprint restrictions imposed during and after World War Two, the most admired skill of a journalist, on popular and quality papers alike, was to report the main news of the day in the most vivid and innovative way, using the fewest possible words. Scoops tended to be fresh angles on the most widely reported stories, rather than the result of investigations into areas untrodden by others. Until then the papers had no incentive to try to extend the range of their coverage because they had been used to the frustrations of trying to squeeze the news they felt obliged to cover into space that was really too limited even for that. Thus the investigative traditions of reporting – that had led, for instance, to exposés of poverty and exploitation in Victorian Britain – had fallen into disuse in the serious newspapers. They left that kind of thing to the populars, mainly the Sundays, with their regular 'I made an excuse and left' revelations about prostitution, or 'I name the guilty man' pieces on small-time fraudsters.

The increase in the size of papers from the late 1950s, coupled with the new generation's reaction against what they saw as the prevailing lethargy and lack of curiosity of the Macmillan years, had convinced both Hamilton and Berry that it was time for intelligent Sunday papers to experiment with a new, analytic form of journalism. Reporting, especially of politics, had lost its inquisitorial edge through years of being filtered through various publicity machines and other devices for distortion. They believed that newspapers should now probe beyond the superficial, tracing events to their source, as Irving and his team had been doing on *Topic*. To take a seven-day rather than a one-day perspective on the news, hoping thus to illuminate aspects that the daily papers had left unclear, seemed a logical role for a Sunday paper.

Even without the element of original investigation for which Insight was later to become noted, this represented, for its time, a radical shift in the conventional approach to journalism, and if he was to be the agent for it Clive Irving wanted to have the aid of his two most sympathetic lieutenants on *Topic*: Ron Hall, the chief sub-editor, and Jeremy Wallington, managing editor. All three were in their late twenties and had already notched up experience in Fleet Street. (In the 1950s it was quite common for a bright graduate to move straight from university on to a national paper, scarcely bothering to stop off in the provinces on the way. The all-powerful and glamorous *Daily Express* was an especially potent lure. But the National Union of Journalists disapproved and tried to ensure that nobody was hired in Fleet Street without prior experience in the regions.) The trio were keen that the team that had come together so recently should stay together if they could find a single employer willing to engage them. They quickly rejected the ITN approach because of their lack of television experience and their belief that their future lay in newspapers.

Michael Berry's idea was for a single page of 'news in depth' in the *Sunday Telegraph* every week. When he had launched the paper the previous year, he made much of the fact that it would be in many respects a seventh-day version of the *Daily Telegraph*, sending reporters out on Saturday to find that day's hard news – in contrast, by implication, to the rival Sundays which, he maintained, made no real attempt to report up-to-the-minute news, except on the sports pages. He soon discovered that part of the reason for this failing was that precious little happened on Saturdays. His idea of a one-page in-depth digest of the week was a way of counteracting this without too seriously compromising his original concept. Irving, Hall and Wallington thought it smacked of a ghetto mentality. They wanted to work on a paper where their distinctive handling of a story and their concept of the seven-day news cycle could be shifted to other parts of the paper when appropriate. When they raised this with Berry, the prospect seemed to fill him with alarm.

At the *Sunday Times*, three years after its acquisition by the Canadian Roy Thomson, Denis Hamilton and his colleagues had already been working for some months on the dummy of a section of the paper to contain a digest of the week's news in a condensed news-magazine style, combined with a look at trends in scientific and sociological fields. The plan was for the paper's specialist writers to submit copy, which would then be rewritten and edited into a terse, cogent whole by a specialised team.

That was not quite what Irving and his colleagues envisaged, at least not the sum total of it. They certainly wanted to be able to call on the expertise of specialists but also to do extra reporting themselves, because they would need to uncover facts and details that conventionally trained reporters would not always regard as relevant. Hamilton allotted them two dedicated pages a week – quite a concession in a paper that averaged only forty-eight pages – and said he would consider letting them infiltrate the rest of the paper when a suitable occasion arose.

Irving saw his first task as being to alter the ingrained preconceptions both of writers and readers about the style in which stories should be presented. The familiar technique of getting the guts of the story into the first paragraph, then elaborating it with as much detail as would fit into the space, was inappropriate, they felt, for their purpose. Irving advocated a different rhythm and pacing, what he called the 'delayed drop': starting the item in a narrative style, like a novella, to engage people's interest, and leaving the core of the message until later. This was the basis for many of the pastiche Insight stories written over the years in *Private Eye* and elsewhere, beginning: 'It was 8.30 on a crisp January morning when X turned the brass key in the double lock of his freshly-painted fuchsia-coloured front door in Acacia Avenue, Purley . . .'

Anxious to promulgate his new gospel, Irving, soon after he arrived at Gray's Inn Road, invited specialists and other journalists to a meeting to explain what he was getting at. According to an account in *The Pearl of Days*, the official history of the *Sunday Times* published in 1972, many of the staff did not take kindly to the pompous wording of the invitation, with its talk of 'new frontiers' and 'new dimensions' to the news. Nor did they relish being lectured about their trade. Maurice Wiggin, the television critic, said that he did not need Insight to explain to him what news was, and he found Irving and the other two 'so rude, so insensibly rude'. Yet although some of their older colleagues dismissed the brash young men as 'teddy boys', others were willing to co-operate with them.

Hamilton knew that the arrival of the trio was bound to be regarded with trepidation by many of the existing staff, and it is a measure of his commitment to innovation that he was prepared to take the risk. The *Sunday Times* in those days was run to some extent like a military under-taking. Much of its reputation in the 1950s had been built on serialising military memoirs, notably of Field-Marshal Montgomery. Hamilton had been a brigadier during the war and retained the stamp of the officers' mess, as did many of his colleagues.

In this company, Irving, Hall and Wallington were very much other ranks, and were slapped down as they began to tread on the highly polished toecaps of their betters. Hamilton grew nervous when they sought to tackle diplomatic and political stories that were the province of the traditional specialists on the news pages. He could not allow the new men to ride roughshod over the old. He therefore ordained that Insight should stick largely to the kind of items that appeared in the back half of *Time* and *Newsweek*, such as latest developments in the '-ologies' – sociology, archaeology, technology, etc.

The first Insight pages, solemnly sub-headed 'The news in a new dimension', were a patchwork of items of moderate length, mainly about such topics. The stories on the first Sunday, 17 February 1963, included news of a setback for the Big Bang theory, the battle of British and American tri-jets (the Trident and the Boeing 727), delays in building motorways, London's new Post Office tower and a single foreign story – the emergence in Germany of a new politician, Franz-Josef Strauss. The following week there were items on the Brain Drain, astronauts' pay, the new-look *Guardian* and an investigation into why the best people were leaving the BBC. There was nothing that could properly be called a scoop, and nothing that suggested a break in the mould of British journalism.

The trio soon found this format limiting and were anxious to get their teeth into something more contentious and something they could write at greater length. The chance came when the Profumo scandal broke in the spring and summer of 1963. The latest developments in this

'The news in a new dimension': part of the *Sunday Times*'s first 'Insight' section, 17 February 1963.

absorbing saga were trumpeted over the front and many of the inside pages of the daily papers, but Irving felt there had been no attempt to put all the pieces of the jigsaw together to give a cogent account of what happened and why it was important, distinguishing between details that were significant and those that were merely trite.

In reporting such delicate matters of state there was still a sense in which the rest of the press gave the impression that it was doing its utmost to reveal all the facts despite severe restraints – although in truth the restraints were mainly self-imposed, as they had been during the abdication crisis twenty-five years earlier. Thus when the Profumo story began to surface in March, the *Daily Express* had printed a photograph of the young Christine Keeler just below a lead story about Profumo, with no apparent connection between the two. Only those in the know could break the code.

Insight's reconstruction of the case broke these artificial barriers to understanding. The story occupied about three-quarters of the regular two pages on the weekend after Mr Profumo's resignation, with another page the following Sunday. It provided a model for treating other major stories – and was also developed into the first of many Insight books, *Scandal '63*. The style was based partly on Theodore White's admired book about the 1960 US presidential election, *The Making of the President*, the first of a series that was to run for more than twenty years, using the minutiae of events to build a vivid picture for readers and carry them along with the narrative. (After the 1968 election the Insight team produced its own US election book, *An American Melodrama*.) Later in 1963 Irving used the same technique to report the machinations surrounding the struggle for the leadership of the Conservative Party after Harold Macmillan's resignation – itself an indirect consequence of the Profumo affair.

The team's first original investigation – original in that it was not a development of a story already published somewhere else – was Ron Hall's account of the career of Peter Rachman, the slum landlord, whose name had cropped up in the Profumo case as the lover of Mandy Rice-Davies, one of the women involved. Rachman had developed a technique of buying run-down property cheaply because it was partly occupied by statutory tenants who were hard to remove legally. He filled the empty flats with West Indian immigrants of the kind who enjoyed noisy parties. This would provoke the 'stats' into moving elsewhere. Rachman would then get rid of the West Indians and be left with empty properties that he could sell at a large profit.

It was the first real exposé the *Sunday Times* had ever printed but the level of daring needed to run the story was sharply reduced by the fact that Rachman died some months before it appeared, ruling out the risk of a libel action. All the same, it caused a stir. Harold Wilson, the new leader of the Labour Party, used it as the basis of a campaign on security of tenure and a new word entered the language: Rachmanism.

It soon became clear that the Insight style could be adapted successfully to the coverage of major international stories, such as the assassination of President Kennedy and crises in the Middle and Far East. After only a year it was beyond argument that the format was a success and Hamilton decided to take up Irving's initial suggestion that the paper's entire news coverage should be restructured on Insight lines. Irving and Wallington were given executive positions on the news side of the paper while Hall took over the editorship of Insight, hiring as his assistant Bruce Page, a young man who had spent much of his life in Australia and who had been working on the *Daily Herald*'s gossip column.

More exposés followed: fake wine labelling, bogus car insurance and illegal 'rings' of antique dealers, and, in later years, probes into the

Thalidomide tragedy, Robert Maxwell's publishing empire and the DC-10 air disaster in 1974. This part of the team's work owed much to the paper's lawyer, James Evans, rare among newspaper lawyers in that his instinct was to try to find ways of getting stories into the paper rather than keeping them out. He was especially supportive of Harold Evans, who embraced the Insight concept enthusiastically when he succeeded Hamilton as editor of the paper in 1966. (James Evans later climbed to senior executive positions in the Thomson organisation.)

Veterans of the early Insight days insist that, initially at least, they were not motivated by any burning desire to change the world by exposing all that was corrupt and conspiratorial. It was more a youthful urge to prick bubbles and, like a high-spirited illusionist, to demonstrate that things were not necessarily as they seemed. The phoney wine-labelling exposure, written by Nicholas Tomalin, was satirical rather than worthy, bringing as it did the full weight of strict investigatory techniques to bear on a deception of great interest but scant global significance. It was Harold Evans, who had won a reputation as a campaigner on the *Northern Echo*, who turned Insight into the equivalent of a caped crusader, dedicated to righting wrongs. He saw an investigation not solely as a piece of journalism, but as a cause to be lost or won.

These Insight campaigns had a profound influence on a generation of journalists. The concept of journalist as hero had previously applied, in the main, to intrepid foreign correspondents and war reporters, who often put themselves into positions of grave danger for the sake of bringing back the news. They were inevitably a restricted, select band. Now here was a new heroism in which anyone could take part, given a doggedly persistent nature, a persuasive telephone manner and an ability to extract vital information from documents such as official and company reports and columns of figures. It afforded, at times, a sense of excitement and danger that was lacking in conventional reporting. (A parallel development across the Atlantic was to culminate a decade later in the Watergate affair, investigative journalism's apogee.)

Although its campaigns gained the *Sunday Times* many plaudits, not everybody was convinced it was the right way for journalism to go. Ron Hall wondered whether this emphasis on campaigning was not over-political, identifying the newspaper as wedded to a particular philosophy, rather than staying aloof and impartial, above the fray. He thought campaigns distorted pure investigation, since they invariably placed undue weight on only one side of the case. He also thought that the most effective Insight pieces were those where it was possible to be both truthful and funny, and to include elements of nefariousness, glamour and absurdity. This could be done in areas such as espionage, high finance and the antiques trade, but was less easy when the subject was something more earnest, such as birth defects, air crashes or hospital mental wards.

Insight was one of the few successful examples in British journalism of the team approach working effectively. By the end of the 1960s there were reporters working on the *Sunday Times* who had spent almost all their careers as members of a team rather than working on their own in the conventional manner. Their patent success, in the context of that paper and at that time, inevitably fuelled an arrogance that their colleagues learned how to tolerate but that grated on outsiders. One such was the playwright Arnold Wesker, who spent some weeks in the paper's offices in 1971 to get material for a play about journalism.

As well as the play, Wesker wrote an extended essay about his experience called *Journey into Journalism* and, before having it published, conscientiously sought permission from the people who had helped him. Some on Insight declined to give it. The section about them in the essay suggested that their working practices were haphazard, not at all the incisive, surgeon-like approach of legend. It is probable, too, that they objected to Wesker's portrayal of journalists in general as less than heroic, as self-satisfied, vainglorious, scheming, ambitious and given to vicious internal rivalries. These are all qualities that people who work in newspapers will recognise readily, but they prefer to keep word of them to themselves. Wesker's attitude to journalism is encapsulated in this extract:

> Newspapers are not boring so much as they induce a sense of futility. After the first sentences I think: what the hell! The language is predictable, the facts likely to be inaccurate and contradicted in another newspaper, or if not inaccurate then specially selected or incomplete, or the situation will change tomorrow or something else is more important or there's just too damn much of it anyway. I'm simply reading what someone else has been interested in for the space of a couple of hours spent interviewing and typing.

The objections from a few journalists to this heresy meant that its publication was delayed for five years, until Harold Evans was prevailed upon to give the go-ahead during a television discussion of press freedom with Melvyn Bragg.

Other papers responded to Insight with ersatz versions: the *Observer* ran an occasional feature called Daylight, analysing a particular event of significance, and devoted pages to what it called 'news background'. Later the *Sunday Telegraph* countered with a feature called first Close-Up and then Telescope. But none of these copycat enterprises matched Insight in verve and commitment, or in the staff and resources devoted to them.

One of the difficulties of changing newspapers – as the Insight team discovered – is that each paper always has a strong body of people committed to the way things have been done hitherto. Journalists, like actors, thrive on the approbation of their peers. They like to be told regularly that theirs was, at the very least, a 'nice piece this morning': the journalists' equivalent of 'You were wonderful, darling.' When they are overseas their morale needs to be boosted by frequent 'herograms' telling them that their coverage has made the opposition look puny. Such an atmosphere of mutual congratulation makes it hard for an editor to suggest to his staff that there might, after all, be a better way of doing things. The line of lesser resistance is to carry on in the time-honoured way, refining established techniques.

Starting a new paper, therefore, offers a rare chance of bringing in fresh thinking and experiment without the trauma of disturbing an existing structure. The first chance to incorporate the lessons of Insight into a newly conceived national paper came in the autumn of 1964.

*　　*　　*

There was nothing particularly wrong (as Insight might have begun) with the Café Royal, the historic restaurant at the Piccadilly end of Regent Street, but there was no denying that it did not, in 1964, have quite the cachet of, say, the Savoy, half a mile away along the Strand. Many of the hundred or so journalists who trooped to Regent Street one hot Saturday night, towards the end of the summer, could not escape the suspicion that they were being palmed off with second best. If, they felt, Hugh Cudlipp was really devoting 100 per cent of his prodigious energies to transforming the listless *Daily Herald* into the sparkling new *Sun*, 'the newspaper born of the age we live in', he would have chosen for the pre-launch dinner and pep talk somewhere with a bit more . . . well, with a bit more class. But the choice was unwittingly symbolic, because at that particular point in its history, the Café Royal shared many of the negative qualities of the old *Herald* itself. It had seen better days. Its old clientele was fading away and it had yet to make the adjustment to the 1960s.

The middle market between the tabloids and the quality press is notoriously difficult to define and to serve. In 1960 the *News Chronicle*, very much in the *Herald*'s kind of market, had been closed down as unviable with a circulation of more than a million. One reason was the difficulty of convincing advertisers that its readers represented a coherent market that could not easily be reached through other media. A more important reason was the high labour costs involved in producing papers in Fleet Street.

Over the years the newspaper proprietors had made concession after concession to the print unions to head off threats of strikes and go-slows. The newspaper industry is exceptionally vulnerable to industrial action because a lost edition or part of an edition can never be recovered. The product has a shelf life of only a few hours until superseded by the next day's issue. Moreover, in the heat of newspaper competition in the 1930s and again in the 1950s, proprietors of the most successful papers would sometimes agree to union demands simply in order to set a precedent for their weaker rivals, who could scarcely afford to pay the new rates or employ the extra men demanded.

The result was chronic overmanning, restrictive practices and exorbitant extra payments. The most graphic description of how the system operated prior to 1986 is given in Linda Melvern's book *The End of the Street*, published that year. She tells how some pay scales involved extra money simply for walking across a room, how machines had a habit of 'breaking down' at times of industrial tension, how union chapel officials frequently ignored and defied management and sometimes demanded changes to editorials and cartoons.

Although such practices had been among the reasons for the failure of the *Herald*, Cudlipp's *Daily Mirror*, operating under the same restrictions, still made plenty of money. Thus it was not in his interest – nor indeed in his power – to challenge the system and risk damaging a most profitable newspaper. He and Cecil King, the *Mirror* group chairman, had decided that the only feasible answer to the problems of the *Herald* was a painless mercy killing, followed by instant reincarnation as the *Sun*.

Nobody in Fleet Street was better qualified to start a new national paper than Cudlipp, the acknowledged master of British popular journalism. A fiery Welshman with a tousled shock of hair, he had left school at fourteen, so had seven years' experience of journalism when he joined the *Daily Mirror* as Assistant Features Editor in 1935, at the age of twenty-one. King, then a director of Mirror Newspapers and later its chairman, wrote of him: 'Cudlipp at that time had little education, no foresight but a galaxy of journalistic gifts.' Six months after joining the

'A painless mercy killing, followed by instant reincarnation': the final issue of the *Daily Herald* and the first issue of the *Sun*, September 1964.

Mirror he became Features Editor and two years after that he was made editor of the *Sunday Pictorial*.

He had an extraordinary talent for popular journalism. He understood the tastes of working-class readers, especially their fascination with sex, relationships and personal issues that affected their daily lives. Technically, he had prodigious skills of condensation and projection, of hitting on a headline and a layout that would encapsulate the sense of the piece and demand readers' attention because of its sheer audacity. For three decades his reputation was unrivalled and today's tabloids still reflect his influence, in terms of style and, to a lesser extent, of content.

At the Café Royal on that September evening, Cudlipp did his best to be upbeat – it was not in his nature to be otherwise – but everyone in the room knew that he was doing no more than make the best of a bad job. The *Mirror* group had not much wanted the *Herald* in the first place: it had come as part of the package with the acquisition of Odhams Press in a hotly contested takeover battle in 1961. As Cudlipp made clear in his rip-roaring memoir, *At Your Peril*, Cecil King wanted Odhams for its stable of magazines: the lacklustre *Herald*, with a declining circulation of about one and a half million, was something of an embarrassment, especially since the Trades Union Congress had a controlling interest in the paper and insisted that it gave the Labour Party its unstinting support.

The *Mirror* bid provoked questions in Parliament about the concentration of media ownership. King, asked in a television interview whether it was not dangerous for so much power to be in one man's hands, replied: 'No, I think it is admirable if the hands are mine.' The takeover provoked the Government into appointing a Royal Commission on the Press, under Lord Shawcross, which reported inconclusively in 1962.

Now, two years later, Cudlipp was telling us that extensive market research endorsed the idea of a paper that, like the *Herald*, supported the Labour Party but, unlike the *Herald*, would not be committed to doing so automatically. It would also shake off the formal tie with the Trades Union Congress and the grey, cloth-cap connotations that went with it. Apart from that, though, it appeared that it was not going to differ all that radically from the *Herald*, which, Cudlipp told us, had been essentially a fine paper that failed only because it had become trapped in an inexorable cycle of circulation decline.

If he really thought that the *Herald* had declined by accident it was a bad omen. More hopefully, he suggested that the new paper would pick up and develop some of the latest trends in journalism, including the

Sunday Times's Insight feature. He spoke as convincingly as he knew how of his plans to introduce a regular Insight-type slot on the *Sun* and invited us to think of names for it. (The choice finally fell on Probe, quickly earning the irreverent nickname Grope.)

Cudlipp gave us a sketch of his ideal *Sun* reader, as defined by him and Bert Hardy, a young advertising executive who had done most to create the 'born of the age we live in' concept, and who was later to become a senior executive with Rupert Murdoch and with Lord Rothermere's Associated Newspapers. The *Sun* reader would be young, working his (in those days the assumption of masculine gender was acceptable) way up in business, weaned on the *Daily Mirror* – then selling more than five million copies a day – but feeling that the breezy tabloid was not a serious enough paper to be seen carrying to the office in the morning.

The *Sun*, then, would be the acceptable face of the *Mirror*. The readers would be young, radical and interested in consumer issues. They would be among the growing numbers who took their holidays abroad – so the *Sun* would carry plenty of foreign news. Since Alfred Harmsworth had produced the first popular newspaper, the *Daily Mail*, in 1896, selling papers had come to be seen as an exercise in marketing as much as journalism. I do not recall whether the phrase 'gap in the market' was current in 1964 but twenty-five years later, steeped in the jargon of market research, Cudlipp would certainly have employed it. Beware market researchers bearing gaps.

That was certainly the view of Brian Doody, a sub-editor on the *Herald*. Towards the end of the evening he stood up and announced to the assembled company that he was so appalled by what he had heard that he was resigning forthwith. It is possible that he was offended and depressed not so much by the presentation as by Cudlipp's dispiriting after-dinner attempt to launch a sing-song of suggestive ditties – scarcely in accord with the upwardly mobile image he had been telling us so much about. In the cold light of the following week Doody was persuaded to rescind his resignation; but his initial instinct was to prove sounder.

Others were reading the warning signs, too. In the dying days of the *Herald*, dummy issues of the *Sun* were produced. Key journalists – mostly from the *Herald* but some hired for the new paper – were invited to the office of the editor, Sydney Jacobson, to discuss the dummies, one of which had its main front-page headline about the Queen. This depressed James Cameron, the paper's best-known reporter and columnist. On his way out of the meeting, he observed bitterly: 'This is supposed to be a brand new paper and there we go leading on a story about the royal family.'

Cameron was wrong if he thought that press coverage of royalty was going to diminish over the next decades: the very reverse was the case. Yet his instinct was reliable when it told him that the prospectus for the *Sun* was essentially phoney. No new thinking had been done about what kind of paper the young, progressive, intelligent readers of the 1960s would like on their breakfast table. It was the *Mirror* formula of the 1950s, thinly disguised in fashionable clothes. Eventually, after it changed hands in 1969, the *Sun* would be the agent for a revolution in British journalism, but not of the sort that Cudlipp had intended or Cameron would have approved.

*   *   *

Roger Wood, a former editor of the *Daily Express*, was put in charge of the *Sun*'s Probe page, with two writers who would work primarily for him, one of them the ex-*News Chronicle* veteran Tom Baistow. It never worked as Cudlipp envisaged – or at least not as he described it to the Café Royal gathering – partly because of the pressures of daily journalism and partly because the people in charge found it impossible to shake off the instincts and priorities of the popular press. Although the Probe team were occasionally given time to develop their own stories, too often they were under pressure to write them prematurely, so as to fill the space that had been allotted in the next day's paper.

The subjects chosen for the page were worthy rather than arresting, the tone explanatory rather than vivid. A 'Probe into Exports' ran for three successive days in November 1964. It was true that the trade gap was the biggest economic problem then facing Harold Wilson's new Labour Government, but it is doubtful if even those people who read to the end of the third instalment were really any better informed about its cause or solution. Other topics were the stuff of women's magazines rather than investigative journalism. 'When should children go to bed?' one Probe headline asked. 'How long should shops stay open?' enquired another. An item began: 'Books for coffee-table decoration rather than reading have become the fashion this year ...' Sometimes the space was devoted to an examination of the background of an item in that day's news – a coup in the Sudan, for instance – inevitably stitched together in the office from press cuttings and agency reports, given the time constraint.

The range of subjects chosen for Probe reflected the eclectic approach of the *Sun* as a whole. Examining children's bedtime alongside the reasons for the trade gap was no doubt intended to be evidence of across-the-board appeal, but equally it could be seen as a lack of any fixed focus, an uncertainty about the precise audience the paper was trying to address. Strong political and diplomatic coverage competed for space with stories about entertainment personalities and photographs of attractive young women. There was a variety of both regular and occasional big-name columnists – Clement Freud, James Cameron, Jon Akass, the novelist Edna O'Brien and even the American Walter Lippmann, whose measured prose about world affairs was admirably lucid, but scarcely the stuff to excite readers of a British popular newspaper. Nancy Banks-Smith wrote about television and Jean Rook was fashion editor.

What the paper chiefly lacked was an unambiguous commitment to its success from Cudlipp and his chairman, Cecil King. Both were wedded to the *Daily Mirror* and put its interests first in all strategic decisions. One possibility, which might in the long run have benefited both papers, would have been to position the *Mirror* slightly lower in the market, removing its more serious elements and concentrating on the frivolous. This would have allowed more earnest readers to switch to the more respectable *Sun*, while strengthening the *Mirror*'s defences against an assault from beneath – bound to come sooner or later, even though Rupert Murdoch was not yet a threat.

When Cecil King became chairman of the *Mirror* group in 1951, he had formed a profitable alliance with Cudlipp, who was made editorial director of the daily and Sunday papers. King, although he understood tabloid journalism, always hankered after something that would do more to improve the minds of the *Mirror*'s millions of readers. He felt himself engaged in what Peter Jay, in the context of television some years later, was to call a 'mission to explain'. He wanted to run a paper that took a more serious approach to the world and it had been his idea for the group to launch three heavyweight magazines devoted to public affairs – *Public Opinion*, the *London Magazine* and the *Statist* – all of which proved expensive failures under the company's ownership. Cudlipp, although always aware of his roots and fiercely protective of tabloid values, was persuaded to support King in the general aim of improving human knowledge. 'I always thought Hugh would have made a natural lecturer for the Workers' Educational Association,' said a colleague.

There was another consideration. King regarded the *Mirror* as his ticket to the confidence of ministers. As his diaries show, he much enjoyed his consultations with the mighty, who would have taken him less seriously if the *Mirror* became a less serious paper. Thus it had its daily World Spotlight page where in the early 1960s readers could inform themselves on changes in company law, or political problems in Malaysia, Uganda, Algeria and Laos. It had foreign correspondents such as Donald Wise patrolling the world's trouble spots – never as many as its circulation rival the *Daily Express*, but certainly more than a modern tabloid would deem necessary. It campaigned assiduously for British entry into the European Economic Community. Much of this went over the heads of readers but they had no alternative paper except the lack-lustre *Daily Sketch*, which never sold more than a million copies. Encouraged, Cudlipp introduced in 1968 a twice-weekly four-page pullout section of political and foreign news called Mirrorscope, as well as the Inside Page, a gossip column with an eye for politics rather than scandal.

The *Sun*'s lack of any clear focus showed in its circulation figures. The initial two million or so – nearly double that of the old *Daily Herald* in its final days – quickly slid to 1.25 million, back to what the *Herald* had sold a couple of years earlier. Cudlipp decided that Sydney Jacobson, the editor, had got the mix wrong, that he did not have the populist flair to attract readers in the numbers needed for the paper to survive. Jacobson was promoted in the group and replaced as editor by Dick Dinsdale, a former *Mirror* executive and a tabloid journalist of the old school. He took the *Sun* down towards the *Mirror*'s market while the *Mirror* itself moved up towards the *Sun*'s. With the bulk of the group's promotional resources devoted to the *Mirror* – including, in 1969, a midweek colour magazine that made huge losses – the weaker sister was at a growing disadvantage. Cudlipp, sniffing the unaccustomed stench of failure, distanced himself further and further from the debacle.

3

1966: Romance among the Wart-hogs

The man must have a rare recipe for melancholy, who can be dull
in Fleet Street.

Charles Lamb, 1802

Golden ages exist only in retrospect, so it is arbitrary to try to pin down
where they begin and end. For working journalists, the golden age is
usually the one that ended just before they joined the profession. The
legendary bylined writers of a generation ago, setting standards to which
their successors aspire, were without a doubt regarded as callow, un-
talented upstarts by the generation – equally revered – which preceded
them.

It would be misleading, then, to speak of any period as being Fleet
Street's supreme era. In the light of what has happened in the last
quarter of a century, however, it is possible to pinpoint with some pre-
cision its final stage of vigour before the diaspora of the 1980s. And if
we are looking for a single year in which a snapshot of Fleet Street
would reveal that ultimate flowering, we can settle on 1966: the year
when Lord Thomson was permitted by a condescending establishment
to sink his millions into its ailing house journal, *The Times*, and the year
Harold Evans came down from Darlington to become assistant editor
of the *Sunday Times*, preparing to take over the editor's chair from Denis
Hamilton a year later.

In 1966 the *Mirror* was virtually at the peak of its success and the
Express, two years after the death of its 'principal reader' Lord Beaverbrook, was at the start of a decline which, twenty-five years later, we
can see was irreversible. The *Mail* and *Telegraph* had not varied significantly over the previous decade while the *Sun* – in its 1966 form – and
Sketch were not to be long for this world. *The Times* was about to have
its fortunes restored, at least in terms of circulation.

34

3.1 Audited Circulation of National Dailies

	July–Dec. 1966	July–Dec. 1991
Daily Mirror	5,077,548	3,641,269*
Daily Express	3,953,612	1,518,764
Daily Mail	2,381,223	1,683,768
Daily Telegraph	1,354,146	1,058,082
Sun	1,247,818	3,665,006
Daily Sketch	849,396	–
Guardian	282,709	409,660
Times	273,148	387,386
Financial Times	151,806	287,120

* includes Glasgow *Daily Record*, not included in 1966
(see p. 287 for full list of current national newspaper circulations)

It happens, too, that 1966 saw the appearance of a revealing portrait of the dying days of a distinctive journalistic culture, in a book called *Fleet Street*, published by Macdonald. It was made up of short contributions from fifty-two people who made their living from newspapers, mainly journalists but a few proprietors, managers and advertising people. It had a foreword by Prince Philip, Duke of Edinburgh. Its purpose was to raise money for the reconstruction of the Press Club, a much-loved but run-down institution then housed in a back alley just off the Street and especially companionable after midnight.

Several contributors to the book captured the Edwardian spirit of Fleet Street as encapsulated in the Press Club. Dennis Castle, described as 'novelist, actor and a club member for twenty-five years', wrote a chapter called 'Up the Press Club Stairs' mentioning veteran variety stars – Arthur Askey, Bud Flanagan, Tony Hancock, Maurice Chevalier – and their spontaneous ripostes and anecdotes at Press Club functions that no doubt seemed hilarious in their time. There was the rickety piano with a wobbly loud pedal 'as inconsistent as a woman reporter'. (Sexism in Fleet Street has a long – some would say a continuing – history.) Horace Sanders, the club's president, told of japes and hoaxes involving the impersonation of an African potentate and the ordering of a hansom cab for Buckingham Palace. It was all reminiscent of Evelyn Waugh's *Scoop*. 'No romance in a newspaper?' asked J. A. Jones, who used to write a touching daily piece about courtroom scenes in the *Evening News*. 'It is all romance.'

Like many members of the Press Club in its latter days, Horace Sanders was not really a journalist at all, as John Marshall, former editor of the *Evening News*, pointed out in his contribution, self-consciously entitled 'What Characters We Are'. He described Sanders as 'Fleet Street's sage and courtly G.O.M. [Grand Old Man], who succeeded Lord Astor of Hever as President of the Press Club and who, in fact, has much to do with the *objets d'art* trade as public relations adviser to the Antique Dealers' Association . . . with his winged collar, striped trousers and judicial air.'

It was these 'characters' on the fringes of the trade who deterred younger journalists from joining the Press Club. Vivian Brodzky, formerly of the *Daily Herald* and *News of the World*, who edited the book, wrote: 'At any given moment in a Fleet Street public house, or the bar of the Press Club, you can find someone without boredom or nostalgia telling others of Fleet Street present and past: it is part of the mystique of the training and making of a full-rounded journalist.' By 1966, though, many preferred to forgo that particular part of their training, as being arduous beyond the call of duty.

Many contributors wrote warmly of the club's annual Christmas party for children. That was its single genuflection to the concept of the family. Apart from that, as Dennis Castle had hinted, the sweaty, chauvinistic world symbolised by the Press Club scarcely included women, except as topics of conversation. Female journalists were beginning to make their mark in Fleet Street but much of the terminology in the book assumed that its leading lights would continue to be men for the rest of time, with references to 'staff men' and 'Lobby men'. There were only two women among its contributors. One of them, Ann Leslie, then of the *Daily Express* but later better known on the *Daily Mail*, addressed the topic of her gender head on:

> The spirit of Fleet Street is still as ineradicably masculine as the old-style men's club. The solid core of it remains untouched by the vague ambi-sexuality that has crept over other publishing media . . . It stays as solidly male as beer and sawdust and battered sheepskin jackets. Above all, what at first appears to be one of the most democratic, flexible institutions possible, has yet to be conquered by ambitious womanhood . . . Women are basically honoured guests in a masculine fortress. All the standards have been set by men, all the power ultimately rests with them.

It turned out that she did not disapprove of this condition – 'personally, I am happy it should remain that way' – which was lucky, for it was to be another twenty-one years before Fleet Street had its first woman editor. Today, Leslie's view has not changed significantly. She believes that the virtual impossibility of combining a career in a national daily with bringing up children means that men will always dominate. Significantly, the first three women editors of nationals were all on Sunday papers, where the time pressures are not as great.

Women who do succeed tend to do it on the men's terms, Leslie believes. 'I didn't want to become like other Fleet Street women,' she says today, 'the ones who began as ordinary human beings but then became as drunk and foul-mouthed as the men and lost their looks early. There has always been a double standard. It's entertaining if a man reels in from El Vino's, falls over and crumples his car, but not a woman.' Yet now that Fleet Street has dispersed and sobriety is rampant, she is nostalgic for the days she described so luridly in 1966: 'I miss the shambolic creatures, the wart-hogs I found so repulsive. Young journalists, especially in America, are much more earnest. Computers have done something very peculiar to them. They're all super-efficient and terribly boring.'

Ann Leslie had begun her career on the *Daily Express* in Manchester, where the beer-and-sawdust atmosphere was undiluted by even the modest level of sophistication imported into Fleet Street by a handful of university graduates (she was one herself). Yet even in Fleet Street the sophisticates were in a permanent minority: the cultural tone was set by people who had themselves started in the provinces and were proud of it. They mocked her 'la-di-da accent'. They believed that the tabloid press had been created by such as themselves, who came from the same working-class roots as their readers and therefore had an instinctive understanding of how to capture their interest. Leslie and her like could never, they believed, acquire that understanding and were only playing at journalism as a short-term fad.

Yet it was their own macho culture that was dying. Dennis Castle concluded his essay in *Fleet Street* by describing the scene at the Press Club: 'You will see that it still goes on, the new cliques surveyed by the old contemptibles, each at their corners of the counter, all making unimportant history.' It was not to go on for long. Ten years later the Press Club moved from its down-at-heel premises by St Bride's church, to take over a couple of floors of the new International Press Building, a skyscraper in Shoe Lane. It was not the same. It included a restaurant, serving late meals for reporters and sub-editors on night shifts; but food was never high on their list of priorities and it could not pay its way.

The young journalists beginning to take the reins had less time for making 'unimportant history' at the bar, as their hard-pressed proprietors demanded more and more of their energy and commitment. Increasingly, the bar of the new Press Club became a haunt of people in the public relations industry, like Horace Sanders, and to keep the place afloat it was let out for publicity functions, which did nothing to make the atmosphere more attractive. It piled up debts and closed down as the papers began to move to their new headquarters elsewhere, leaving only a rump, known as the London Press Club, that met in a wine bar off Ludgate Hill.

Archaeologists of the written word would find, in that commemorative 1966 volume, more tangible evidence of a disappearing civilisation. From the proprietors who contributed to it came a sense of great complacency, at least for public consumption. Viscount Rothermere, owner of the *Daily Mail, Daily Sketch* and *Evening News* (and father of the present viscount), attempted to rationalise the irrational when discussing why modern production techniques had not reduced staffing levels:

Exactly the opposite has happened because new inventions have multiplied production, created new necessities and enlarged human horizons beyond previous imagining. An older economic order would have been unable to cope with these fast, massive developments which have therefore called into being equally massive concentrations of financial power to handle them.

There was even more extravagant optimism from Rothermere's main rival Sir Max Aitken, son of the first Lord Beaverbrook and his successor as chairman of the *Daily Express, Sunday Express* and *Evening Standard*. He revered his father so much that he refused to inherit his title, saying there could be only one Lord Beaverbrook. (Sir Max's son, Maxwell, had no such inhibitions, and took his seat in the Lords after his father died.) Sir Max also tried to emulate his father's curt style of tycoonery, but the performance was unconvincing. He wrote:

I think the present is fine and the future is glorious. Newspapers have their detractors. We must be aware of them and beware them. How to treat 'em? Shoot 'em down. They generally have no idea of our problems and the exertions we make to overcome them. A lofty commission, reporting on questions of finance and manpower, has spread the impression that the newspaper industry is inefficient. Nonsense. The British newspapers are unparalleled in their speed of reaction to news and their flexibility in switching from point to point under the pressure of hourly events.

With his head comfortably embedded in the sand, Sir Max declared: 'I do not foresee any sudden changes in the general production of newspapers.' And he concluded: 'I am sure that the future of our industry will be happy and secure.'

Like most of the other proprietors, Sir Max was dismissive of the potential impact of television on the press. By 1966 commercial television had been in existence for a decade and, although there had been only a small decline in total newspaper circulations, it was at the very least a powerful competitor as an advertising medium. But Sir Max wrote: 'Radio, television and all the new networks have been proved not to menace us. They enhance us. This is because of human nature and that very distinct form of it – British human nature – which Fleet Street understands so well. There is a superficial and flighty element in the new modes.'

Lord Rothermere noted only that television was forcing newspapers to print 'more matter with an entertainment value'. L. Marsland Gander, television and radio correspondent on the *Daily Telegraph*, pointed out that in 1920, before the arrival of radio, there were 2,293 daily and weekly papers in Britain; by 1966 the total was down to 1,434. He was reluctant to attribute this totally to television: after all, the circulation figures for the surviving titles had increased markedly since the 1920s. He said that the impossibility of competing with the broadcasting media to be first with the news had led to a greater concentration on features and vivid descriptive writing: 'A two-way traffic in ideas and methods has steadily developed. Television has adopted the ways and been fired by the energies of journalism; the newspapers have adjusted themselves to a world in which they are no longer the fastest purveyors of intelligence to the public.'

The newest press baron, the Canadian Lord Thomson, had hedged his bets and taken a large stake in Scottish commercial television, characterising it famously as 'a licence to print your own money'. His contribution to the *Fleet Street* book was more sanguine than that of the other proprietors, exposing a more realistic view of new technology and the future:

We have to learn to use these new tools of our trade, and I hope the efforts to do so will not be hamstrung by restrictive practices or managerial sluggishness, of which we have seen too much in the recent past . . . If we are to move hopefully into the future to produce better newspapers more efficiently we require a change of heart in the unions and an end to restrictive practices which still stick like leeches.

Again anticipating what was to become increasingly apparent over the next twenty years, Lord Thomson noted 'a strong anti-press feeling' among many sections of the community, 'due mainly to the policies which have bought circulation by pandering to those who delight in pornography, shady biographies, scandal and intrusion into personal affairs that are better left alone.' (This was three years after the Profumo affair and the publication of the memoirs of Christine Keeler, its central figure.) But on this matter Thomson's crystal ball was clouded with optimism. He foresaw 'the great advance in the expansion of quality newspapers and a falling-away of support for some of those that set lower standards'. The first part of that prediction came true only slowly, the second not at all.

The roseate view that press standards had improved, were improving and would continue to improve cropped up time and again in the book. Trevor Evans (later knighted), the industrial correspondent of the *Daily Express*, detected that 'managements and editors and their executives realise that dependability of their news standards is a far better investment for securing public support than ill-informed, easily disproved speculation'.

Evans set great store by the Press Council, formed in 1953 in response to growing concern about newspaper inaccuracies and intrusion into privacy, and about news being doctored to conform with the political prejudice of press proprietors. The idea of the council, made up of people from inside and outside the industry, had been floated originally by the National Union of Journalists (who were later to boycott it for some years). It was endorsed in the report of the first Royal Commission on the Press, in 1949. At first, editors and proprietors opposed it because it seemed to amount to an encroachment on their precious privileges. They reluctantly accepted it through fear that, if they did not, Parliament would impose legally binding constraints. And since it was to be established by the industry itself, they would be able to dictate its terms of reference.

Once in operation, it was apparent that the Press Council provided a useful safety valve through which outraged readers could let off steam, while the papers took on no formal obligation except to print its adjudications on complaints against themselves. Thus the council would sternly rail against 'cheque book journalism', the practice of bidding ever higher sums for people's stories, especially the confessions of criminals or their close relatives. Nothing would happen as a result of these strictures. Editors of the offending papers, mainly the national tabloids, would argue that while they personally would like to see the practice cease, they would not unilaterally eschew it while their rivals kept it going. The result was that editors continued to do virtually as they pleased in this and every other respect while declaring, for public consumption, that the council was forcing them to apply beneficial self-discipline. So by 1966, Trevor Evans could write: 'The public is becoming increasingly conscious of the range of complaints that it may now submit to the Council, and the newspapers are increasingly aware both of the care given by the Council to these complaints and its candour in expressing its conclusions.'

Sir Linton Andrews, former editor of the *Yorkshire Post* and chairman of the Press Council from 1955 to 1959, was even more convinced that it was a powerful force for good:

> A healthy new element has been brought into journalism by the Press Council. It wields increasing influence ... The outcome so far has been entirely encouraging to those who thought a Press Council would tend to banish injustice and ill-will ... The furious atmosphere of horse-whip threats is a memory of long ago. How much better is the calm, thoughtful justice of the Press Council.

Better, certainly, for those who might have fallen victim to the horse-whip; but down the years, as the essential impotence of the council to control declining standards became apparent, there were those who, in their impatience, wanted to take the whip down off the wall.

The falling standards of the press, noted by Lord Thomson in 1966, became worse in the next two decades. The growing stridency and irresponsibility is sometimes attributed to intensified competition, especially among the tabloids; but this is an over-simplification. There has been intense competition among London newspapers since they began in the eighteenth century. The 1960s saw the closure of the *News Chronicle*, *Daily Herald* and *Sunday Dispatch*, followed to the graveyard in 1971 by the *Daily Sketch*.

The survivors spent huge sums on editorial innovation and promotional campaigns to keep their circulations buoyant. The weapons they chose to deploy were different, though, from those of today. The *Daily Express*, for instance, persisted in believing through most of the 1960s that it was vital to keep its reputation for having its reporters first

'A major news story would be handled as a military operation': the *Daily Express* front page on 22 August 1968, the day after Soviet tanks rolled into Czechoslovakia.

on the scene when a foreign news story broke. Lord Beaverbrook and, to begin with, his son Max Aitken invested large sums to keep nineteen staff correspondents resident all over the world, ready to fly to trouble spots at a moment's notice.

A major news story would be handled as a military operation. In 1968, when the Russians sent tanks into Czechoslovakia, the *Express*'s Moscow correspondent was already there. Support staff were flown to Vienna and Germany to be on hand as reserves and to help with communications if it became difficult to get the stories out. Apart from the overseas-based corps, there was a team of star writers based in London, 'visiting firemen', that included, over the years, men such as Sefton Delmer, Donald Seaman and, for a while, James Cameron. One of them, René McColl, described in the *Fleet Street* book how he customarily kept a bag half-packed, ready for the next urgent summons to the airport. (Today, any *Express* reporters who did that would like as not find that the moth had got to their safari suits before there was a chance to use them.)

The *Daily Mail*, with fewer resources, tried to keep pace with the *Express* and so did the *Daily Mirror* up to a point, although it placed more emphasis on vivid photographs and gripping headlines than on the text. The reward for what would today be regarded as over-extravagant expenditure on foreign news was, for the *Express*, a circulation that for some years exceeded four million. But readership surveys, increasingly used by managements to replace the traditional journalistic instinct for what readers wanted, never put overseas coverage very high on the list of items people actually read in popular newspapers.

Foreign dispatches in the tabloids are like the lavish scenery and costumes made for an ambitious musical: it is nice to know they are there, although it is hard to be precise about what they contribute to our enjoyment of the evening. So when the financial controllers became more influential in Fleet Street management in the 1970s, foreign expenditure was slashed to the bone. The process was encouraged by the sale of the *Sun* in 1969 to Rupert Murdoch, who has never believed that foreign news contributes usefully to the mix of a tabloid newspaper.

The populars felt an obligation to provide a basic news service, but had also long vied with one another in the murky areas of sensation and revelation. Sensationalism, as a rule, is less expensive than foreign news and more immediately effective in increasing circulation. With the cuts in serious news coverage, competition for scoops on racier matters became more acute. Despite the Press Council's disapproval, tactics grew rougher and the old inhibitions were breached. The book *Fleet Street* shows that, in 1966, discretion was very much part of the journalist's stock-in-trade. It contains several anecdotes about reporters heroically refraining from publishing stories when they were persuaded that to do so would be against the national interest. Some of these incidents involved the royal family, which, from the 1960s on, has been the victim of numerous true, half-true and untrue 'revelations'. Louis Wulff, the former court correspondent of the Press Association, wrote:

> When a specialist uncovers a story, or part of a story, which official-dom does not want published at that time or in that form, the most effective (and honest) procedure is not to issue a denial. It is to take the press into official confidence, preferably before the specialist concerned has had time to make his final formal inquiry. If all the press is told all the story at the same time, and asked not to publish it before a certain date, it is rare for such an embargo to be broken.

Today there would be no such self-sacrificing regard for the niceties. The procedure would be to print the story first and ask questions afterwards. The incident in April 1989, when someone tried to sell the *Sun* some personal letters stolen from Princess Anne, contrasts with the article in the book by Arthur Tietjen of the *Daily Mail*, about the Welsh gold ring, which happened more than forty years earlier.

In 1947, shortly before the wedding of Princess (now Queen) Elizabeth and Prince Philip, Tietjen acquired four letters concerning the offer of a Welsh gold ring to the bride. Tietjen did some research on the man who had made the offer and found he had been 'associated with questionable companies'. The *Mail* decided not to print the story but to warn Buckingham Palace instead. Not a word appeared in the paper.

In 1989 the *Sun* (which some months earlier had apologised to the Queen for publishing one of her family photographs without permission) congratulated itself on giving Princess Anne's letters back to the palace and not revealing who had signed them. It trumpeted its rectitude in a front-page story and the identity of the letter-writer was revealed in another tabloid a few days later.

The cosy relationship between the press and officials that prevailed in the 1960s was embodied in the Parliamentary Lobby system and the subsidiary lobbies by which specialist correspondents conduct their relations with government departments. Stuart Robert de la Motihière of Agence France Presse disclosed in the book details of the groups of 'trusty' diplomatic correspondents who go every day to the Foreign Office to be briefed by a member of the News Department. Geoffrey Wakeford of the *Daily Mail* wrote a contribution called 'Parliamentary Men' (although even then there were one or two women in the Westminster press gallery). Loyally, he did not disclose the existence of the then less widely known 'secret' political lobby briefings, but did write:

> A code of conduct enforced by the Lobby itself governs the generally pleasant business and social relationship between the House, its Members and officers and some fifty or sixty full-time Political Correspondents, as Lobby men are usually known to their readers. This relationship owes much to the mutual tolerance with which the facilities provided are controlled by the House authorities and exercised by the journalists.

Even then, there were those who thought the system Wakeford described was too cosy by half.

*   *   *

Fleet Street appeared just before Lord Thomson acquired *The Times*. He had already owned the *Sunday Times* for seven years and the *Scotsman* for thirteen. He had earned his peerage, but did not hide the fact that he wanted to possess a national daily paper. His article in the book was a thinly veiled – indeed not really veiled at all – appeal to the Government to ease its restrictions on bulk ownership of newspapers by tycoons such as himself. He described the Monopolies and Mergers Act as 'misconceived' in its aim of restricting further acquisitions of newspapers by groups already owning papers commanding an aggregate circulation of 500,000 copies: 'No one is more aware than myself of the hostility in some quarters to large press groups, but I am equally well aware that it was only the strength, expertise and financial resources of our group that kept alive several important and now prospering regional papers that otherwise would have gone to the wall as so many others have done in the recent past.' If I'm prepared to take on the dross, he was arguing, can it be fair to deny me the gold?

There was a guarded contribution from the Hon. Gavin Astor who, if he guessed he was in his final months as the proprietor of *The Times*, did not let on. Most of his essay was a potted history of the newspaper, from its foundation in 1785 by John Walter as the *Daily Universal Register*. Astor stressed that the paper was not, as some believed, controlled by a trust: in retrospect, the implication of that was that he was free to dispose of it if he liked, subject to the approval of a five-man committee of the great and good that had been established in 1922 after the death of the previous owner, Lord Northcliffe, to prevent its falling into such unsuitable hands again. Indeed, Astor had already been engaged in exploratory talks with the *Guardian*, the *Observer* and the *Financial Times* about possible link-ups.

In May 1966 the paper, edited by Sir William Haley, made its last bid for viability under independent ownership by bringing its appearance into the mid-twentieth century, putting news instead of classified advertisements on the front page, introducing an intellectual gossip column and allowing staff correspondents to be identified by name. The changes succeeded in generating a modest increase in circulation to around 290,000, but they cost money that was not readily available from Astor's resources. In the final sentence of his article he left his options open: 'The aims of the proprietors are still to maintain the highest standards of integrity and journalism, printing and technical excellence, and to ensure the continuance of *The Times* as it has evolved over the years as an objective, professional organ of the press, respected for its integrity, free from all bias and growing in pre-eminence as a national institution.'

That word 'still' had an ominous resonance: he pointedly did not say that his aims as chief proprietor included maintaining his own proprietorship.

Thomson had let Astor know of his interest in the paper in February 1965 but negotiations did not begin in earnest until September 1966, when other available options had been investigated and rejected. Despite the Canadian's pleas in the *Fleet Street* book, the Government insisted that his bid must be referred to the Monopolies and Mergers Commission, who approved it on condition that Thomson promised to play no direct role in running the paper. The committee of five moral watchdogs were replaced by four independent 'national directors' on the board, chiefly to ensure the editor's independence from the dictates of an alien proprietor.

Those who insisted on such safeguards were, without wholly appreciating it, introducing a new – and, as it turned out, short-lived – principle into the British press, that of an editor's right to dictate the policy of a newspaper even against the wishes of the proprietor. The concept of freedom of the press had until then meant freedom from statutory control by the authorities. Now here were these very authorities intervening to prevent a proprietor from influencing the editorial line of a newspaper that he owned, and no voice was raised to question their right to take such high-handed action.

As it happened, the safeguard was superfluous in respect of Lord Thomson, a self-effacing man and the only important newspaper proprietor in recent years genuinely willing to let his editors follow their own inclinations. On the rare occasions that he did make his views known to them, or to his editor-in-chief Denis Hamilton, there was no sense of handing down instructions about the editorial line. (When Rupert Murdoch bought *The Times* fifteen years later he was made to give similar undertakings to Thomson's, but showed how meaningless and unenforceable they were when he dismissed Harold Evans as editor a year later.)

Despite these humiliating conditions imposed on his purchase of *The Times*, Thomson thought the deal 'the summit of a lifetime's work'. And despite establishment doubts about his credentials, the prospects for British serious journalism seemed secure enough. The country's most renowned paper – if still one of its least read – had been acquired by a multi-national group with tremendous resources and a willingness to invest long-term in boosting circulation. It seemed that if anybody could break the industrial deadlock and change the antiquated production methods that characterised Fleet Street, Lord Thomson could. It was true that the new owner was not British, but then neither was he mad,

May 1966: *The Times* brings its appearance into the mid-twentieth century, putting news instead of classified advertisements on the front page. The first story in the new-look paper, announcing that London would be the new NATO headquarters, turned out to be untrue.

as Lord Northcliffe had been, nor possessed of political ambition, like Lord Beaverbrook.

Denis Hamilton, the editor of the *Sunday Times*, was appointed editor-in-chief of the two sister papers. As editor of *The Times* Hamilton appointed William Rees-Mogg, a senior *Sunday Times* editor who, even at thirty-eight, adopted an appropriately donnish mien. He set himself a target of increasing circulation by 50,000 a year, which would have meant that by 1970 it would have reached half a million – a figure which, by general agreement, represented the approximate break-even point. Rees-Mogg proved an energetic innovator: one of his first introductions was a separate, self-contained section for business, emulating a formula that had worked well on the *Sunday Times*. The paper's policy remained securely Conservative (Rees-Mogg had once stood as a Conservative candidate), broadly espousing the progressive, Heathian wing of the party.

Rees-Mogg made one of the several attempts in the 1960s, none really successful, to transfer part of the *Sunday Times* Insight formula to a daily paper. Like Insight, *The Times* News Team was instituted to plug a gap in the paper's coverage. Insight had been created chiefly as a means of solving a problem more acute on Sunday than on daily papers: the lack of much hard news at the weekend and the need to provide a format for making sense of current issues within the framework of the past week, or even longer. The problem at *The Times* was more basic: there was scarcely any coherent coverage of major news stories in the manner that had become standard on other papers during the previous decades.

Times writers believed that their special quality lay in judicious weighing-up and assessment of events – 'pipe-sucking', as the process was characterised by its detractors. They did not ignore the facts that made up these events but they felt no obligation to ferret out every last detail before their competitors did, or to write them up in colourful, dramatic prose. Although *The Times* had made its reputation in the nineteenth century by being first with significant news from distant parts, as well as with revelations from Westminster, this was not, in the view of many of its staff, what their great newspaper should concern itself with in the 1960s.

(I had personal experience of this when, as a reporter for the *Sun*, I was in Rawalpindi, covering a short and localised skirmish between India and Pakistan in 1965. *The Times* was the only major national paper unrepresented for several days until their North of England correspondent showed up. He had, he believed, been chosen for the assignment because of his service in the Territorial Army, but by the time the decision to send him was taken, international flights into Pakistan had been suspended. He had therefore undertaken part of the journey by sea.)

'*The Times* didn't value news very highly,' recalls someone whose career there straddled the Astor and Thomson ownerships. Hamilton thought this the paper's most serious weakness and pressed this view on Rees-Mogg, by instinct a pipe-sucker himself, a thinker rather than a doer. To cure the failing, Rees-Mogg lured Michael Cudlipp (Hugh Cudlipp's nephew) from the *Sunday Times* news desk, to become joint managing editor with special responsibility for news. But Cudlipp found it hard to exert much influence on long-serving *Times* journalists.

There was tension between the old *Times* people and the relatively few journalists who had been brought from the *Sunday Times* or from other papers. Many *Times* writers were averse to change. They were convinced of the intrinsic value of the work they had been doing and frankly suspicious of the young men – especially Cudlipp – who were telling them that from now on they would have to do it differently. Some foreign correspondents, in particular, resented being telephoned late at night with requests for hard news stories, often about hurricanes, crashes and other disasters that required merely factual reporting, with none of the thoughtful analysis that was their forte.

The notion of the News Team arose from the 1966 Aberfan disaster, where 144 people, mostly children, died when a slag heap engulfed a Welsh village school. While other newspapers sent teams of their best writers and photographers there, some in chartered planes, *The Times* relied on its South Wales correspondent, Julian Mounter, who happened to be suffering from flu. The coverage was the worst of any paper, because Mounter could not possibly cover all the aspects himself. Most of the front page was taken up with a stilted description of the disaster, which showed signs of being heavily edited. Eyewitness reports were taken from news agencies. The news editor had not brought greater resources into play because there was no tradition in *The Times* of the exhaustive and emotional reports of tragedies that by then were commonplace in its rivals.

Cudlipp believed that it was time to introduce such practices but recognised that the political structure of the paper prevented him from making any impact on the existing news desk operation without risking dissent. He therefore created a flying squad of six reporters, operating independently of the news desk, who could be assigned as shock troops in teams of varying numbers to give big stories the big coverage they needed.

Disasters were high on their agenda. When trains or planes crashed, the News Team would amaze their colleagues by leaping on to aeroplanes and hurrying to the spot. They excited the envy of other staff by being given their own News Team car, a Morris Oxford. They also aroused distinct irritation, especially when they moved into someone else's cherished patch. In 1968 four of them flew to Paris in a chartered plane to help Charles Hargrove, the resident correspondent, cover the Sorbonne riots. He made it clear as soon as they arrived that he did not, in his judgment, require any help. He banished them to a room away from his office and left them to do first-hand reports on sit-ins and street troubles while he concentrated on the political ramifications. Neither he nor the News Team felt able to consult each other or co-ordinate their coverage.

Because the flow of stories requiring their attention was not constant, the News Team kept themselves busy with background reports on contemporary subjects such as pirate radio stations, which again was not the kind of topic that traditional *Times* reporters had much appetite for. This was the sort of ground that the *Sunday Times* Insight team was covering, although the News Team never regarded itself primarily as an investigative unit.

The one piece of original investigation that *The Times* did undertake during this period involved it in a great deal of controversy but was not the work of the News Team at all. It arose by chance from an article that Gary Lloyd, a former News Team reporter, wrote advising readers how to protect their houses from burglary. He had taken expert advice on the question from a former professional burglar. A few months later the informant telephoned Lloyd and told him that a young friend was being pressurised by the police, who were demanding money. Lloyd and Julian Mounter carried out an investigation that included the use of a secret tape recorder, authorised by Michael Cudlipp. When Rees-Mogg heard about the story he asked: 'Do you mean that *The Times* should be running a lot of words about a corrupt detective-sergeant or two? Shouldn't we leave that to the *Sunday Times* or the *News of the World?*'

He agreed to publication after hearing the tapes. 'London Policemen in Bribe Allegations' was the main front-page headline in the issue of Saturday, 29 November 1969, above a story that began: 'Disturbing evidence of bribery and corruption among certain London detectives was handed by *The Times* to Scotland Yard last night. We have, we believe, proved that at least three detectives are taking large sums of money in exchange for dropping charges, for being lenient with evidence offered in court and for allowing a criminal to work unhindered.'

After a long enquiry and eventual trial, two policemen were convicted. The judge, Justice Sebag Shaw, instructed the jury: 'You have not got to decide whether the matters which have emerged in this trial would have been better investigated in New Scotland Yard and not in Printing House Square.' After the verdict, explaining why he had allowed the tapes as evidence, he commented: 'I was impressed by the manifest truthfulness and reliability of the two reporters on the staff of *The Times* who arranged for the recordings to be made and for their subsequent safe custody.'

Yet many old-style readers and staff members agreed with Rees-Mogg's original instinct that this was not a proper story for their paper to be handling. It seemed to them almost subversive that the newspaper of the establishment should be engaged in subterfuge aimed at discrediting authority – behaviour surely more appropriate to an organ of the far left. Evidence of the disquiet surfaced on 2 December, just three days after the exposé, in one of the most remarkable front-page stories ever to appear in *The Times*. It was written by David Wood, the political editor, a stalwart of the pre-Thomson *Times* and a guardian of the values it represented, who had clearly been greatly disturbed by this evidence that his beloved paper was moving into new and, to him, unwelcome areas of journalism. Under the headline 'Tory Chiefs Fear Trial by Press', his report began:

Deep disquiet was expressed by leading members of the Shadow Cabinet when Mr Heath presided last night at the Commons over a discussion that turned upon the allegations of bribery and corruption made by *The Times* on Saturday against detectives of the Metropolitan Police. I understand that there was a general feeling in the Shadow Cabinet that *The Times* report represented a serious portent in two quite different respects. First, it was considered deeply disturbing that to trial by television . . . there might now be added trial by newspaper, with *The Times* leading the way. This was thought to be a development that editors of newspapers should carefully contemplate before they went any further. Secondly, it was agreed that *The Times* appeared to have put the printing of allegations against the police above the public interest.

This was the authentic voice of Wood – who had excellent contacts in the Conservative Party – and of the old guard at Printing House Square. The message was that, having discovered that something scandalous was going on, *The Times* should not have let the information

51

pass into the hands of the general populace, where it might provoke resentment and disaffection against 'the public interest'. The establishment was closing ranks in an attempt to make Rees-Mogg and Hamilton reconsider the direction in which Michael Cudlipp (who never managed to forge a fruitful relationship with Wood) and his eager young newshounds were taking the paper. Rees-Mogg defended himself and his reporters adroitly, but he was sensitive to the criticism and no similar adventures in this brand of reporting were undertaken during his fourteen-year editorship.

What was coming to be dubbed 'investigative journalism', although much admired by younger members of the profession, was not universally welcomed elsewhere, as that incident made clear. In the late 1960s Britain was coming to the end of one of its comparatively infrequent periods of Labour government. It was bad enough for the Conservatives and their natural allies to be out of power for the first time since 1951 – a setback they attributed in part to the intrusiveness of the press in reporting the Profumo affair. It was even worse that sections of the press were now taking it upon themselves to question the motives and actions of big business, the police, politicians and other pillars of society. For them, investigative journalists were dangerous radicals. It was understandable – just – that they should be nurtured by Denis Hamilton's raffish, slightly unsound *Sunday Times*, but not by the hitherto sturdy *Times*. This was taking permissiveness too far.

Most editors would have ignored such criticism as being a predictable response to change: people like their newspapers to be comfortably familiar, like a faithful family dog. Yet Rees-Mogg, despite his declared commitment to the half-million circulation target, felt some sympathy for the internal critics. He was far from being the kind of editor who thinks it benefits people to have shocks administered to their complacency on a regular basis. His own instinct, like that of the staff he had inherited, was to seek to preserve time-honoured values. Although he was one of the newcomers, his conservative inclinations led him increasingly to identify with the old hands. The result was that the revolution he was supposed to be leading was seldom more than a half-hearted affair.

That was why he was especially hurt when, some three years into his editorship, a group of thirty senior journalists – dubbed the White Swan group after the pub where their leaders had met – drew up a petition calling for the restoration of *The Times*'s traditional values and authority, its calmer way of doing things. By then the circulation had gone up to nearly 450,000 but the petitioners were concerned that this had been achieved through a serious drop in standards.

It had in fact been achieved largely by a promotional campaign that was becoming too costly to sustain. Although Rees-Mogg was angry at what he came to regard as the White Swan conspiracy, the combination of that evidence of staff unrest with the paper's economic difficulties provided an insuperable argument for modifying the strategy, ending the drive for continued circulation growth and concentrating on producing a high-quality paper for the elite. Symbolising this switch, the News Team was disbanded, although by now the paper's main news desk, under a former News Team leader Colin Webb, bore a greater resemblance to that of its contemporaries. It would take another decade and a further change of owner and editor before *The Times* would shake off the last traces of its elitism – and in doing so, some even then believed, sacrifice its individuality and charm.

*   *   *

In 1966 the tabloid press, as defined by its page size, amounted to only two daily papers, the *Daily Mirror* and the *Daily Sketch*. The mid-market *Daily Mail* and *Daily Express* were still broadsheets and the *Sun* was neither one thing nor the other, a size somewhere between the two. As a group, the five titles constituted the popular daily press. Overall, their prospects looked healthy. The *Sun* and *Sketch* were struggling but the rest prospered.

The atmosphere at the *Mirror* group's headquarters in High Holborn, in the words of a senior executive, was one of 'effortless superiority', inspired by the total self-confidence of Hugh Cudlipp. With the exception of the *Sun*, which Cudlipp did his best to ignore, the papers in the group were bounding ahead, especially the flagship daily itself, which had no real opposition at the bottom end of the tabloid market. Associated Newspapers' *Daily Sketch* was slickly produced but, compared with the *Mirror*, it had a demure quality, lacking a powerful, pulsating heart. It made no appeal even to those put off by the *Mirror*'s growing earnestness, and it never managed to take its circulation into seven figures for long. This persuaded Cudlipp to inch the *Mirror* up-market with Mirrorscope and the Inside Page.

Cudlipp and King were not blind to the danger that somebody would try to slip in below the *Mirror* with a less serious tabloid with more flair and conviction than the *Sketch*. They discussed starting one themselves as a pre-emptive strike – the tactic Northcliffe would employ when he established rivals to his own magazines to dissuade other publishers from doing so. If the *Mirror*'s readers did begin to desert, it would make commercial sense to keep them within the group. In the end they decided that this would be a defeatist tactic and there was simply no need for the mighty *Mirror* to resort to it.

King, in particular, was convinced that the future belonged to the mighty, that as powerful papers grew bigger they would squeeze their weaker rivals out of existence. He predicted that before the end of the century there would be only two or, at the most, three national daily papers: the *Mirror* in the mass market, one serious broadsheet and possibly one middle market title. (Lord Thomson, in a speech in the House of Lords in 1967, was a bit more optimistic: he said maybe four papers could survive. But he did not think closures were necessarily a bad thing if they made the remaining papers more efficient and profitable, pointing to the United States, where most people had a choice of two morning papers at the most.)

Hugh Cudlipp's contribution to the *Fleet Street* anthology reflected the *Mirror* stable's tremendous confidence. The ailing *Sun* was not mentioned in it at all. Cudlipp wrote instead a glowing – some might say fawning – eight-page tribute to Cecil King. For instance: 'Gaiety isn't everything: the *Mirror* would not be the world's most notable popular newspaper if there were not a lot more to it than that. It is King's *thinking* that has particularly benefited the *Mirror* as a newspaper. He strives to make sure that his newspapers talk sense, durable sense.'

Less than two years later Cudlipp was one of the *Mirror* directors who conspired to oust King from the chairmanship. Although he recognised that, as a paid executive rather than a proprietor, he was ultimately vulnerable, King's hurt and shock have been recorded in his diaries. It was probably not a premonition of his own fate that led him to say, in the last of a series of three Granada lectures on popular communication he delivered in 1966: 'As for those of us who run successful papers, let us take pains to avoid pride. It is as hard to stay on top as it is to get there.'

Fleet Street was a playground for proprietors but never a safe place for mere executives, however thoughtful, however exalted.

4

'Your saviour is here'

There is some very amateur management in Fleet Street. It is a
delicate matter to discuss the management of your opposition, but
what appals me is that some of them don't even seem to realize
their shortcomings, let alone what they should do about it.

Lord Thomson, House of Lords, January 1967

On 16 July 1969 all members of the *Sun*'s staff received a three-page
typewritten statement from the board of the International Publishing
Corporation, its parent company. It said that the board had met the
previous day 'to consider, and finally resolve, the future of *The Sun* daily
newspaper'. It went on:

> The financial and other implications of a number of proposals put
> forward by the newspaper division at the request of the board were
> fully considered. The proposals covered every conceivable arrange-
> ment under which *The Sun* could be continued in its present form as
> a competitive national newspaper. I have to inform you, with great
> regret, that the directors, bearing in mind the tremendous losses
> which have been sustained over a period of eight years, decided that
> IPC is unable to continue publication after the stipulated period which
> expires in January of 1970.

This referred to the undertaking given in 1961 to keep the *Daily
Herald* going for seven years and not to merge it with the *Daily Mirror*.
The guarantee period was extended by two years when the *Herald* was
relaunched as the *Sun* in 1964. The statement disclosed in detail how
much it had cost IPC to fulfil those pledges:

> The average losses of the *Daily Herald* each year from 1962–1964 were
> just under £1,000,000. In the year ending February 1965, when the
> *Sun* was launched, these losses rose to £2,969,000, because of the costs

of the relaunch. In the following year this loss was reduced to £1,826,000. In the year ending February 1967 the loss came down to £1,730,000, but rose again to £1,968,000 in 1968. In the financial year ending February 1969 the loss was £1,270,000.

The forecast loss for the current year shows another increase in loss to £1,997,000. The reasons are: (i) increased operating costs; (ii) a decline in revenue from sales and advertising. The paper has been vastly improved editorially, but the praise of the professionals has not been reflected in public demand. Over the past eight years *The Sun* (formerly the *Daily Herald*) has lost £12,702,000.

Faced with such figures, and given his over-riding commitment to the *Daily Mirror*, it is not surprising that Cudlipp turned down the various survival plans for the *Sun* put to him by his colleagues and others. The Free Communications Group, a briefly prominent left-leaning pressure group aimed at securing journalists' control for newspapers, suggested converting it into a weekly. Robert Edwards, editor of its sister Sunday paper the *People* with its circulation of more than five million, suggested combining the two titles as effectively a seven-day paper, which would mean popularising the *Sun* and aiming it at the *People*'s market. Cudlipp saw this as dangerous competition for his beloved *Daily Mirror*.

Cecil King, had he stayed at the helm, might have closed the *Sun* even earlier. In his 1966 Granada lectures he was already dropping barely concealed hints that he felt the future of the lower-circulation popular press was in jeopardy.

'The *Mirror* and *Express* are so far ahead, and command such a large share of the market, that the others must regard the future with foreboding,' he said, and concluded: 'Some serious newspapers and some popular papers have a difficult commercial future and some titles, alas, may disappear.'

In discussing employment prospects for the staff of the *Sun*, the 16 July statement referred to an approach 'by Mr Robert Maxwell, who has a plan to continue publication of *The Sun* on a more modest commercial basis'. It added that negotiations with Maxwell would begin at once.

*   *   *

Robert Maxwell was a flamboyant but in some respects a mysterious figure. Born Jan Ludvik Hoch in 1923 in Ruthenia – then in Czechoslovakia but now part of the Soviet Union – he left just before World War Two and joined the British army. Later he assumed his English name.

His foothold in publishing was secured at the end of the war, when he was appointed the head of the press regulatory section for the British occupying forces in Berlin. Among his contacts were members of the Springer family, eager to re-establish their pre-war scientific publishing firm. Through them, Maxwell acquired the rights to distribute their publications in Britain, where scientists and scientific libraries had for years been starved of access to the fruits of German research.

By 1951, despite several arguments with his German partners, he was an established businessman and publisher. That was when he set up Pergamon Press, the core company for many of his future enterprises, and bought Simpkin Marshall, a book distribution company, which went bankrupt three years later. But Pergamon thrived and in 1959 the restless Maxwell launched a second, parallel career, in politics, by being adopted as the Labour candidate for north Buckinghamshire. He entered Parliament five years later.

Apart from being the year of his debut as an MP, 1964 saw two other momentous developments in Maxwell's rise. He floated Pergamon on the stock market, giving his own holding a book value of some £10 million. And he made his first attempt to buy a national newspaper. Cecil King, having decided to launch the *Sun*, offered to dispose of the *Mirror* group's interest in the *Daily Herald* title to the trade union movement, which was already the paper's majority shareholder. Maxwell produced a plan by which the Trades Union Congress would keep majority control of the paper and he would publish it for them at a site away from high-cost central London. The unions were not interested, the *Herald* vanished and the TUC forfeited its interest in the national daily press.

For the next four years Maxwell sought ways of becoming the proprietor of a paper committed to the Labour Party. When the Co-operative movement's *Sunday Citizen* (formerly *Reynolds News*) closed in 1967 he was again hovering around the death-bed to examine the feasibility of effecting a miraculous resurrection. The following year he made his first attempt to buy into a mass-circulation paper when he made a takeover bid for the *News of the World*, the racy Sunday paper that sold more than six million copies every week and had been selling a phenomenal eight million twenty years earlier.

The paper had been owned for generations by the Carr family, but in 1968 one of its members put his shares on the market, representing a quarter of the equity. Maxwell offered 37s. 6d. a share for them – 9s. 6d. more than the then listed price. His move terrified the Carr family and the paper's editor, Stafford Somerfield, who wrote a leading article attacking Maxwell on the grounds that he was a foreigner, whereas the *News of the World* was 'as British as roast beef and Yorkshire pudding'. He feared, too, that Maxwell would turn the Conservative paper into a mouthpiece for the Labour Party, although Maxwell had promised to give up his seat in Parliament if he won control.

To defend his family's interests against the bid, Sir William Carr brought in Rupert Murdoch, a young Australian newspaper proprietor then little known in Britain but keen to establish a base there. Murdoch came in as a 'white knight'. The idea – the Carrs' idea, at least – was that, having bought enough shares to prevent Maxwell taking control, Murdoch would run the business in effect in partnership with the Carrs. When the news of his involvement broke, Somerfield was telephoned by a friend on another paper who told him: 'Your saviour is here.' Murdoch and Carr did a deal under which Murdoch would shore up the company in return for a 40 per cent holding in it. Although many commentators agreed with Maxwell that the deal seemed to violate the rules of the City Takeover Panel, it was allowed to go ahead. The dispute began two decades of rivalry between the Australian and the Czech, with Murdoch, as on this occasion, usually emerging victorious.

*   *   *

Rupert Murdoch, at the age of thirty-seven, had already been a newspaper and television proprietor for fifteen years when he came to London to buy the *News of the World*. His father, Sir Keith Murdoch, had been managing director of the Melbourne *Herald* group and one of the most respected newspapermen in Australia until his death in 1953. But he was the outright owner of only two small newspaper groups, one in Brisbane and one in Adelaide. The Brisbane papers were sold for death duties so Rupert, who had graduated from Oxford and then worked briefly as a sub-editor on the *Daily Express* in London, went to Adelaide to take over what remained of the family business.

During his time in Britain he had come to accept the conventional Fleet Street wisdom that Hugh Cudlipp's and Cecil King's *Daily Mirror* represented the epitome of popular tabloid journalism. He tried to absorb some of its style and spirit into the *News*, his Adelaide daily paper, although its readership profile had more in common with the British middle market represented by the *Daily Mail* and *Daily Herald*. Murdoch particularly admired the *Mirror*'s radical campaigning zest and he deployed it in Adelaide in defence of Rupert Max Stuart, an aborigine convicted – wrongly as Murdoch thought – of murder. The campaign raised his paper's profile in South Australia but provoked the enmity of many of the state's most influential figures, some of whom withdrew their advertising.

It was almost the last populist liberal campaign of this nature conducted in any of Murdoch's papers. He appears to have drawn from the experience the moral that, however much credit such activities gained him among the progressive left, there was little profit in them. Originally a socialist, a member of the Labour Club at Oxford, Murdoch's views swung to the right as he established himself as a newspaper proprietor, and his papers' support was generally given to those politicians he thought could create the most suitable economic and social climate for his enterprises to flourish.

For the first few years he was content to remain in Adelaide and learn his business, although he did make a cheeky and unsuccessful attempt to take over the rival – and larger – newspaper group in the city. In 1956 he made his first, modest, out-of-state acquisition when he bought the *Sunday Times* in Perth, Western Australia. Two years later came his entry into television when he gained control of an Adelaide station. Then, in 1960, he moved into the big time nationally – and into the kind of tabloid wars he would come to relish – when he bought the Sydney *Mirror* from the Fairfax group. The Fairfaxes were the city's most powerful newspaper family: they owned the redoubtable *Sydney Morning Herald* and the evening tabloid the *Sun* – then more successful than the rival *Mirror*, which they had acquired from its previous owner chiefly to prevent their great competitor, Sir Frank Packer, from controlling it. After some disagreement within the board, Fairfax agreed to sell the *Mirror* to the ambitious Murdoch, some directors believing that, since·he was bound to fail with it, any long-term threat he might pose to the Fairfax empire would be neutralised. Throughout his career, Murdoch has repeatedly been underrated by his opponents.

Two years later Murdoch became the dominant tabloid proprietor in Sydney when he bought the *Daily Telegraph* and *Sunday Telegraph* from the Packers. This ensured him full economic use of his Sydney presses and, for the first time, made him an influential figure in national politics. Still restless, in 1964 he launched Australia's first national daily paper, the *Australian*, in Canberra. By 1969 it had made him no money but he was determined to stick with it. By now he also had a television station in the Sydney area and Australia was beginning to feel too small for him.

London, where he had already worked in his youth, was the natural place to seek expansion. Despite a reputation for impetuousness, he thinks in the long term, and he had been quietly accumulating a holding of shares in the *Mirror* group, against the day when it might become vulnerable to a takeover. At the same time he had asked his friend, the banker Lord Catto, to look out for other possible British acquisitions. It was Lord Catto who had given him the original tip-off about the *News of the World*.

*   *   *

The announcement of the *Sun*'s imminent demise came six months after Murdoch's defeat of Maxwell over the *News of the World*. Maxwell had taken the rebuff badly and nobody was at all surprised when, even before the formal announcement of the *Sun*'s closure, he expressed interest in acquiring the ailing paper from IPC and so fulfilling his ambition to own a journal that supported Labour. He would aim for a low circulation of about half a million which could, he calculated, be viable if overheads were pared. The paper would therefore operate with a staff of less than half its former strength and be printed overnight on the presses that produced the *Evening Standard* by day. Cudlipp, anxious to assuage his conscience over the closure by ensuring that the paper and some of the jobs would be saved, was prepared to hand over the title and the goodwill to Maxwell for nothing: it seemed clear, after all, that the new paper would not be a rival to his flagship, the *Daily Mirror*.

Maxwell summoned *Sun* journalists to a meeting where he explained his plans and introduced his potential editor, Mike Randall, the deputy editor of the *Sunday Times* and a former editor of the *Daily Mail*. Randall stressed that he had as yet made no formal commitment to Maxwell and the hostile attitude of the journalists, who doubted the feasibility of the scheme, must have accentuated his doubts. In fact the journalists' lack of enthusiasm could have been overcome, but what thwarted Maxwell in the end was the opposition of the print unions, who would not agree to a low-cost operation that would certainly be used by other Fleet Street proprietors as a pretext for rationalising their own expensive production arrangements.

Enter Rupert Murdoch. Over at the *News of the World*, Sir William Carr's white knight had quickly turned into a poisoned pawn. Murdoch had lost little time in stripping the Carr family of all power. He had initially given two undertakings: first that he would not seek to increase his 40 per cent holding and secondly that a member of the Carr family should remain as Chairman. Less than three weeks after shareholders had approved his rescue scheme, he wrote to Carr saying he was going to buy more shares. Six months later Sir William, under pressure, resigned as chairman and Murdoch took over.

Murdoch pays no heed to conventional theories of business prudence, whereby one acquisition has to be 'digested' before another can be considered. In cricketing terms, he is not the kind of batsman who needs to play himself in. After his successful boundary hit with the *News of the World*, he sought to give the next ball comparably rough treatment. Murdoch's plan for the *Sun* was more ambitious than Maxwell's. He would turn it into an uncomplicated tabloid, competing with the *Daily Mirror*, printing on the *News of the World* presses in Bouverie Street, which hitherto had been idle for six out of seven nights a week.

It was quickly clear that his offer commended itself to the unions much more than Maxwell's. Murdoch was proposing a paper published in Fleet Street on traditional Fleet Street lines – with all the feather-bedding and restrictive practices that implied. He would need something approaching the existing number of staff to run it. It was true that Murdoch did not have Maxwell's Labour Party credentials, but at least he was not going to upset the industrial status quo.

A few of Cudlipp's colleagues warned him against selling to Murdoch – just as some of the Fairfax board had been averse to selling him the Sydney *Mirror* – but Cudlipp felt he had little option. He could not simply let the paper die and if he disposed of it against the unions' preference he laid himself open to retaliatory action at the *Mirror*, which could quickly cripple the company. So he agreed to sell Murdoch the title for a paltry £800,000, paid by instalments. And Cudlipp commented, in one of the many hostages to fortune he has offered up in a controversial career: 'This is obviously the end of Mr Maxwell's dream of being the proprietor of a national newspaper.'

*   *   *

Murdoch had clear ideas about the sort of paper he wanted the *Sun* to become. He is a hands-on proprietor and his experience with the Sydney *Mirror* and *Telegraph* had convinced him that he knew as well as anyone how to run brash tabloids: he would often irritate editors by rewriting headlines or suggesting a new front page layout at the last minute. In a competitive market, where the spoils go to the paper that makes the most impact day after day, he saw no virtue in restraint.

He believed, too, in giving readers what they wanted, and judged what they wanted by the papers they bought. Thus he was by temperament opposed to the kind of intellectual uplift that Cudlipp and King were seeking to infiltrate into their *Daily Mirror* in London. The idea of journalism as a social service was alien to him. He simply did not believe that many tabloid readers were interested in analyses of foreign and economic matters; even if you thought that to improve the national level of awareness was a proper role for a tabloid, he considered such articles were unlikely to have the desired effect because they simply would not be read. When an interviewer for the *Sunday Times*, talking to him about his plans for the *Sun*, asked what he thought of the Mirrorscope feature, he plucked it from the day's *Mirror*, held it at arm's length and silently let it drop to the floor.

It is probable, too, that Murdoch's attitude to Cudlipp's *Mirror* was partly shaped by his brief stint on the *Daily Express* in the 1950s. In that era, before journalists began switching from paper to paper almost as a matter of routine, their loyalty expressed itself in the conviction that their own paper was the very best. By extension, therefore, the rival sheets – and those who produced them – were inadequate and incompetent. When Murdoch worked in Fleet Street, the circulation contest between the *Express* and *Mirror* was at its height. No professional journalist could call Cudlipp's *Mirror* incompetent – there was a great deal to be learned from it. Yet the competitive atmosphere could not but colour the attitude of an enthusiastic newsman in his early twenties, leading him to question the reputation of the rival paper's mastermind.

In 1969, while he recognised the *Mirror* as the pace-setting tabloid, Murdoch knew from his Australian experience that Cudlipp and King were not infallible. In 1949 the *Mirror* group had bought the *Argus* in Melbourne, seeing it as a possible foundation of an Australian chain. But the journalistic mix was never right. The paper lost money consistently under the *Mirror* ownership and was eventually closed. In an interview in the *Guardian* in 1968, during his fight for the *News of the World*, Murdoch had told Terry Coleman: 'Coming here, you begin to think – is Cudlipp all that damned good? You know, they all think he's God . . . Maybe one could mix it over here.'

To lead his editorial team to the *Sun* he hired two men who had worked for the *Daily Mirror* but had left because they felt that their talents had been insufficiently recognised by Cudlipp. Larry Lamb, from the *Daily Mail*, was editor and Bernard Shrimsley from the *Liverpool Daily Post* his deputy. They shared Murdoch's views about tabloid journalism in general and the *Mirror* in particular. As tabloid traditionalists, they saw great virtue in the daily pin-up to excite hot-blooded male readers and Lamb saw no reason why, in the permissive 1960s, the model should keep her breasts covered. There were topless pictures from the beginning, although they did not become a regular daily fixture on page three until some time later.

The value of the page three girl was not simply that it attracted many readers but, equally important, it got the paper talked about. Murdoch set great store by promotion. An important reason why the *Sun*'s circulation took off so quickly – it nearly doubled, reaching 1.6 million in its first year – was that Murdoch was willing to invest heavily in television advertising, which had been used sparingly by its competitors until then. The *Sun*'s commercials were pacy and racy, reflecting the paper's own style. Although the effect of promotion campaigns is notoriously short-term – many of the new readers stop buying the paper once the campaign is over – some stayed each time, and the circulation climbed steadily.

In a typical gesture, Cudlipp threw a party on the night of 17 November 1969, to mark the first issue of the Murdoch *Sun*. (He has always denied the highly coloured recollection of some guests that the table decorations included dead sunflowers.) When copies of the first issue arrived at the *Mirror* building in High Holborn, Cudlipp glanced at it quickly and told Lee Howard, the *Mirror* editor: 'Lee, we've got nothing to worry about.' Yet soon the *Mirror* was forced to drop its improving features such as Mirrorscope, and even flirted briefly with topless pin-ups. Howard did not last much longer. By 1973 the *Mirror* was beginning to lose money and Cudlipp stepped down as chairman, aged only sixty. In 1977, the circulation of the *Sun* overhauled that of the *Daily Mirror*, which only began to narrow the gap in 1988, when it introduced good run-of-press colour two years earlier than Murdoch could.

Larry Lamb's *Sun*, although chirpy and outspoken, was less shrill, less harsh than the paper that has developed since Kelvin MacKenzie became editor in 1981. Between the stories about royalty and entertainment personalities, the *Sun* of the 1970s found space for adequate – in tabloid terms – coverage of political and other serious news. It supported Labour in the 1970 election, mainly because Murdoch, in the early months of his proprietorship, wanted to keep as many of the old *Sun* readers as he could. By 1974, with circulation climbing healthily, he could afford to follow his instincts and switch to the Conservatives, although it was not until Margaret Thatcher became Prime Minister in 1979 that the paper developed the strident devotion to the Tory cause that became its hallmark in the 1980s.

One reason for this sharper political direction was the engagement in 1979 of Ron Spark as the chief leader-writer. Spark, an Oxford history graduate, is a Fleet Street veteran who had spent most of his life with the *Express* group, mainly on the *Sunday Express*, writing leaders and the Crossbencher political column. There he had developed a talent for political invective on behalf of the right-wing causes dear to the heart of the proprietor, Lord Beaverbrook, and, after Beaverbrook's death in

1964, of the sprightly John Junor, the Sunday paper's long-serving editor. After falling out with Junor he was hired by Murdoch to give an edge to the *Sun*'s leader-writing in the run-up to that year's general election.

During the Falklands War in 1982, Spark's leaders augmented the impassioned support for the British cause in the news columns, most famously exemplified by the front-page headline 'Gotcha' over the story on 4 May about the sinking of the Argentinian battleship *Belgrano*, with heavy loss of life. When Peter Snow, on the BBC2 programme *Newsnight*, sought to be even-handed in weighing up the claims made by the British and Argentinian publicity machines, he was denounced by the *Sun* on 7 May as a 'traitor', in its most vehement editorial of the war: 'What is it but treason to talk on TV, as Peter Snow talked, questioning whether the Government version of the sea battles was to be believed? We are caught up in a shooting war, not a game of croquet. There are no neutral referees above the sound of the guns. A British citizen is either on his country's side – or he is its enemy.'

Spark's editorial went on to attack the *Guardian* and *Daily Mirror* for similarly raising questions about the wisdom of the war effort, and ended: 'We are truly sorry for the *Daily Mirror*'s readers. They are buying a newspaper which again and again demonstrates it has no faith in its country and no respect for her people.'

The *Mirror* responded under the heading 'The Harlot of Fleet Street': 'The *Daily Mirror* does not believe that patriotism has to be proved in blood . . . We do not want to report that brave men have died so that the *Sun*'s circulation might flourish.'

Despite the patent absurdity of the *Sun*'s charge against Snow, there was little doubt that it and the great majority of the papers were reflecting, more than the *Guardian*, the patriotic mood that the war had inspired, which swept Thatcher back into power the following year. People who had their doubts about the war, however, wondered how far the Conservative papers were reflecting a mood that they themselves had created: for a tone of strident jingoism mixed with sneering triumphalism had already begun to creep into the tabloid papers – led by the *Sun* – at the end of the 1970s, and it intensified during the 1980s.

*   *   *

It is impossible to define precisely when such trends begin, but a benchmark was the headline 'Hop Off You Frogs' over a story in 1986 about one of Thatcher's periodic disputes with the French over matters relating to the European Community. The editor, Kelvin MacKenzie, clearly

The *Sun*'s famous headline during the Falklands War, 4 May 1982.

'A tone of strident jingoism mixed with sneering triumphalism': an article in the *Sun* in July 1989.

felt that such chauvinism struck a chord in his readers, for the word 'Frog' was used whenever there was a suitable story about Anglo-French rivalry. In the *Sun* of 15 July 1989, the day after the two-hundredth anniversary of Bastille Day, the word was used in three headlines: 'Fury as the Frogs Tear into Maggie' on page two, 'History Lesson for the Frogs' over the lead editorial on page six and 'Frogs Hop in for Harford' as the main headline on the sports page.

For good measure, that day's paper contained a cartoon about the Japanese buying into the British car industry, showing a giant sumo wrestler being introduced to the workers as a new supervisor, while a newspaper in the drawing carried the explanatory headline: 'Japs Get Slice of Rover'. The cartoonist must have been suffering from a rare bout of tolerance because the *Sun* calls the Japanese 'Nips' as often as 'Japs', even when the story is not especially vindictive. 'Nips Are Drips' said a headline in the issue of 1 August 1989, over a story (derived from the previous day's *Daily Telegraph*) about the way Japanese take baths.

When Emperor Hirohito was about to die in September 1988, the headline over the leading article was 'Hell's Waiting for This Truly Evil

Emperor'. It began: 'There are two reasons for sadness as Emperor Hirohito lies on his deathbed. The first is that he lived as long as he did. The second is that he died unpunished for some of the foulest crimes of this violent century ... When he goes, he will surely be guaranteed a special place in Hell.'

The Japanese Foreign Ministry complained, as they had become accustomed to doing about the work of the xenophobic Ron Spark. When I interviewed him for *Tatler* in 1988, Spark insisted that the words 'Frog' and 'Nip' do not appear in his leaders 'unless they're used in a jocular sense'. Even when they are, it is unlikely that the French and the Japanese see the joke. In 1987, in the course of a trade dispute between Britain and Japan, Spark wrote:

> The *Sun* today has an important warning for the trade war lords of Japan: don't make an enemy of our country once again. There are still many British ex-servicemen alive who remember only too well the agony of the prisoner-of-war camps and how their comrades were tortured and murdered by sadistic Japs. Last time we ended our argument with Japanese imperialism in a perfunctory way ... This time the argument will have to be settled a different way. Mrs Thatcher saw off the Argies. She must now see off the Japs.

In our interview Spark, a soft-spoken man whose calm and rational manner belies the ferocity of his writing, explained such outpourings of venom:

> Sometimes you have to remind the Japanese of the past. So much obloquy attaches to the Germans – and quite rightly – but the Japanese, who committed just as dreadful horrors in the Pacific war, we forget. We see them coming into this country with all the money in the world, and we think what great chaps they are. I don't believe in visiting guilt on countries, especially more than forty years after the war, but at the same time they've had an easy ride compared with the Germans. We do get correspondence from former Japanese prisoners-of-war complaining about Japanese cars and television sets, etcetera.

The Spanish committed no comparable wartime crimes against Britain, but they also get the sharp end of Spark's pen, especially when they have the effrontery to inconvenience British people going about their lawful business of flying off for a holiday in the sun. When in

1987 many were impeded in doing so by a strike of Spanish air traffic controllers, Spark wrote: 'If you don't like your job, señor, why don't you quit and take up bull fighting, bird strangling or donkey torturing?'

Not only foreigners are the victims of the *Sun*'s prejudices. Homosexuals are not much liked, either. 'Pulpit Poofs Can Stay' was a front-page headline over a report that the Church of England had decided not to bar homosexual men from the ministry.

Sometimes Ron Spark's invective is deployed to pursue campaigns in which Rupert Murdoch has a direct interest. In January 1986 Murdoch, in a carefully planned overnight manoeuvre that I describe in Chapter 5, moved his four national daily and Sunday papers to Wapping, east of Tower Bridge, and some 6,000 print workers lost their jobs. For more than a year, demonstrations were mounted outside Wapping, and few were neutral on the issue. Sir John Harvey-Jones, the chairman of ICI, said on *Question Time* on BBC Television that it was 'monstrous' to put 6,000 people out of work. For the *Sun* this was unforgivable disloyalty. A scalding editorial said that Sir John 'appears to have gone off his double-barrelled rocker' and concluded viciously: 'Next time you step into the minefield of Wapping make sure your mouth and brain are connected.'

* * *

The Wapping move made it doubly certain that Murdoch would occupy a place in the pantheon of entrepreneurs who have made a significant and lasting impact on the British newspaper industry. He was already a figure of stature in Fleet Street as the publisher of a paper that had, under his ownership, developed from a fragile weakling into the country's best-selling tabloid. And in 1981 he became the most important national newspaper proprietor when he bought the venerable *Times* and the flourishing *Sunday Times* from the Thomson Organisation.

Under Thomson the *Sunday Times*, edited first by Hamilton and then by Harold Evans, had continued to thrive throughout the 1960s and 1970s, setting a standard for innovative investigative journalism in its Insight pages, for creative photo-journalism in its magazine and for increasingly authoritative coverage of books and the arts. *The Times*, however, deliberately forfeited the impetus of the Thomson ownership when, in 1970, Hamilton and William Rees-Mogg decided under pressure to retrench and abandon the target of a half million circulation. Since then it had languished and stagnated. An almost continuous economic squeeze throughout the 1970s meant that scarcely any significant new staff were recruited – people who might have brought the paper the freshness and drive it so lacked.

The paper's losses mounted. Denis Hamilton, in his book *Editor-in-Chief*, puts part of the blame on Rees-Mogg. 'William undoubtedly lacked the sort of drive which would have made *The Times* take off,' he wrote. He is less inclined to blame the management but, to the extent that they failed, along with all other Fleet Street managements, to challenge the unions' control over the newspaper industry and the consequent inflated costs, they also bear a heavy responsibility.

The lack of unity among newspaper proprietors was an important reason for Fleet Street's appalling labour problems. Meetings of the Newspaper Publishers Association (NPA) in the 1960s and 1970s were, according to people who attended them, rancorous and unpleasant occasions. Max Aitken and his colleagues from the *Express* group would constantly be at loggerheads with Lord Rothermere's representatives from the *Mail*; executives from the *Mirror* and *Sun* were similarly quarrelsome. Instead of presenting a united front – which after all was what the NPA was for – they took the opportunity to score points off each other. They would agree to nothing that might benefit their rivals, even if it would benefit them equally.

Thus the unions were increasingly and shamelessly able to use their power to disrupt production to gain ever more concessions from management on pay and conditions. The infamous 'Spanish customs' grew up over the years, involving flagrant over-manning, absurdly restrictive working practices and even the deceit of signing in for work under a false name to collect the pay packet of a non-existent person. As each abuse became institutionalised, there was no way of ending it short of agreeing to another and possibly more expensive concession to the wish of the unions to keep the maximum number of men in work and to extend their earning power. Agreements were made and then unilaterally abrogated by the unions, often at a late stage in the production process, when the management had the choice of agreeing to their workers' demands or losing an edition of the paper. The *Sunday Times*, with only one publication night a week, was especially vulnerable to such blackmail.

The leaders of the 'chapels', the in-house union branches, established their own alternative management structures. In the mid-1970s, Esther Rantzen and a BBC television crew came into the Gray's Inn Road headquarters of *The Times* to make a programme about the diary column. In order to film in the machine room, Miss Rantzen had to get the permission of the chapel. She found the atmosphere tense to the point of unreality. As she was ushered from one office to another to see senior chapel officials, she felt as though she were making a film about the

Mafia, penetrating a time-worn bureaucracy before being allowed into the presence of the Don of Dons. (Permission was finally granted but it came on the night of an industrial dispute, when no paper was produced. The crew had to come back a couple of nights later.)

Roy Thomson was convinced that the only way *The Times* could be made viable was to introduce computerised typesetting, but he was pessimistic about the prospect of achieving it. In a speech to the House of Lords in January 1967 he said:

> The number of men employed in Fleet Street is so large as to have no relation to the amount of work required to be done. This has come about through the years as the result of union demands and proprietor capitulations. If a new piece of equipment is to be installed, before it is accepted – if it is accepted at all – irrespective of how many men are reasonably required, the union demands more, many more; so that no existing jobs can be eliminated and no savings can accrue to the publisher.

He went on to explain why it was usually more sensible to give in to union pressure than to fight: 'When we are confronted with a last-minute demand for more money, however unreasonable it might be, that would cost us perhaps less than £1,000, whereas to miss a single issue of the *Sunday Times* would involve a loss of £150,000, what are we expected to do? It is all right to be a martyr, but one cannot be at that kind of cost.'

One reason why Thomson did not feel able to take decisive action lay in his attitude towards ownership of *The Times*. He felt, uncharacteristically for an otherwise hard-headed entrepreneur, that some kind of sacred trust had been vested in him, that he was in some way privileged by being allowed to pour his personal fortune into sustaining so venerable an institution. Thus the normal rules of profit and loss did not apply. Because a showdown with the unions, quite apart from the short term loss, might put the future of the paper in peril, he shunned it. Although a direct input typesetting system was purchased for Times Newspapers in his lifetime, the unions would not agree terms for its use.

When he died in 1976, control of the group passed to his son Kenneth, who did not share his father's emotional attachment to *The Times*. He wanted to make the unions change their ways. Instead, in pursuit of a pay dispute they stepped up their sabotage of the production of *The Times* and the *Sunday Times* in the first months of 1978. Under pressure

70

from Kenneth Thomson the management of Times Newspapers gave
the unions an ultimatum: unless they agreed terms for the introduction
of new technology and an end to industrial disruption by November
1978, both papers would close and remain closed until agreement was
reached. According to Hamilton, Marmaduke Hussey, chief executive
of Times Newspapers (and later chairman of the BBC Board of Gov-
ernors), had no plan of campaign:

> We thus went to war with the chapels with no estimate of how much
> the war would cost us – no idea that within a year we would be facing
> losses of between £40m and £60m. In fact it was in some ways like
> the start of the first world war, with everyone predicting that it would
> be over by Christmas. Hussey predicted that the shutdown would be
> a short one. 'After a fortnight,' he said, 'the TUC will have been
> brought in, and there'll be pressure on the fathers of the chapels to
> bring them to heel.'

In fact the closure lasted for eleven and a half months. The high costs
mentioned by Hamilton were incurred largely because all the journalists
had been retained on full pay. At the end of it, hardly any progress had
been made in resolving the matters under dispute. The demoralisation
of the management infected the journalists and the papers faltered:
during their year's absence, their rivals had naturally lured away many
of their former readers. There had been a tentative offer before the
closure of a 'gentlemen's agreement' that no other paper would print
extra copies to take advantage of Times Newspapers' misfortune but, in
what some of his colleagues saw as a curious decision, Hussey chose
not to seek any such self-sacrifice.

Before the closure *The Times* and the *Guardian* had been roughly
level-pegging with sales of around 310,000. When *The Times* reap-
peared, the *Guardian* was above 400,000 and remains there to this day.
The Times returned at a high circulation briefly but quickly fell away and
took two more years to get back to its level before the closure. During
the *Sunday Times*'s absence, the *Observer* went up from 700,000 to
1,120,000 but was soon well below a million again. The *Sunday Times*
initially recovered rapidly although it went into a slow decline for a few
years afterwards.

In August 1980, a strike by journalists on *The Times* gave the Thomson
management the excuse they had been seeking to get rid of the troublesome newspapers. From the beginning Gordon Brunton, chief executive
of Thomson Newspapers, was clear who he wanted to buy them.

Although he invited offers from anyone with a serious interest, Murdoch, despite his down-market reputation, was his favoured contender from the time that Hamilton first raised the possibility with him on a flight to Bahrein for a board meeting of Reuters news agency in October 1980 – the same month that Brunton announced that the papers were for sale. At first Murdoch said he was not interested in them, but it soon became apparent that this was only a tactical manoeuvre and that he was waiting to see whether he could pick them up at a knockdown price. They were not as cheap as he had hoped but nor was the final price of £12 million exorbitant.

On 12 February 1981, Murdoch became the owner of *The Times* and the *Sunday Times*. John Biffen, the Trade and Industry Secretary, agreed to waive an enquiry by the Monopolies and Mergers Commission – which had puffed so hard about the Thomson takeover fifteen years earlier – on the grounds that both papers were losing money: a suspect contention in the case of the *Sunday Times*, as Harold Evans maintains in a detailed analysis in his *Good Times, Bad Times*. Murdoch had been adamant that he would pull out of the deal if it was referred to the MMC, with all the delay that would incur. He easily convinced the national directors of *The Times* that his intentions towards the paper were honourable.

At the time, there were two main puzzles about the Murdoch takeover. First, why did he want to buy a company that included a chronically unprofitable daily paper, even one whose losses were partly balanced by the potential profits of the *Sunday Times*? After all, his world-wide holdings – not just newspapers but interests in television and film and even an airline – were already so enormous that Times Newspapers would never be more than a small droplet.

The second question was why Thomson and the Government were so keen to hand over control of the house organ of the establishment to a man with his record. His demonstrated skill was to gain circulation for his tabloids by appealing to readers' lowest common denominator: that did not instantly mark him down as the ideal owner for *The Times*.

The first mystery is easier to solve than the second. Few newspapers come on the market that Murdoch does *not* want to buy. In Australia he had launched a serious broadsheet Sunday paper as long ago as 1964 and his ambition to own a quality paper in Britain had come to the surface in 1976, when he had all but won control of the *Observer* but was thwarted by the opposition of the staff. There was, too, certainly an element, however small, of revenge for the way he and his wife Anna perceived themselves to have been snubbed by London society when they first came to Britain in 1969, especially a drubbing he received from David Frost in a television interview. These effete, snobbish members of a dying class, who had laughed at him and tried to freeze him out, would now have to kowtow to him as the proprietor of their prized house journal.

Finally, although his Wapping coup was still five years away, he must already have sensed that he would at some stage need to act decisively to overcome those very trade union strategies that had brought the two papers to their knees and allowed him the chance of acquiring them. When the showdown came, the more papers he owned the stronger would be his position.

As for the motive of the Thomson board, Denis Hamilton indicates in his memoirs that they, too, were driven to a large extent by the desire to teach the unions a lesson after the years of humiliation that had been imposed on the management. They thought – and in this they proved right – that Murdoch, uniquely among the current crop of newspaper proprietors, had the determination and ruthlessness needed to tackle the unions head on. Gordon Brunton went through a show of inviting other bids: the most credible came from Rothermere's Associated Newspapers, who were keen to have a Sunday paper, but Brunton doubted their commitment to *The Times*. For a while, Brunton indulged the editors of the two papers, Rees-Mogg and Evans, in their ill-starred efforts to build consortia to take over the papers, involving members of their staff. Yet the papers were always Murdoch's for the asking, as Hamilton makes clear in his description of the Bahrein flight, on which he had arranged that he should be seated next to Murdoch:

> He believed, I think, that he was quietly extracting what he could from me. In fact I had known I would be travelling with him and had come prepared, hoping to plant as much of a seed as possible – for my fellow-directors felt that only a strong owner who would be prepared to take savage measures, and of whose determination the unions could have no doubt, had any hope.

The no-contest takeover had all the external appearances of an establishment 'fix' of the kind that Murdoch affects to despise. Conspiracy theorists were convinced that the speed with which it was decided not to refer the sale to the Monopolies and Mergers Commission – although the case for doing so appeared strong – was a recognition of the staunch support given by the Murdoch press to the Thatcher Government. It is also possible that ministers sensed that high noon was approaching in

Fleet Street and, like Brunton, thought Murdoch the man best equipped to aim his six-gun at the unions when it did. Whatever the Government's motive, its haste to endorse the sale contrasted sharply with the reluctance with which a Labour Government had approved the Thomson acquisition fifteen years earlier, although on the face of it Thomson had fewer apparent disqualifications than Murdoch for the role of proprietor of *The Times*.

Biffen denies that any improper or partisan considerations came into play. Under the Fair Trading Act, the decision on whether to waive a reference to the MMC is personal to the Secretary of State. Because it was a subject of public controversy, the Cabinet Office convened a meeting of senior ministers to discuss it. Although conceding that Thatcher was sympathetic to Murdoch's bid, Biffen does not recall any pressure on him to decide in favour of the Australian. Accountants at the Department of Trade and Industry had assured him that both papers were, at that time, making a loss. (Even Evans concedes that in 1980 the *Sunday Times* did no better than break even, but argues that a longer period should have been taken into account.)

His accountants' view meant that Biffen was empowered, but in no way obliged, to waive a reference to the MMC. Given Murdoch's threat to withdraw if the MMC was brought into play – a threat which, after meeting Murdoch, Biffen found credible – the issue was whether the Government would be justified in preventing the Thomson Organisation from selling the papers to the buyer of its choice.

Biffen did not feel he had a right to take account of Murdoch's controversial reputation as a proprietor, but only to consider whether the extent of his newspaper holdings amounted to an undesirable concentration of ownership. Gordon Brunton, managing director of the Thomson organisation, showed officials at the DTI a letter from Hamilton stating that he and the two editors of the papers preferred Murdoch to all other outside bidders, although Evans's first preference was naturally for the consortium that he was establishing.

For Biffen, it was a finely balanced decision but ultimately, given the Thomson threat to close *The Times* if it was not sold by March, and the fact that he could not force Thomson to consider other bids if Murdoch's was blocked, the Secretary of State decided that he did not want to risk going down in history as the man who killed *The Times*.

Hamilton was rewarded for his part in initiating the deal by remaining as chairman of Times Newspapers, although he insisted that his salary was still paid by Thomson, because he did not want to work directly for Murdoch. (Hamilton resigned after less than a year in protest against

Murdoch's ultimately unsuccessful attempt to vary the safeguards built into the sale agreement by transferring the titles of the two papers into the direct ownership of his holding company, News International.)

Murdoch even hired Marmaduke ('Duke') Hussey, who resigned as chief executive of Times Newspapers soon after the debacle of the year-long stoppage but had remained as Hamilton's vice-chairman. One of the tasks Murdoch gave Hussey was to organise the celebration of *The Times*'s bicentenary in 1985: despite his republican pretensions he wanted high-level representation from the royal family, and it had not escaped him that Hussey's wife was a lady-in-waiting to the Queen. Sure enough, the Prince of Wales was persuaded to attend the celebratory banquet at Hampton Court.

*   *   *

The initial changes to *The Times* under Murdoch were attributable more to its new editor than its proprietor. Rees-Mogg had announced some time previously that he would resign as soon as a new owner took over and Murdoch had decided to switch Harold Evans from the Sunday to the daily paper. It was in some respects a puzzling appointment, taken against the advice of people who knew Evans, including Hamilton. Although Evans was acknowledged as the most accomplished broadsheet editor in the country, he was not at all the kind of journalist who excites Murdoch's admiration: far from being ruthless, he worked through instinctive flair and was always changing his decisions. Nor can Murdoch have approved of his politics, for Evans is the epitome of the 1960s liberal – a fact that would prove one of the many causes of subsequent friction between them.

What probably weighed most heavily with Murdoch was the necessity, as he saw it, of prising Evans away from the *Sunday Times*. If he had stayed there as editor, surrounded by the loyal team he had built over the years, it would have been virtually impossible for Murdoch to exercise any control at all over the Sunday paper. Evans would have been an alternative centre of power. Murdoch did not relish the thought of owning an institution that he could not, in any real sense, be said to possess. Moving Evans to *The Times* – an offer he correctly calculated Evans would not be able to refuse – was a solution to both of his immediate problems, for the alternative candidates for *The Times* editorship were members of the paper's existing staff whom he knew only by reputation, and did not admire.

Evans has given his own detailed version of his turbulent year as editor of *The Times* in *Good Times, Bad Times* and I have given an account in *Barefaced Cheek* that naturally differs in emphasis. Although his skittish, clannish and sometimes secretive manner angered many of the existing staff, some of his changes to the paper, making it more accessible and giving it a sharper news sense, have been maintained by his successors. When he left, after a cataclysmic public row with Murdoch, he had lifted sales from around 270,000 to more than 300,000, with scarcely any of the television and billboard promotion that Murdoch pioneered for the *Sun* in the 1970s and which is today regarded as vital for a serious circulation drive by both tabloid and quality newspapers.

Sales of the *Sunday Times* drifted downwards following Evans's departure, under the editorship of his former deputy Frank Giles, seen by almost everyone except himself as a stopgap appointment. In 1983 he was summarily replaced by Andrew Neil, an aggressive Scot cast much more in Murdoch's mould. Neil brought to the position some passionately held political convictions, including a loathing of restrictive practices, that were substantially to the right of those held by most of the existing *Sunday Times* staff. There were clashes and some key people left. Neil was particularly scathing about the Insight team, which he said was politically motivated and had produced no worthwhile investigations for some time. He kept the team going but changed its personnel.

As for *The Times*, the change in its basic nature occurred under the next two editors after Evans, leading to a useful increase in circulation accompanied by what many saw as a decline in its authority. Charles Douglas-Home, who had been Evans's deputy, succeeded him. His task, as he saw it, was first to restore morale after Evans's tumultuous year, then to maintain what he could of the old paper's qualities, while taking account of Murdoch's views on serious journalism. Murdoch, he ascertained, regarded the *Daily Mail* as the perfect quality newspaper, combining an essentially serious approach with techniques derived from the popular tabloids, and with none of the intellectual pretension that, in Murdoch's view, disfigured *The Times*.

Douglas-Home, who had worked for a time on the *Daily Mail*'s main mid-market rival, the *Daily Express*, thought that the best way to take account of this view was to hire key people from the *Mail*. Chief among them was Charles Wilson, an outspoken Scot whose principal foray into quality journalism until then had been as editor of a failed Sunday paper launched in Glasgow a few years earlier. Wilson brought other *Mail* journalists with him and soon the emergence of mid-market news values became apparent. Stories that the old *Times* would have thought trivial began appearing on the front page. Tabloid journalese started to creep into the paper. 'Consumer' stories would be given greater prominence

– a report on possible moves to make the motor trade improve its repair service led one of the home news pages in July 1985: five years earlier that would have been regarded as a *Telegraph* rather than a *Times* news judgment. Yet *The Times* still kept the look and many of the characteristics of a serious text paper. It was a curious hybrid.

One of the journalists hired from the *Daily Mail* was Anthony Bevins, a political reporter who would later become political editor of the *Independent*. Interviewed by Andrew Dickson in the *Listener* in April 1988, he gave some examples of how *The Times* had become '*Mail*ised', citing a lead story which said that 'the Prime Minister led a withering Parliamentary onslaught' (on Neil Kinnock). Said Bevins: '"Withering" and "onslaught" are sheer *Daily Mail*.' And he recalled an argument during his time there about whether to angle the latest development in the Westland helicopter affair on the prospect of Leon Brittan resigning as Secretary of State for Trade and Industry, or on the wider ramifications for the Government as a whole. He lost the argument and *The Times*, like the tabloids, led on the Brittan aspect, while the other broadsheets covered it less sensationally, concentrating on the issue rather than on personalities.

In 1982, again at Murdoch's insistence, *The Times* introduced its own up-market version of the tabloid pastime, bingo. Called Portfolio, the lucky numbers were selected by reference to the previous day's gains and losses in the stock market, adding a cloak of respectability, albeit a thin one, to a mindless pursuit. The introduction of Portfolio by Douglas-Home (although it had been discussed in Evans's time) was the most vivid symbol of the changes that Murdoch made and was to make on *The Times*, for it marked the end of the paper's high-minded era, the erasure of the heritage of such editors as Sir William Haley, for whom items justified their inclusion in the paper because of their importance rather than their mere interest. *The Times* had never had as many 'entertainment' aspects as the other papers and those it did tolerate, such as the crossword and the Diary, had a hint of intellectual rigour about them. Portfolio did not.

Among other changes were a sudden spate of editorials attacking the BBC, supporting the opening of the airwaves to greater competition. There were suspicions that this could be connected to Murdoch's imminent intention of starting a satellite television service, but such improper thoughts were vehemently denied by Douglas-Home, who wheeled the independent directors into action to refute them. When Douglas-Home died in 1985, aged only forty-seven, Charles Wilson succeeded him, and hired more people from the *Daily Mail*, increasing the pace of the

'Poverty' led nurse to prostitution

A hospital nurse was struck off the nursing register yesterday because she had been convicted of loitering for the purpose of prostitution.

After the nursing disciplinary hearing Miss Susan Ling, aged 29, of Luton, Bedfordshire, said she worked at night as a prostitute because her National Health Service wages were so low.

The hearing in Marylebone, central London, was told that Miss Ling had received 28 vice convictions in London, Norwich, Nottingham, Stoke-on-Trent and Luton before her employers discovered her double life.

Miss Ling, a State-enrolled mental nurse, resigned from the Saxondale Hospital, Nottingham, after the authorities there were told of her last conviction, when she was fined £150 by magistrates in Luton for loitering.

Alsatian ate baby as drunk mother slept

A drunken mother slept while her baby son was savaged by the family alsatian dog in bed beside her, an inquest in Bury, Greater Manchester, was told yesterday.

The coroner, Mr Bryan North, said that Mrs Alma Bradley, aged 34, must have drunk so much she was "totally oblivious and unconscious" not to realize what was happening.

He said that it "stretched credulity" that the father, Mr Roger Rankine, was sleeping in a room below and was not disturbed while the dog dismembered Dean, his son, aged 11 weeks.

Mr North said that both parents had shown a total lack of concern by drinking so much that they were incapable of looking after the child.

He was told that the parents 'ad taken it in turns to visit a 'ublic house near their home in 'rkhills Road, Bury, on the 'ht Dean died, two days 're the new year.

Mr Rankine had arrived home at 9.30pm, when Mrs Bradley went out, returning two hours later when she had some more to drink before going to bed at about 2am.

The inquest was told that Dean's body was found later that morning in the bloodstained bedroom. Police Constable Terence Cross saw the baby on the floor with one leg severed and the other missing.

Mrs Bradley, who did not know the that the baby was in bed with her, is undergoing treatment in a psychiatric hospital and was unable to give evidence at the hearing.

She was said to have told the police: "I was tipsy and in a good mood. I was giddy. I had a lot to drink. I was enjoying myself. Roger was looking after the baby."

Mr North recorded a rarely used verdict of "lack of care by another or others".

No charges are to be brought.

Hamburger rivals grilled in court

The American hamburger "war" came to the High Court yesterday when McDonald's Golden Arches Restaurants asked a judge to ban its rival, Burger King, from running a "knocking" advertising campaign.

McDonald's claims that advertisements displayed on the London Underground with the slogan: "It's Not Just Big, Mac", libels the company by hinting that Big Mac hamburgers are not made of 100 per cent pure beef.

In an action set to last six days and likely to cost £100,000, McDonald's is seeking injunctions to stop Burger King making "disparaging mis-statements" about (its) best-selling burger and "passing off".

Mr Robin Jacob, QC, for McDonald's, which has 119 restaurants in Britain, told Mr Justice Whitford that the Burger King advertisement was "a masterpiece of ambiguity".

He said that some people might also take the advertisements, which ran briefly from September 1983, as meaning there was a commercial link between McDonald's and Burger King, whose largest burger is called The Whopper.

The hearing continues today.

Two girls died after sniffing deodorant cans

A coroner is to write to aerosol companies after the deaths of two girls, who sniffed the contents of deodorant cans.

The girls died within five weeks of each other in north Devon in separate incidents. The two inquests were held in Barnstaple yesterday.

The coroner, Mr Brian Hall-Tonkin, recorded verdicts of accidental death on Tracey Thomson, aged 14, of Lanrig Road, Fauldhouse, West Lothian, and Denise Blake, aged 13, of Chanters Hill, Barnstaple.

A coroner's officer, Mr Robert Clements, said that both aerosols contained warnings not to inhale excessively or use near the face and mouth.

Examples taken from July 1985 when consumer stories began to feature more prominently in *The Times*.

vulgarisation, as some saw it, of the news pages. Wilson's interest in horse racing ensured that stories on the subject occasionally appeared on the news pages instead of only on the sports pages. Circulation continued to increase and Murdoch's cynical view of the tastes of broadsheet readers would have gone unchallenged were it not for the event in 1986 that changed many preconceptions about the British press: the launch of the *Independent*.

5

The Great Escape

In a minute-to-minute industry, when they've got you by the balls, you've got to listen. Well, they haven't got us by the balls any more.

Kelvin MacKenzie, editor of the *Sun*, addressing his staff on the eve of the move to Wapping (reported in Linda Melvern, *The End of the Street*)

London Docks became redundant in the 1960s when giant container ships, too big to be handled there, took over world trade from smaller freighters. In a remarkably short space of time, acres of riverside land to the east of Tower Bridge were abandoned. For a decade most of it lay disused, while the property market stagnated in the economic downturn of the 1970s. It was a buyers' market with few buyers: precisely the circumstances that appeal to entrepreneurs such as Murdoch. In 1978 he bought a thirteen-acre site at Wapping, the most westerly of the dockland communities and a place with a lurid history. Ratcliffe Highway, which runs through it, was a notorious haunt of footpads and the scene of a sensational set of murders in the early nineteenth century. In 1936 Cable Street, just inland, saw a historic clash between Oswald Mosley's Fascists and local residents, mostly dock workers, who successfully prevented a Fascist march through the East End.

Fifty years later, Wapping was to see turbulence sparked by political convictions no less passionately held. The name of the Thames-side settlement was to become synonymous, depending on your point of view, either with a ruthless disregard by employers for the rights of their workers, or with a daring break for freedom by an industry that had for years been shackled by a corrupt workforce.

It required no uncanny gift of foresight to recognise that Fleet Street, the traditional centre of newspaper production for two centuries, could no longer be sustained as such. The sight of elongated trailers piled high with giant rolls of newsprint, manoeuvring in the narrow streets between Fleet Street and the Embankment, was an industrial anachronism, as well as an intense irritation to drivers stuck behind them. In the hellish basements of the grubby, overcrowded newspaper buildings still greater incongruities were to be seen: men setting type on Linotype machines that in many other countries had already been consigned to printing museums; lines of type being moulded from vats of molten lead, then placed by hand into the frames of the pages. Scarcely anything had changed since the turn of the century.

These archaic processes were occupying acres of prime space in central London, in low-rise, uneconomic buildings surrounded by sky-scrapers producing fortunes for their owners in rents. On the floors above the presses, journalists pounded the life out of ancient, battered typewriters to produce words for publication – and this in the 1980s, when computer-based techniques for newspaper production had been available for more than a decade, if only the print unions would have let the London proprietors use them.

In 1978 more than four million copies every weekday of Murdoch's *Sun*, and nearly five million of the *News of the World* on Sundays, were being produced from a rambling building in Bouverie Street completed in 1930. Its value as a site for development was enormous. The purchase of the land at Wapping was part of Murdoch's long-term objective to realise that value and to rationalise production using modern methods.

Building work at Wapping began in 1980. In 1983, when it was nearly completed, Murdoch began negotiations with the unions on the terms for moving there. By now he had two more papers, *The Times* and *Sunday Times*, but initially the negotiations concerned only the two tabloids. It was soon clear that they were unlikely to make progress. From Mur-doch's point of view there was no point in new technology if it did not involve job losses. The unions still felt themselves strong enough to resist meaningful cuts in manning – or as the triumphant proprietors would declare in retrospect, they refused to accept that the party was over. Long after the band finished the last waltz, the reluctant dancers had to be collared and hurled out of the hall.

The first sign that the music was about to stop had come two years earlier, at the end of 1983, from an unlikely venue: Warrington, near Manchester. Eddy Shah, the English-born son of an English mother and an Indian/Persian father, had, after a chequered career in theatre and television, launched the *Messenger* group of free local newspapers in the Manchester area. Opening a new plant at Warrington, he had decided to use non-union workers, because he was incensed at the extravagant manning levels demanded by the National Graphical Associ-ation (NGA).

Shah had been encouraged to take on the union by two Employment Acts introduced by Margaret Thatcher's Conservative Government, which had gained office in 1979. The acts outlawed both the closed shop and secondary action. Secondary picketing had been a powerful weapon of organised labour, where people not directly involved in a dispute would beef up the picket lines of those who were. And by organising strikes at other plants in the same ownership, the unions were able to exert damaging economic pressure on an employer.

Shah's showdown was the first proper test of the Act. When the NGA ignored its provisions against secondary action he pursued them through the courts to such effect that, after a series of mounting fines, all the union's assets were confiscated. On 29 November 1983 came what was to prove the decisive confrontation, when the police showed that they were prepared to uphold the law by breaking up a picket of several thousand NGA supporters, allowing Shah's papers to leave the print works and be distributed.

His victory turned Shah into a national celebrity. One of his strongest supporters had been Andrew Neil, the outspoken young Scot from *The Economist* who had, to everyone's surprise, just been made editor of the *Sunday Times*. He had caught Murdoch's attention because of his support for breaking the television duopoly of the BBC and the ITV network – an issue that highlighted his fervent opposition to cartels and restrictive practices of all kinds. He saw the Warrington dispute in the same light. Even more than his proprietor, he was appalled at Fleet Street's labour practices and the cynical exploitation by the print unions of their monopoly position. In fact he would try to goad Murdoch to move against them. Murdoch said there was nothing he could do on his own, but Neil persistently sought to persuade him otherwise.

Neil had been editor for only a few weeks when the *Sunday Times*, like other national papers, was stopped by a strike in support of the NGA in Warrington. Neil phoned Shah, who apologised for having caused the trouble. Neil advised Shah not to give in to the pressure to settle that was bound to come from what he called the Fleet Street establishment, anxious to end their labour troubles. Shah seemed touched. 'You're the first person from London who's phoned me about this,' he said. Neil supported Shah editorially, brought his battle to the attention of the Cabinet and gave him moral support over the telephone.

The two met for the first time in February 1984. That was when Neil suggested that Shah might carry his crusade a stage further and start a national newspaper using modern technology and non-union labour. At that stage Neil believed that the only way out of the Fleet Street log-jam was for an outsider to launch a competing national paper with such a low cost structure that the other papers would be forced, for the sake of survival, to stand up to the unions and slash their overheads. Only such outside intervention, he believed, could tip the scales in favour of the proprietors in the inevitable showdown with the workforce.

Neil was surprised that his advice was apparently taken on board so readily. Soon after that meeting Shah, an imaginative and resourceful man, began to draw up plans for just the kind of newspaper they had discussed. He commissioned an accountant's report which calculated that he would need £18 million in start-up capital. It took the best part of a year to persuade City institutions to put up the money but it was all in place by February 1985. By chance that was also the month when Rupert Murdoch, whose lieutenant had planted the idea in Shah's mind, began a process that would make it hard for the new paper to flourish.

*　　*　　*

When Murdoch was formulating his plans for making the Wapping plant operational, Shah's victory at Warrington played a part in his calculation. It showed that the courts were able to enforce the government's new employment legislation. His awareness of Shah's plans for a national daily provided another spur for rapid, hopefully pre-emptive action. Accordingly he did not wait for Shah's financing to be completed before deciding on his own strategy.

Linda Melvern, in *The End of the Street*, has related in compelling detail how Murdoch, his patience with the unions exhausted, began planning early in 1985 for the extraordinary industrial coup he was to engineer a year later. His lieutenants spread the word that he was proposing to launch a new London evening paper, the *London Post*, based in Wapping. This provided a handy pretext for increasingly frequent visits there by his senior executives. A modern direct-input production system was bought from Atex in the United States and initially installed in great secrecy at a warehouse at Woolwich, in south-east London.

Because the machines had little in common with traditional production methods, Murdoch felt that he did not necessarily need members of the print unions to man them. Instead, towards the end of 1985, he hired electricians from the EETPU (Electrical, Electronic, Telecommunications and Plumbing Union) whose leadership was further to the right than most in the labour movement. With London a notable hotbed of rumour and gossip, the men were recruited in Southampton, seventy-seven miles away, and taken to Wapping every day by bus, to be trained in the utmost secrecy to operate the new machinery.

Murdoch was now planning to move all four of his papers to Wapping, because he knew that if just the two tabloids were moved (assuming, as he did, that it would be done without the agreement of the print unions) then crippling action would be taken against the other two. No detail was overlooked. He assumed the unions would seek support from other workers in the distribution chain, particularly railway workers, so he established a complete road distribution system by-passing the rail network – so effectively that before the end of the decade the railways, which had formerly enjoyed a monopoly of national newspaper distribution, had been entirely superseded by road transport. Murdoch knew, too, that union pickets were certain to try to stop workers entering the new plant and to halt the trucks leaving it. He installed barbed wire and elaborate security arrangements, so that the plant quickly became known as 'Fortress Wapping'.

To justify transferring production to the fortress without the print unions, the management had, for public relations purposes, to provoke industrial action at the papers' present plants. They knew that if they simply moved the whole operation to Wapping unprovoked, most of their journalists – at that point the key to the enterprise – would refuse to move with them. If they could plead justification they had a chance of winning the journalists round. The National Union of Journalists was likely to recommend solidarity with the print unions, but the NUJ is ineffective at disciplining its members and can easily be defied.

Orchestrating a showdown with the print unions proved a little more difficult than might have been expected in an industry with such turbulent labour relations, for the union leaders had sensed that something dramatic was afoot – without knowing precisely how dramatic – and were behaving with more circumspection than usual. Even when, on 19 January 1986, an advertising supplement to the *Sunday Times* was produced at Wapping, and was inserted into the paper produced traditionally at Gray's Inn Road, the unions did not react immediately. The following Thursday, at a meeting with Murdoch, the print union leaders offered unprecedented concessions on work practices and manning but Murdoch told them they were too late: Wapping was going to be operated without them and there would be heavy job losses at Gray's Inn Road and Bouverie Street. After the talks had broken down Brenda Dean, general secretary of the print union SOGAT, remarked: 'I rather got the feeling that the company did not want a settlement.'

She was right. The company wanted a strike and that, in the end, is what they got. It was clear that there were going to be strikes at all four News International papers on Friday but the action was not made official until early evening. Once the strike was called, Murdoch could legitimately dismiss all the print union members without compensation on the grounds that they had broken their contracts. With the journalists, he had less trouble than he anticipated. He offered them all a bonus of £2,000 plus free health insurance as a lure, but most would probably have agreed without the bribes.

Five years earlier, had anyone suggested to journalists on *The Times* that they would find themselves participating in so daring and rapid an attempt at union-busting, they would not have credited it. They had a historic tendency to regard themselves as a special breed, responsible citizens who weighed events up carefully and responded in measured terms, not given to hasty decisions. Yet by now they had already been exposed to the cold draught of reality during five years of ownership by Murdoch, to whom such notions were elitist and wet. After an emotional address by the new editor Charles Wilson, appointed after the death of Charles Douglas-Home, they voted by three to one to go to Wapping, with only a handful preferring to quit their jobs rather than make the move.

At the *Sunday Times* the vote was much closer and a group of 'refuseniks' held out for a week in Gray's Inn Road. Andrew Neil was upset and baffled by the extent of the opposition. Since his appointment as editor he had become increasingly infuriated by the blatant exploitation of management by the unions, both for practical and political reasons, making it difficult to produce the kind of paper he wanted. It amazed him that many of his staff could not see how much more bearable their life would ultimately be with this major irritant removed. But the collectivist tradition of the British left, even the centre left, was deeply ingrained. The Wapping move went directly against that tradition.

All but six of the refuseniks finally succumbed. The most important of the holdouts were Don Berry, managing editor for news and a key member of the senior editorial team (now with the *Daily Telegraph*) and Claire Tomalin, the literary editor. In the succeeding months many other stalwarts, depressed at the embattled atmosphere at Wapping and at having to defend their actions to liberal friends, found other jobs. On the two tabloids, there was much less resistance.

The Murdoch titles missed only one day of publication, Saturday 25 January. On the Sunday the *Sunday Times* and *News of the World* both appeared from Wapping, with some editions of the latter being printed at Murdoch's plant in Glasgow. Rather fewer copies than usual were produced but the nut had been cracked. The following day *The Times* and *Sun* duly appeared, and none of the papers has missed a day since. The print unions were able to attract considerable support in the labour movement for their anger at the way they had been treated. Mass picketing of the plant – sometimes leading to violent clashes with the police – continued for thirteen months. It made for an unpleasant, contentious atmosphere but workers were never prevented from entering or trucks from leaving. That weekend in January 1986 marked the effective end of Fleet Street as a newspaper publishing centre and the dawn of a new age for the national press.

*   *   *

The enormous cost savings generated by Wapping allowed the ever-restless Murdoch to raise loans to invest in other projects. In the first full financial year after the moonlight flit, ending in June 1987, the profits of News International, his British company, rose to £111.5 million, from £11.7 million the previous year (although that lower figure was partly accounted for by the £67 million cost of the Wapping move). During that year he had secured domination of the Australian newspaper scene by acquiring the *Herald* and *Weekly Times* group in Melbourne, where his father had once been managing director. He bought the *South China Morning Post* in Hong Kong for £180 million and, for about the same price, the publishers Harper and Row in the United States. In the US, his main interest was now the Fox television network, which he had formed from the Twentieth-Century Fox film company, bought in 1985 for $575 million, and the Metromedia network of six television stations acquired a year later for $1,500 million.

In July 1987 he bought his fifth British national paper – and surely his last, unless he sells some of the others. The irony of his purchase of *Today* for £38 million was that he was adding to his stable the paper that his man, Andrew Neil, had helped persuade Eddy Shah to launch, but whose thunder he had stolen by moving to Wapping two months before the new paper began publication. With cost-saving technology already in place in part of the established press, and certain to spread to the rest of Fleet Street before long, *Today* had forfeited the intrinsic commercial advantage that had attracted investors to it.

That was not, however, why it initially failed. Shah has many of the necessary qualities of a press magnate – drive, energy and commitment among them. He came to national newspapers with high ideals, which he proclaimed to all who would listen, but with little relevant experience and indeed with a measure of contempt for Fleet Street's values and traditions. He was certainly right to be contemptuous of its labour relations, but his almost equal scorn for its journalism, as compared with what he saw as the solid virtues of regional reporting, led him to hire too inexperienced a staff.

Shah's vision was of a middle-market tabloid with full colour printing, that did not engage in titillation or gossip or uncomfortable business exposés. He didn't like what he thought of as the Fleet Street mafia, and rented offices in Vauxhall Bridge Road, Pimlico, deliberately distant from Fleet Street with its social temptations for journalists. He spoke dismissively of 'Fleet Street fat cats' and vowed to have none on his paper. His choice of editor seemed defensible at the time but was, in retrospect, a fundamental mistake.

He first approached Andrew Neil, who was too canny to let his enthusiasm for the project lure him from one of the highest-profile jobs in British newspapers so soon after he had taken it over. On the advice of both Neil and Charles Wintour, former editor of the *Evening Standard* and a leading authority on newspapers, Shah next sounded out Brian MacArthur, who had spent much of his career on *The Times* and had been the launch editor of *The Times Higher Educational Supplement*. For some years he had been working on the *Sunday Times*, where it was assumed he would be made editor; but he had been pipped by Andrew Neil and left to edit the *Western Morning News*. MacArthur's sole experience of tabloid journalism was a brief stint as deputy editor of the *Evening Standard*, to which Wintour had appointed him.

In his touching book describing the terrible time he had with Shah, *Eddy Shah: Today and the Newspaper Revolution*, MacArthur quotes the daunting blueprint that Shah presented to him for a newspaper that would, if followed to the letter, have been something akin to a revivalist tract. Some of its provisions were:

> To support true democracy and not the false democracy of collectivism;
>
> To operate a truthful and fair free press not influenced by the intimidation and subterfuge of extremists and their ideologies;
>
> To produce an attractive and entertaining newspaper without reliance on scandal, sexual and financial titillation and sensationalism;
>
> To support freedom of religion and worship;
>
> To support freedom from all coercive monopolies;
>
> To criticise the law of the land but never to support those who are defiant of the law by use of force, intimidation and subterfuge;

To support the right of those who wish to join a trades union as well as those who do not;

To protect those who suffer from an irresponsible invasion of privacy;

To protect the right to engage in private enterprise and pursue the trade or profession of one's choice without harassment.

Many of these principles were inspired specifically by Shah's own experiences with the Warrington pickets and they seemed an eccentric prospectus on which to launch a newspaper. But as the deadline of March 1986 approached, worries about the editorial content were overtaken by fears about whether the paper could be produced at all. The modern machinery was unfamiliar to nearly everyone, so nobody knew how to cure its teething troubles. The colour registration was never as good as Shah and MacArthur had anticipated and printing in several different centres was another unfamiliar technique that had to be mastered. Two weeks before the launch all the wiring under the floors and in the walls of the office had to be ripped out and replaced to higher safety specifications.

Yet Shah remained unshakeably optimistic, at least in public. With the figures he was quoting it was impossible to see how he could fail. Break-even would come on a circulation of a little over 300,000 – surely a conservative target for a ground-breaking full-colour tabloid – and that was at advertising rates 50 per cent lower than existing papers. In a speech to the Royal Society of Arts in January 1986, a few days before the Wapping move and six weeks before *Today*'s launch, Shah said that with no advertising at all his paper could make money with a circulation of 1,500,000.

He sketched, too, his vision of a future paradise for small newspaper owners like himself:

Low cost production means a more varied press with a multiplicity of titles. The base of ownership of national newspapers will be widened from a handful of rich barons to professional newspaper businessmen who will create products for the market gaps that they see. Why not a daily sports paper – or a fashion paper? Why not a variety of business and money newspapers? By contract printing, break-evens could be based on 60,000 to 100,000 circulations . . . It is, I am sure, going to be an expanding, exciting and profitable future, as long as those in this industry, including those in this room, are prepared to step into tomorrow. The jibes of the doubters will follow us, but they are running out of time. Our product, and those who are creating and producing it, will speak for themselves in the next few weeks.

When they did, it was with a weak and muddled voice. The first issue of *Today*, on 4 March, was fatally late in reaching the shops, partly because of delays in production and partly because the distribution system had not been properly thought out. After a botched launch, the paper never acquired the necessary impetus. Initial 'curiosity' sales of around a million – Shah's original target – soon declined sharply. By the end of April the figure was down to 500,000 and a month later 400,000, diving towards Shah's break-even figure before any of the launch cost had been recouped.

Senior staff started to leave. Its two middle-market competitors, the *Daily Mail* and *Daily Express*, were selling about 1,800,000 each. They were both much sharper, more carefully targeted products and they countered the threat of their new rival with heavy expenditure on promotion. They certainly did not intend to sit back passively and watch their market being invaded. *Today* had a flabby feel which, combined with insipid colour reproduction and an overall sense of disorganisation, gave it the character of a plump, overdressed bag lady, wearing a grubby rainbow quilt and murmuring disjointed phrases. By June a rescuer was needed. He appeared in the shape of 'Tiny' Rowland, chairman of the conglomerate Lonrho, which owned the *Observer*. Lonrho put in £24 million to take a majority shareholding.

Shah, still effectively running the paper as chairman, hired Sir Larry Lamb, former editor of the *Sun* and the *Daily Express*, to write a report on the editorial organisation of the paper. According to MacArthur he concluded that the people who ran it were 'a team of amicable amateurs'. Lamb's recommendations for reform included MacArthur's removal and, although most of the rest of the report was ignored, it was clear that his brief tenure as editor was drawing to a close. Returning from holiday in July he learned that his job had been offered to David Montgomery, editor of the *News of the World*. Montgomery turned it down and MacArthur was reprieved. But Shah was still determined that he should go and in December, when he received an offer to rejoin the *Sunday Times*, MacArthur resigned. In a cordial letter to him afterwards, Shah pin-pointed the reason for the paper's failure: 'I never felt that we ever identified the market we were aiming at.'

MacArthur's replacement, his former deputy Dennis Hackett, was no more successful. The paper continued to lose circulation and money – some £28.5 million in its first year. In June 1987, with sales below

300,000, Rowland was in a mood to sell. After both Rupert Murdoch and Robert Maxwell had expressed strong interest, and after it seemed that Maxwell was going to clinch it, the title passed for £38 million to Murdoch, who had outflanked his old rival once again.

It was a surprise that the Government allowed Murdoch to buy it without an enquiry by the Monopolies and Mergers Commission. Even the Press Council, which did not often express a view on such matters, issued a statement pointing out that 'there could hardly be a more obvious increase in concentration than the acquisition of a fifth national newspaper by a group that already owns four'. Lonrho, encouraged by the example of Thomson Newspapers six years earlier, said it would close the paper unless Lord Young, Secretary of State for Trade and Industry, waived a reference to the commission – and declared within twenty-four hours that he would do so. It was argued on Murdoch's behalf that no monopoly consideration arose because *Today* occupied the middle market, the ground between Murdoch's existing up-market and down-market titles, where he was hitherto unrepresented.

Murdoch appointed David Montgomery, who had turned down the editor's job a year earlier, as both editor and managing director of *Today*. He gave the paper a needed sense of direction and purpose and the circulation soon responded. As well as a gifted editor, Montgomery proved an implacable enemy: he boycotted the Press Council for more than a year because of its temerity in calling for the reference of the sale to the MMC, removing the ban only when Murdoch himself ordered it.

It is tempting to trace a pattern of deviousness in the story of Rupert Murdoch and *Today*. A Murdoch editor suggests to an ambitious and courageous entrepreneur that he starts a new non-union paper at a time when Murdoch himself is contemplating a showdown with the unions. Is Shah the stalking horse? A former executive from Murdoch's *Sunday Times* is made editor of the new paper, then goes back to his old job with Murdoch when he resigns ten months later. Finally, when the risks, costs and trauma of the launch have been undergone, Murdoch picks up the paper, if not exactly at a bargain price, at a modest one.

The conventional wisdom about Murdoch, though, is that he does not usually go in for forward planning on that scale. In 1982 *Newsweek* quoted an associate of his as saying: 'He keeps a stable of acquisitions guys in his office. I used to think they did things according to some grand design, but really they're just a bunch of guys with suitcases and airplane tickets.'

Six years later the *Sunday Times* reported Martin Singerman, President of Murdoch's US subsidiary News America, thus: 'There are no set global figures or ratios. We look at each situation as it arises.'

A clinching reason for going ahead with the *Today* purchase was that Montgomery was keen. Ever since being approached by Shah a year earlier, the Ulsterman had been thinking about *Today* and the opportunity it presented. By 1990 he had taken the circulation up to 600,000 but there it stagnated, still a long way behind the *Mail* and the *Express*, then started to slide. By March 1991 it was little more than half a million and Murdoch's new chief executive Andrew Knight decided it was time for a change. A day after giving an interview to the *Independent* about his plans for the paper, Montgomery had been moved to an ill-defined executive job within News International and replaced as editor by Martin Dunn, the deputy editor of the *Sun*. Dunn took it back to being a conventional middle-market newspaper like the *Express* and *Mail* but the circulation continued to fall, down to 430,000 by the end of 1991.

* * *

After buying *Today*, Murdoch could not test the tolerance of the Monopolies and Mergers Commission further – at least not just yet – and his next major corporate acquisitions had no connection with the British press. He took full control of Collins, the publishers, where he had held a 41 per cent stake for some years. And he paid a phenomenal $3,000 million for Triangle Publications in the United States, including the *Daily Racing Form* and *TV Guide*, the largest selling weekly magazine in the world. He was regularly criticised for borrowing too heavily from banks to finance his deals – as opposed to issuing new share capital, which he resisted because it would have diluted his family's ownership of the group. But the fact that the banks continued to lend to him proved that, in their view, the scale of his debt was not unreasonable.

In any case, he was not totally averse to selling properties. He sold the shares in Reuters that he had held on to when the agency was floated in 1984. He even sold the *News* in Adelaide, the first paper he ever owned, when his purchase of the *Herald* and *Weekly Times* group gave him the *Advertiser*, the largest paper in the city. For Murdoch, business and sentiment are seldom mixed.

The *New York Post* – his first American paper – and Chicago *Sun-Times* were sold because he was not allowed to own newspapers and television stations in the same city. He had made these sales unwillingly but the US Congress had refused to grant him dispensation from the rules, largely because of a campaign conducted by Senator Edward Kennedy of Massachusetts. Murdoch's papers had a long history of criticising the liberal Kennedy, sometimes in abusive and personal terms. This was a rare case of the political disposition of Murdoch's papers having an adverse impact on his commercial interests.

But it soon became clear that he needed the money for a huge debt restructuring in 1991. He sold a group of American periodicals for $185 million – including the *Star*, a weekly paper he founded as one of his first US enterprises. Back in Britain, he sold a substantial quantity of shares he had acquired in Pearson, the conglomerate whose holdings included the Westminster Press regional press group, the Penguin publishing empire, Royal Doulton china, a stake in British Satellite Broadcasting and, most interestingly, the *Financial Times*. By 1988 he had secured a 20 per cent holding in the *Financial Times*. He had always been envious of the lucrative vein of financial advertising that was its exclusive preserve and believed that if properly marketed in North America the paper could make inroads into the circulation (nearly two million) of the *Wall Street Journal*. But there was no chance that the Government, supine though it had been in the matter of *Today*, would have allowed him to own both the *Financial Times* and *The Times* and, recognising this, he liquidated the holding.

His most expensive gamble was with his satellite television service, Sky, which lost him around £10 million a week in the financial year ended June 1990, its first full operating year. Losses were reduced to about a sixth of that after November 1990, when he merged Sky with the rival British Satellite Broadcasting to form British Sky Broadcasting. This cut his stake in the merged company to about half. With a virtual monopoly in satellite TV in Britain, and with the service watchable in more than three million homes by the spring of 1992, the investment looked set to make him a profit within a few years. Indeed in March 1992 it was reported to be operating at a profit, although this did not take into account the huge debts still to be repaid.

* * *

After Shah, the next proposal to launch a new daily paper, taking advantage of advanced technology, came from an equally improbable quarter. Andreas Whittam Smith was city editor of the *Daily Telegraph* and, at forty-seven, had a reasonable chance of succeeding the veteran William Deedes as editor. A few days after Shah announced his plan in March 1985, Whittam Smith received a telephone call from another business journalist canvassing his view on whether the new paper would ever clear the launching pad. Like most people in whose lifetime there had been only one way of producing national newspapers – the inefficient and expensive way – Whittam Smith was at first sceptical about whether

Shah's scheme would work, and especially about whether this outsider from Warrington would be able to raise the necessary capital.

As he thought about it, though, the idea seemed increasingly feasible, and he began to wonder whether he might be able to start something of that nature himself. A national newspaper produced on a low cost base would have a significant competitive advantage over existing titles which, at that time, seemed neither able nor willing to find a rapid means of escape from the restrictive practices of the print unions. Although Shah was going to establish his own printing plants, Whittam Smith saw no need for this. Most newspapers outside London were published only in the evenings, so they had spare capacity overnight. Facsimile transmission meant that made-up pages could be transmitted to the printing plants down the telephone line from London.

As his plan developed Whittam Smith drew in two younger colleagues on the *Telegraph* – Matthew Symonds, an economics leader-writer, and Stephen Glover, a feature writer. They engaged Douglas Long, former managing director of the *Mirror* group, to help on the business side. (Symonds knew him through his father, Lord Ardwick, who as John Beavan had been political editor of the *Daily Mirror*.) Saatchi and Saatchi, the advertising agency, did some market research which suggested that there was a demand for a quality broadsheet principally aimed at people below forty-four. This was the 'gap in the market' that the existing papers were not filling – although, as Hugh Cudlipp discovered to his cost in 1964 and as Eddy Shah and others were to find in 1986, a market gap is a notoriously treacherous concept.

In the autumn of 1985 Whittam Smith initiated soundings in the City about raising the £18 million he believed his project would need. Shah's earlier trawl around the capital markets meant that a new newspaper was no longer a totally novel proposition for the money men, who were still impressed by any new paper's prospective cost advantages over its rivals. By December £2 million of seed capital had been found, enabling the planning to begin seriously. Details of the project were disclosed publicly for the first time in the *Financial Times* on 27 December 1985. By the new year the three founders had left the *Daily Telegraph* and were installed in offices of their own. The aim was to launch in October 1986.

Murdoch's move to Wapping at the end of January proved a setback to raising the remaining £16 million. Overnight *The Times*, sure to be one of their principal rivals, had reduced its cost base to something comparable with that proposed for the new paper. Moreover, once the Wapping move was seen to have worked, despite the continuing picketing outside the News International plant, other papers could be expected to protect themselves by moving towards comparable savings. It meant the evaporation of the one tangible advantage that the *Independent* was seen to enjoy over the established newspapers. Most potential investors had always been more impressed by that cost differential than by all the speculative research about gaps in the market. Of the sixty-five prospective investors who showed serious interest, only thirty converted that interest into an actual stake in the paper, many of the others defecting soon after Wapping.

Whittam Smith was able to convince the remaining thirty that the weakening of the print unions' grip on the industry could in the long run contribute to a climate in which the *Independent* could thrive. In March another external development momentarily threatened the last stages of the financing plans. The disastrous launch of Eddy Shah's *Today* showed that newspapers were inescapably risky undertakings and that failure was at least as likely as success. Yet by April the required money had been raised, most of it from City institutions. Preliminary work – most importantly the staffing – could begin.

When it came to finding editorial staff, the Wapping trauma worked in Whittam Smith's favour. Many journalists on *The Times* and *Sunday Times*, some of whom had been unhappy ever since Murdoch bought the papers, found the circumstances of the Wapping move objectionable and working conditions there barely tolerable, involving the daily necessity of crossing a line of aggressive pickets. It was with some relief that they grabbed the chance of escape, even to a project involving so high a level of risk. Scores of job applications came from the Murdoch papers to the new City Road offices of the *Independent* and several key appointments were made from them.

The name was chosen partly as a result of market research, and it made an important contribution to the paper's success. The researchers had detected resistance among readers of other papers to the predictability of their political positions. There appeared to be a demand for a paper prepared to think issues through, untainted by preconceptions or by the influence of a strong-willed proprietor. The first issue of the *Independent*, on 7 October 1986, was produced smoothly and on time, in notable contrast to *Today*. Whittam Smith had insisted that it should be preceded by a full month's run of dummy issues, which ensured an unusually confident and snag-free launch. Because it had borrowed stylistic devices from existing papers, especially *The Times* and *Telegraph*, it had an oddly familiar feel to it from the first day. Critics of the launch issue had to fall back on the charge that it was 'boring', an empty word used by people who can find no obvious shortcomings or *sottises* to provide easy targets.

The launch plan envisaged circulation settling at about 375,000 after the initial ups and downs that accompany any such enterprise. Sales for the first week averaged around half a million a day, until they predictably began inching downwards. The *Independent*'s impressive circulation growth from mid-1987 has tended to obscure those difficult early months. Sales hit a low of 256,923 in January 1987 but by the spring they were perking up. The June figure was 327,122 and by the end of the year that had gone up by a further 50,000 to reach break-even point. The figure stayed fairly stagnant in the first half of 1988 but before the end of that year the 400,000 landmark had been achieved.

The number of readers, like much else in the launch, was thus very much on target. Where Whittam Smith and his colleagues had miscalculated, though, was in the source of those readers. Since all three founders came from the *Telegraph*, most people assumed that they would be aiming to penetrate their former paper's market, and the trio shared that assumption. Yet the paper they produced was substantially up-market from the *Telegraph* and gained most of its readers from *The Times* and the *Guardian*.

Comparing the first six months of 1987 with the first six months of 1986 (pre-*Independent*), the *Telegraph*, under its new editor Max Hastings, was down by fewer than 10,000 copies. *The Times* and the *Guardian*, with their much lower circulation base, had lost about 30,000 each. There was evidence that some readers had found *The Times* more abrasive, less user-friendly since the Murdoch takeover, and switched gladly to this more contemplative organ, or at least added it to their daily paper diet. Bearing in mind that sales of the *Financial Times* had actually gone up by 28,000, from Jan.–June 1986 to Jan.–June 1987, the arrival of the *Independent* appeared to have swelled the quality daily market by close to a quarter of a million copies.

If the three founders had miscalculated about which papers their readers would chiefly come from, their forecasts about their demographics were spot on. They were aiming to attract young, prosperous people and succeeded spectacularly in doing so. The proportion of readers in their thirties and forties was higher than for any of its rivals. The paper's name and uncommitted attitude appealed especially to independent-minded youngsters, perhaps taking a daily paper regularly for the first time in their lives. It was they who had been the target of the teasing advertising slogan based on the paper's name: 'It is. Are You?'

In the first six months of 1987, 23.4 per cent of *Independent* readers were aged between fifteen and twenty-four, and 25.8 per cent between twenty-five and thirty-four. The business plan had predicted that the proportion of readers between twenty and forty-five in the A, B, and C1 categories would be 50 per cent: in fact it was 56.3 per cent – more than one per cent higher than its closest rival the *Guardian*, and double the proportion of *Daily Telegraph* readers in that category.

The *Independent*'s early success made it easier for Whittam Smith to attract big-name writers. William Rees-Mogg, the former editor of *The Times*, had been a columnist since the first issue but during 1987 Peter Jenkins, political columnist of the *Guardian*, went to City Road, as did Miles Kington, a humorous writer with a substantial following in *The Times*. The *Independent* was named newspaper of the year in Granada Television's *What the Papers Say* awards. On its first anniversary it received almost universal praise from trade magazines such as *Campaign* and *Marketing Week* and from papers including the *Sunday Times* and the *Observer*, whose media editor, Richard Brooks, revealed that both his wife and father had become regular readers – anecdotal evidence of the grip the new paper was beginning to exert over the middle class.

By the spring of 1990 the *Independent* was closing the circulation gap with *The Times* and the *Guardian* but it suffered more than them from the deepening recession, which affected both circulation and, more gravely, advertising revenue. Morale, too, was depressed because of the struggles to establish its new Sunday edition, launched in January of that year into a highly competitive market. By the end of 1991 daily circulation was down to 372,000, more than 15,000 behind *The Times* and 37,000 short of the *Guardian*. Capital from Italian and Spanish newspapers had been injected to keep the company afloat. All the same, bearing in mind the initial boldness of the enterprise, to have become within five years an established title in the national press could be counted a distinct success.

*   *   *

Other post-Wapping launches were a mixed bag and most of them flopped. An exception – of a kind – was *Sunday Sport*, launched just three weeks before the *Independent*. The success of the *Sport* at the very seamiest end of the market is described in Chapter 10, while Robert Maxwell's unhappy experience in 1987 with his well-intentioned but hopelessly botched *London Daily News* is related in Chapter 6.

Whether *News on Sunday* was well-intentioned is still a matter of controversy and depends partly on your political standpoint. The horrifying story of the paper's conception as a left-wing Sunday tabloid controlled by its workers, and the series of appalling misjudgments that condemned it to an early grave, is mordantly told by Peter Chippindale and Chris Horrie in *Disaster! The Rise and Fall of the News on Sunday*. The thinking behind the project seemed valid enough: that the left was seriously under-represented in the British press and there must be a market for a radical Sunday tabloid that aspired to higher things than the *News of the World*, *Sunday Mirror* and the *People*, especially at a time when those papers' excesses were becoming increasingly blatant and vulgar.

That theory has long been the Mata Hari of the British press – seductive but treacherous. Papers such as the *Daily Herald*, *News Chronicle*, *Reynolds News* (briefly the *Sunday Citizen*) and Hugh Cudlipp's *Sun* have perished nobly in its name. Since the 1930s the bulk of the Labour Party's electoral support has come from the tabloid-reading classes but, maddeningly for the theorists, the readers have refused to care whether their newspapers support their political opinions or not. Many readers of the *Daily Express* in its 1950s heyday must have been Labour voters, as are many readers of the *Sun* four decades later. The *Mirror* newspapers are the only Labour supporters among the tabloids, but they – especially the two Sundays – have often kept their politics inconspicuous.

The idea of *News on Sunday* originated in March 1985, the month that Whittam Smith had his first thoughts about the *Independent*. It was a low point for the left in Britain: Margaret Thatcher was midway between her second and third election victories and Neil Kinnock was only just beginning to pull the Labour Party back into a state where it could be perceived as having a viable future.

Because of the political in-fighting and disorganisation that plagues many left-wing bodies, the paper's first issue did not appear until April 1987, two years after it was conceived and two months before that year's general election. By then John Pilger, the only journalist of real stature who had committed himself to the project, had resigned after quarrelling with the editor, Keith Sutton, over an early dummy. Pilger had identified in the dummy the banality and lack of serious journalistic endeavour that was to characterise Sutton's paper. Clive Thornton, former managing director of the *Mirror* group, was one of the many executives who had also been eased out or had given up in despair.

One of the many lessons of *News on Sunday*'s failure was the danger of relying on initial market research to shape a newspaper and predict the level of its sales. With no product to test the market, researchers have to give a general description of the ideal newspaper for which the promoters are aiming. Asked whether you would buy such a paper, from its description a paragon of every journalistic virtue, it would be churlish to reply anything but 'yes please'. Based on the first 'blind' survey a dummy was produced and passed to a sample panel for assessment. The result was almost as encouraging. After they had seen it, 5.6 per cent of the sample group said they would be certain to buy a paper like it. If extrapolated to the twenty million buyers of Sunday papers, that meant a circulation of a million. In addition, a further 9.8 per cent said they would be very likely to buy it. (A hazard of such extrapolation is that, even if the percentages are valid, the target numbers will only be achieved if every single one of the twenty million newspaper buyers is aware of the new product. This implies an expenditure on promotion that would have been way beyond *News on Sunday*'s budget – £6 million for the entire start-up. In fact a sample survey on the day after the launch showed that more than half of respondents had not heard of it.)

Newspapers run by committees have seldom worked. There were endless disputes and endless meetings to resolve them, often resulting in a resignation or forced departure. Just after he quit, John Pilger wrote in the *New Statesman*: 'Committees have failed *News on Sunday*. Committees too often draw comfort from their own procedures and mediocrity; at worst they become cabals.'

There was a strong feminist group on the committees, constantly alert for evidence of sexism. Under their influence one of the paper's launch slogans – 'No Tits, But a Lot of Balls' – was vetoed and the advertising agency resigned the account soon afterwards. The first issue was deplorably weak, prominently featuring details of the menu in the Ministry of Defence canteen, technically an official secret. (Chippindale and Horrie reveal that this was meant to be a jokey stunt, but it was ham-fistedly handled.) After selling only a third of the 1½ million print run of the first issue, the paper was taken over by Owen Oyston, an entrepreneur, two months after launch and closed five months later, in November 1987.

*   *   *

In the autumn of 1988 launch fever, its temperature undiminished by the failures of 1987, spread to the Manchester area. Roger Bowes, a former executive with the *Express* group, decided that what north-west England wanted was a regional – not a city-based – daily quality paper, and that it would need a circulation of around 60,000 to be profitable, 40,000 to break even. He launched the *North West Times* in September with start-up capital of £1.5 million, much of it raised through a tax-efficient Business Expansion Scheme.

The paper's first issue just achieved the 60,000 mark but it was a downhill slide from there and by the time it closed, seven weeks after launch, sales were down to 16,000. Like *News on Sunday*, it had failed in two main respects. First, the editorial content was insufficiently appealing to sustain the interest of those who read the initial issues; and second, not enough resources had been devoted to marketing the paper and making people aware of it.

The short, unhappy life of the *North West Times* was a bad omen for Eddy Shah, just about to embark on his second attempt at testing his theory that the new technology would enable hordes of small independent entrepreneurs to start their own national papers. This time he was planning a mass-market tabloid, competing with the *Sun*, *Mirror* and *Star*, but doing so in full colour, which the other papers could not then manage, and without the notorious tabloid excesses: no salaciousness, no naked women, no intrusion into privacy. It was to be called the *Post* and its editorial office would be in Warrington – partly because of its lower labour costs and partly symbolising Shah's continuing antipathy towards London media folk, even though he had briefly been counted among their number. It would circulate in England and Wales, but not Scotland, and would be printed at five centres across the country. He had raised £5.5 million for the venture.

When I went to see him a few weeks before the launch, Shah was his usual optimistic self. He enthused: 'Nine million mass market tabloids are sold every day. It's a huge market with only three players. With lower costs per unit we can fragment it. We can break even with a sale of 350,000 or so – which means there's no reason why other tabloids shouldn't be launched serving smaller markets.'

Yet that let-a-hundred-flowers-bloom argument contained a major flaw. In a market whose leader was selling four million copies a day, why should advertisers bother with a paper selling less than a tenth of that, however good value and however squeaky-clean? In the event, the proposition was not properly tested.

As editor, Shah had engaged Lloyd Turner, who had recently stepped down from the *Daily Star* after a record award of libel damages to Jeffrey Archer, the novelist. Even disregarding that expensive misjudgment, Turner was an odd choice to edit a paper aimed at setting an example of purity and decency to the other tabloids. Under his editorship the *Star* had scarcely been a model of rectitude.

Once again, the treacherous weapon of market research had been deployed to justify the editorial strategy. The researchers found that 12 per cent of tabloid readers were dissatisfied with their papers and many women were so appalled by the existing tabloids that they would not have them in the house: so Shah would make a push for home deliveries.

Aside, though, from that initial statement of pure intentions, Shah, as he had done with *Today*, became obsessed with the technology at the expense of the editorial content. Such had been the advances in desk-top publishing that he calculated he could print and lay out a daily paper using Pagemaker software on Apple Macintosh personal computers, with no need for a large central mainframe computer. This time the technology worked better but as far as the product was concerned, it was the same dismal story of thirty months earlier. Colour reproduction was poor and the paper lacked any distinctive quality that would persuade people to switch to it from what they were reading already. The promotion budget of £1.25 million proved inadequate to make people aware of the paper and it was almost certainly a mistake for Shah himself to feature in the television advertising – again as he had done with *Today*.

The *Post* was launched on 10 November 1988 with a print run of a million and a settle-down target of 600,000. It did not make it to Christmas. By mid-December Shah was in negotiation with a possible purchaser but the deal fell through and the paper folded ignominiously. It seems unlikely that the engaging Shah will make a third attempt to become a national newspaper proprietor but he can still claim a significant place in press history as one of the catalysts of the tremendous changes that transformed the industry in 1986.

*   *   *

The main national newspaper launch of 1989 was the *Sunday Correspondent*. This was an attempt to emulate the success of the *Independent* on the one day of the week when it did not publish. The *Independent* itself had been thinking of establishing what its founders called 'a Sunday presence' for some time. Whittam Smith had approached 'Tiny' Rowland, owner of the *Observer*, to see if that eminent Sunday title was for sale, but Rowland quoted an unrealistic price of £100 million and the discussion ended. Another thought was to create a seven-day newspaper on the United States pattern, but Whittam Smith returned from a transatlantic visit unconvinced that the formula would work in Britain.

Certainly the quality Sunday market did not then look overcrowded. Increasingly it was dominated by the *Sunday Times*, which, with a circulation of around 1,300,000, was climbing towards the levels of its heyday in the 1970s and had easily outstripped the *Observer* and *Sunday Telegraph*, with around 700,000 each. The *Sunday Times* had been buying circulation by putting on extra sections – for instance a self-contained literary review – that were not by themselves cost-effective. Market researchers often produced findings to show that people thought there was simply too much to read on Sundays and both the *Observer* and *Sunday Telegraph* at different times ran advertising campaigns seeking to exploit the perceived demand for a sharper, more concise product. But the sales figures suggested that, whatever they told pollsters, people actually went and bought the bulkiest paper, because it represented the best value. If they *did* have too much to read on Sundays, they would maybe drop their second paper but stay with the *Sunday Times*.

The other two quality Sundays both seemed vulnerable. The *Sunday Telegraph*, after an initial spurt when Peregrine Worsthorne took over as editor in 1986, had been drifting downwards. It seemed that the audience for Worsthorne's particular brand of High Tory brutalism was fairly stagnant at 700,000, incapable of significant expansion. As for the *Observer*, its reputation as a decent, liberal paper had been tainted by the enthusiasm with which it espoused Mr Rowland's business interests, particularly his feud with the al-Fayed brothers. In the late 1980s the weight of that commercial obligation seemed to be squeezing the paper's erstwhile radical spirit and, despite several changes of design and of key staff, the circulation decline could not be stemmed.

In November 1987 two men, inspired by the example of the *Independent*, decided to try the same trick with a Sunday paper. One was David Blake, a former news editor on *The Times*, the other Gavyn Davies, an economist with Goldman Sachs, the investment bankers. They were soon joined by another Murdoch refugee, David Lipsey, a writer on social affairs for the *Sunday Times* and more recently editor of *New Society*. Another early member of the team was Douglas Long, the former *Mirror* chief executive who had helped launch the *Independent*.

It was not a particularly propitious time to raise money: the stock market had crashed the previous month. By the end of 1988 the £18 million needed had still not been raised, and the failure of the *Post* and *North West Times* deterred investors who had been wavering – notably the *Guardian*, whose deputy editor, Peter Cole, had left a few months earlier to become editor of the new paper. It was touch and go until the end of February, just before the bankers' deadline ran out, when the final slice of money came from the *Chicago Tribune* group. It was announced that the paper would be called the *Sunday Correspondent* and be launched in September 1989.

In the twenty-two months between the initial idea and the launch, the weekend newspaper market had undergone a significant change. Saturday had long been the slowest day for daily papers. Circulations were lower than on other weekdays because many people buy their papers on the way in to work or have them delivered to their offices, and fewer are at work on Saturdays. Yet to introduce leisure and home sections in Saturday papers seemed logical enough, because the week-end is the time for gardening and do-it-yourself decorating and on Saturdays the shops are open for people to buy the implements and materials advertised in that day's papers.

Such sections had, however, never caught on with readers or adver-tisers. Hugh Cudlipp's *Sun* tried something of the kind when it was launched in 1964 and more recently the *Daily Express* had experimented with a section called Express on Saturday. On the other hand, the *Financial Times*, which suffers more than any paper from Saturday droop, had successfully launched a separate leisure section on Saturdays, advis-ing business people and (in particular) their wives how to spend the money they had been amassing during the week. The *Daily Telegraph* followed suit and found that it could, after all, attract readers and leisure-market advertisers to the Saturday paper. By 1988 Saturday was the *Telegraph*'s best-selling day of the week, 30,000 higher than the average weekday.

The *Independent*, then without a Sunday paper, decided to go for a larger slice of the weekend advertising cake by launching a Saturday colour magazine in September 1988. Cleverly edited by Alexander Chancellor, the magazine was less glossy than those of the Sunday papers and less concerned with conspicuous consumption, emphasising stylish, reflective writing. Printed on matt paper, it distinguished itself physically from the other magazines by featuring black-and-white photo-graphs, using colour sparingly. At the same time a separate Weekend section was put into the paper, making a Saturday package that soon sold some 30,000 copies more than the average weekday sale, despite its higher price.

By the end of the year, all the rival broadsheets had retaliated. The *Telegraph* put into effect a long-simmering plan to switch its colour magazine from the Sunday to the Saturday paper. When launched in 1964, the magazine had been distributed with the Friday *Daily Telegraph*, because of its much higher circulation than the *Sunday Telegraph*. In 1976 it was moved to Sunday to put the Sunday paper on a level footing with its two rivals. But with the daily selling 1,139,000 copies a day in the first six months of 1988, against the Sunday's 716,000, the commercial argument was overwhelming for moving the magazine back to a weekday and thus nearly doubling its advertising rates. Saturday was now the obvious weekday to do it. On Sundays the magazine was replaced by a new colour section called Seven Days, specialising in photo-journalism – but it did not have the feel of a conventional magazine and the Sunday paper's circulation fell as a result. *The Times* introduced a sixty-four-page, four-section Saturday paper, with one of the sections in colour (but not a glossy magazine because that would have competed with the highly profitable *Sunday Times Magazine*) while the *Guardian*, a couple of months later, launched an innovative Weekend section in tabloid format, on newsprint.

All this Saturday activity affected the Sunday market. Total sales of Sunday quality papers fell by 130,000 between October 1988 and September 1989. All three were down but the *Sunday Times*, continuing to add sections and value, was the least harmed. The men behind the *Correspondent* believed that the main reason for this contraction of the market was the inadequacy of the existing papers, and their pre-launch research appeared to confirm this. In one respect it tied in with that done for the *Independent*. The indications were that in the Sunday market, too, there was a desire for a paper that was not ultimately answerable to a magnate or an international entrepreneur.

'It is about a return to good writing by journalists freed from pro-prietorial control,' Peter Cole told a publishing conference in June. He developed the theme in numerous pre-launch interviews: 'We know that we are the corner shop to Mr Murdoch's supermarket. We also know that there are plenty of people out there who are suspicious of the conglomerates.'

Two slogans on pre-launch posters cleverly emphasised both the paper's compactness and its freedom from tycoons: 'Great but not Wapping' and 'Concise but not Tiny'.

The *Independent*, meantime, had been blowing hot and cold about whether to start a Sunday paper of its own. Early in 1989, before the *Correspondent* had completed its financing, Whittam Smith had said that there was no immediate prospect of a Sunday *Independent*. However successful a new paper turned out to be, it was sure to prove a drain on the company's resources for a time. The board had been considering floating shares on the Unlisted Securities Market in the spring of 1990 and these new costs would depress the share price.

The final go-ahead for the *Sunday Correspondent* changed the balance of the argument. If the new paper was a success, it would stack the odds against any significant penetration of the market by a fifth quality Sunday. Although there was no chance of launching simultaneously with the *Correspondent*, it would be almost as effective to enter the lists after three or four months when, if the pattern of previous launches was maintained (in particular that of the *Independent* itself), the infant would be at its most vulnerable. After producing a dummy *Independent on Sunday* in August and researching its impact on advertisers, Whittam Smith announced that the paper would appear in January, with Stephen Glover, one of his co-founders, as editor.

The team behind the *Correspondent* were pained, especially when the *Independent* would not accept their advertising. They saw the *Independent*'s announcement as an attempt to strangle their enterprise at birth – as it was. The ferocity of the rivalry between the two teams of pioneers surprised and even upset those who had come to regard the *Independent* as a representative of all that was clean and decent in journalism, not the kind of paper to soil its hands in such no-holds-barred competition. Georgina Henry wrote a pained note to that effect on the media page of the *Guardian*: 'the *Independent*'s image has been irrevocably changed by its Sunday action. It has not been a clean fight, this will we/won't we titillation riding on the back of an honourable title which did so much to change the industry.'

In *New Statesman and Society* Sean French commented: 'It seems to have been a feature of Britain's cultural scene that herbivores have started behaving like carnivores.' The hard fact was that two new quality Sundays were to be launched in the space of four months and the experts predicted that at least one would go to the wall. The battle lines were drawn.

*　　　*　　　*

The first issue of the *Sunday Correspondent* appeared on 17 September 1989. It seemed polished enough if, by common consent, a little bland, lacking bite. With two sections and a magazine its profile most closely matched that of the *Observer*, and politically it seemed to share that paper's centre-left position. Peter Cole had deliberately not stuffed its pages with established fashionable names but perhaps took that self-denying process too far. It could have used a big-name columnist: instead the main political column, long and low-key, was written by David Blake, one of the paper's founders.

The first issue's print run was 667,000 – slightly lower than the *Observer*'s regular circulation of 680,000 – and almost all were sold. But the headlong decline, familiar from other launches, began immediately. Nick Shott, the chief executive, had set a break-even circulation target of 375,000, rising, he hoped, to 425,000 by the end of its first year. That seemed ambitious, seeing that the long-established *Observer* and *Sunday Telegraph* both sold fewer than 700,000. Within five weeks,

Let a hundred flowers bloom: the first issues of three of the newspapers that appeared in the 1980s. The *Correspondent* had closed by Christmas 1990.

despite a £5 million promotional campaign, sales had dropped to 350,000 and were still sinking, to around 200,000 by January.

That was when the *Independent on Sunday* made its bow, to a chorus of approval from the pundits and consequent predictions that the *Correspondent* would not be long for this world. In the week after the *Independent on Sunday*'s launch, twenty-five out of thirty-five advertising executives, questioned in the trade magazine *Campaign*, said they thought the *Correspondent* would close. But in the first weeks, as the *Independent on Sunday* was undergoing its initial slump from the launch sale of some 800,000, the *Correspondent*'s circulation was stabilising at around 220,000.

Whereas the *Correspondent* had produced a conventional package of two broadsheet sections – news and review – plus a glossy magazine, the *Independent on Sunday* came up with a different format. There was only one broadsheet section, for news and sport. Business news came in a plump tabloid – aping the Sunday *New York Times* – while the review section was the most innovative of all, printed in colour on stiff but not glossy paper, slightly larger than conventional tabloid size. It was a hybrid of a magazine and a newsprint review section, with short deadlines that allowed some of the previous week's openings and cultural events to be recorded in it. There was no conventional glossy colour magazine because Whittam Smith did not want to risk taking advertising from the *Independent*'s Saturday magazine.

By March 1990 the *Independent on Sunday* seemed to be heading towards a 'bottoming out' figure of around 340,000, or half as many again as the *Correspondent*. But the total Sunday quality market, which had grown with the launch of the two new titles, was drifting back towards its former level of 2,700,000, despite Whittam Smith's belief that markets expand when acceptable new products are introduced. All five competing papers were faced with a continued squeeze on sales and the *Independent* imposed an economy drive on both its daily and Sunday papers to prepare for hard times ahead.

That March the *Correspondent* received a tangible, morale-boosting expression of faith when it was able to raise £10 million extra investment – £7 million equity and £3 million loan finance. The *Chicago Tribune* provided more and became the biggest single investor, with 17.7 per cent of the equity. An executive of the American group, Michael Pakenham, was sent to London to, as he put it, 'galvanise the newspaper's appearance, content and co-ordination of editorial staff'. The *Guardian*, having wavered and then declined the invitation to be a first-round investor, now plunged in with £3 million, or 16.6 per cent.

Like all papers, the *Correspondent* had been affected by a sharp down-turn in advertising at the beginning of 1990, but this fresh financing seemed a signal that it was not going to expire gently under the assault from its newer rival. Yet circulation continued to drop until by the end of the summer it was down to 150,000. The new backers' final throw was to fire the editor, Peter Cole, and replace him with John Bryant, from *The Times* and before that the *Daily Mail*. Bryant's brief was to convert the paper into an up-market tabloid – an interesting experiment but one that, to have any hope of success, needed more resources than were now available to the ailing title. It closed before Christmas 1990.

6
Masters of the Game

> You must be prepared to put your whole heart and soul, your
> stomach, your liver, your whole anatomy into a task which will
> appear most of the time to be dangerously stimulating and on
> occasion positively revolting.
>
> Lord Beaverbrook, quoted by F. A. Mackenzie

Before the *Independent* was launched, the founders made much of the
fact that the paper would have no single proprietor in the traditional
Fleet Street sense. Part of the reasoning behind the launch was their
belief that people felt somehow soiled at the thought of reading a paper
that was controlled by a ruthless millionaire or a multinational conglomerate – or, in the case of the Murdoch papers, both.

The success of the *Independent* appeared to validate the assumption
behind this strategy. People who own newspapers, the press barons,
have been feared rather than loved, reviled rather than respected, even
when their publications have been popular and successful. Yet attempts
to launch newspapers without a single dominant proprietor, or to dilute
his influence by making him answerable to boards or committees, have,
until the *Independent* came along, mostly proved disastrous, in Britain at
least.

In *Dangerous Estate*, Francis Williams wrote, unprophetically: 'The
age of the strongly individualist newspaper proprietor who himself
impressed an editorial personality on his paper is almost over: we are
moving into the era of the administrators. Only Lord Beaverbrook
remains of the old breed.'

Yet the era did not die with Beaverbrook. As newspapers passed from
hand to hand, it was invariably the prospect of influence that made them
so irresistible to would-be purchasers. With the notable exception of
Lord Thomson, there has not been a significant newspaper proprietor
sufficiently humble to eschew all attempts at influencing what goes into
his papers. Despite that, there is a powerful strand of liberal opinion

that believes such acts of self-denial to be the only way in which freedom of the press can be ensured – hence the insistence that the two latest owners of *The Times* sign hands-off undertakings, and the appointment of 'independent' figures to make sure they kept to them. When Lord Stevens, chairman of the *Express* group, told the *Independent*'s Maggie Brown, in an interview in March 1989, that 'I do interfere' in the papers' policy, there was a shocked disapproval, and the remark was used as the basis for an article by the *Independent*'s political editor Anthony Bevins in *British Journalism Review* (winter 1990) deploring proprietorial influence.

Bevins also threw up his hands in horror at a statement on television by Max Hastings, editor of the *Daily Telegraph*, that his proprietor Conrad Black had a right to influence the policy of his paper. Such attitudes, claimed Bevins, meant that 'the very notion of a free press is a joke'. He argued that journalists should resist the attempts of proprietors and even editors to dictate the nature of political and other coverage, that they should not 'pander to what the editors want'.

If even editors are not to decide what goes into their paper, who is? Bevins appears to believe that the writing journalists, imbued as they are with the spirit of free enquiry, should be allowed the strongest voice. This ignores the historical fact that newspapers without a coherent philosophy emerging from strong central editorial direction (viz. *News on Sunday*) do not succeed.

It is scarcely surprising that proprietors, who have achieved that status through being men of decision and conviction, should contest the view that their role in their organisations is to sign the cheques and keep quiet. Proprietorial vendettas have always been a feature of journalism, although in modern times the sight of a proprietor pursuing his commercial interests through the columns of his paper has been viewed with disapproval. Here the market provides as good a restraint as any. Readers took against the *Observer* in the late 1980s because of its campaigns on behalf of its owner Lonrho, just as those who felt that Murdoch's *Times* was too blatantly canvassing its owner's interests, especially in satellite television, were fortunate to have the *Independent* to switch to.

* * *

In the literal sense, press barons are a twentieth-century phenomenon. The first newspaper owner to be elevated to the peerage was Edward Levy Lawson, owner of the *Daily Telegraph*, who became Lord Burnham in 1903. (The more celebrated Alfred Harmsworth, founder of the *Daily Mail*, did not become Lord Northcliffe until 1905.) But since the late eighteenth century British newspaper proprietors have exercised an influence over politics and society that has made them the subject of awe, envy and abuse.

Paradoxically, when in the twentieth century circulations of popular tabloids grew to seven figures, their actual political influence waned – although this did not usually dampen the political pretensions of their proprietors. They still took an editorial line, which qualified them for favours from politicians, even if it had a dubious impact on the opinions of a mass readership only spasmodically interested in politics. The newspapers that filled the bulk of their columns with less demanding topics were the ones that achieved the most success. When their lack of political influence was recognised, proprietors were still vilified, but now for manipulating and corrupting public taste rather than for trying to secure the election of a particular party. Yet in reality the successful mass-market papers, such as the *Daily Mirror* in the 1940s and the *Sun* in the 1970s, were those that reflected the public mood rather than created it.

The idea that there is something unethical, immoral almost, about a proprietor trying to influence the content of his newspapers is of recent growth. If you had suggested to most newspaper owners, at least until World War Two, that they should have invested in their newspapers only to allow their editors (their hirelings, after all) a free hand to decide what to print, you would have been derided. Until the second half of the nineteenth century, owning a newspaper was primarily a source of influence rather than of fame or profit – certainly not profit. Because the chief motive of the proprietors was to support some particular view or party, news took second place to opinion: the intelligence was often stale and sometimes invented. The proprietors and financial backers were rich men with no pressing need to make profits from the venture. Stephen Koss wrote in *The Rise and Fall of the Political Press in Britain*: 'Today, it is perhaps difficult to recall how intimately newspapers were once bound to political organizations or to factions and individuals within them, and how dutifully they had once served those interests, even to the detriment of their own commercial viability.' In other words, pleasing a paper's patrons took priority over pleasing its readers. And its patrons were almost exclusively the opinion-forming elite.

Significantly, the first newspaper to put news before opinion, and whose proprietor was prepared not to exercise an editorial prerogative, was the first to gain undisputed long-term success commercially. In 1785 John Walter launched the *Daily Universal Register* – soon to become *The Times* – as a means of promoting his new printing process. With no political axe to grind, at least at the beginning, he was able to concentrate on developing a comparatively fast and impartial service of news. To do this he needed to exploit new forms of production and communication. For a hundred years, *The Times* was in the forefront of developing new technology both for printing newspapers and for transmitting dispatches from distant parts. And until Lord Northcliffe bought it in 1908, its editors – notably Thomas Barnes and John Delane – were invariably men of greater prominence than its proprietors.

*   *   *

The influence of the Harmsworth family on the modern British press is incalculable. Not only was the *Daily Mail* the first mass-market daily paper but in the mid-1960s, the period I have chosen for the beginning of this study, the direct or indirect descendants of Alfred and Harold Harmsworth, Lords Northcliffe and Rothermere, still ran two of the largest press groups. A third, the *Telegraph*, was run by a descendant of the Berrys, who had shared with the Harmsworths the ownership of much of the national press in the 1920s. Even Rupert Murdoch, who arrived on the scene five years later, had a dynastic relationship through his father, to whom Lord Northcliffe was a friend and counsellor.

It is perilous to generalise about the motives of newspaper tycoons but, since Northcliffe, most of the successful ones have been inspired initially by considerations of commerce or, quite often, personal gratification, rather than by strictly political ambition. (I use the word 'political' in the sense of believing fervently in a policy and wanting to own a newspaper for the purpose of propagating it, not necessarily out of ambition for political office.)

Of this century's successful proprietors, only Lord Beaverbrook has been so motivated – and the actual political impact of his papers was minimal, despite their wide readership. Most hopeful politician-publishers have suffered the fate of Colonel Arthur Sleigh, who founded the *Daily Telegraph* in 1855 for the purpose of pursuing a vendetta against the Duke of Cambridge. After a few months he had to sell the title to his printer, Joseph Levy. Many have sought to own newspapers because they wanted quick access to the sources of power for social or occasionally personal reasons, including a desire for honours. As for Northcliffe, his ambitions for power and influence were formulated only after he had started his newspaper empire.

Northcliffe was an archetypal press magnate. Starting with nothing but energy, vision and ambition, he launched his first title (*Answers*) at the age of twenty-three and eight years later, in 1896, the *Daily Mail*. In the late Victorian age of mass production it was the first mass-produced newspaper, with all the concessions to popular taste that the term implies. For that reason it was scorned by those who thought that discussion of grave matters of state could only be conducted in the self-important style that the papers had adopted hitherto.

On the other hand, Northcliffe was courted by politicians who, on the brink of the age of universal franchise, were excited by the possibility of gaining hundreds of thousands of votes through the editorial columns of his mass-circulation newspapers. In the ensuing century, this belief in the power of the press, although never incontrovertibly proven, has dominated people's attitudes towards newspapers. While taking every opportunity to seek favourable references to themselves, politicians would, when it suited them, deplore what they characterised as the pervasive influence of the unelected press barons. (This essential contradiction in the attitude of public figures to newspapers helps explain why attempts to control the excesses of the press have generally been stillborn.)

In 1908 Northcliffe bought *The Times*, then well past its nineteenth-century heyday. He succeeded in boosting its circulation and viability, enabling it to survive – albeit often in a debilitated condition – until Northcliffe's spiritual successor, Rupert Murdoch, acquired it in 1981. But Northcliffe was disappointed by the level of political influence he was able to exert. He was defeated for a seat in the Commons and during World War One was given only minor government tasks to perform. He was offended not to have been appointed to the British delegation at the Versailles Peace Conference of 1919.

When Northcliffe died in 1922, virtually insane, the bulk of his Associated Newspapers empire passed to his brother Harold, Lord Rothermere, who had been the unassertive financial genius of the group, as essential to its success as his flamboyant brother but always over-shadowed by him. The *Daily Mail*, the core title of the group, remains in the family's hands: the present Lord Rothermere, the third of the line, inherited it when his father died in 1977. The three-generation line of succession disproves the usually reliable rule that the children of press barons invariably make a hash of their inheritance.

The present Lord Rothermere, formerly Vere Harmsworth, lives for most of the time in Paris. He does not, at first meeting, appear to possess the magnetism or political ambition of a Northcliffe or a Beaverbrook or the cavalier ruggedness of a Murdoch. His marriage in 1957 to an actress, Beverley Brooks, was a traditional liaison for an English aristocrat. Although he was made vice-chairman of Associated Newspapers in 1963 he was not given much to do until his domineering father finally retired nearly ten years later.

He lacks the empire-building instinct of a first-generation tycoon. In 1976 he wooed the *Observer* but it went to the American oil company Atlantic-Richfield. His bid for *The Times* in 1981 was no doubt meant seriously but was seen as half-hearted by the one group it had to impress, the board of Thomson Newspapers. In the 1970s, emulating Murdoch, Vere Harmsworth toyed with expanding the group's activities into the United States. He tried to defend Clay Felker's *New York* magazine against Murdoch's advances but was predictably outflanked. He then set up Felker as editor of *Esquire* and took a share in the *Soho Weekly News*, a rival to New York's *Village Voice*, but both ventures foundered. He journeyed to Wilmington, Delaware, bearing a supply of his favourite mineral water in a heavy wooden cabin trunk, to bid for a group of newspapers there, but they went to the Gannett chain for double what he was prepared to pay. In the end, America was too difficult.

Yet the third Lord Rothermere should not be underestimated. He has the invaluable ability to choose talented lieutenants and keep their loyalty. By placing unqualified trust in his editor, Sir David English, he has succeeded in his principal strategic aim, to establish the *Daily Mail* as the dominant middle-market paper at the expense of its long-time rival and tormentor, the *Daily Express*. Indeed he has come out the victor in all his skirmishes with the *Express* group. The launch of the *Mail on Sunday* in 1982, seen by many then as a potentially expensive gamble, damaged the rival group's main revenue-earner, the *Sunday Express*, whose circulation it had overtaken by 1989. The merger of Associated's *Evening News* with the *Express* group's *Evening Standard* in 1980 was effected on terms that allowed Rothermere to take over full ownership of the monopoly London evening paper when the *Express* group changed hands in 1985. Two years later he cleverly defeated Robert Maxwell's attempt to drive the *Standard* out of business.

*   *   *

The other scion of the Harmsworth family still ruling a Fleet Street roost in the mid-1960s was Cecil Harmsworth King, the son of Northcliffe's and Rothermere's sister Geraldine. He worked his way up in the family business and in 1935 became a director of the *Daily Mirror*, founded by Northcliffe in 1903 and, after a false start, a pioneer in the use of large pictures and bold headlines on a tabloid-size page. In 1935, when Rothermere sold his controlling interest in it, King stayed on and in 1951 became chairman in a boardroom putsch when he ousted Guy

Bartholomew, one of the founding fathers of British tabloid journalism.

King was a taciturn man who, as his diaries abundantly show, shared the Harmsworths' tendency towards unabashed self-esteem. Although a man of refined tastes, far removed from those of the *Daily Mirror*'s mass readership, he formed close working relationships with men who had a talent for popular communication; first Bartholomew and then Hugh Cudlipp. King's own unceremonious removal from office was provoked by his attempt to wield the political influence that many assume wrongly to be there for newspaper owners to exploit at whim. Like his uncle Alfred, he wanted to *take part* in national and international affairs, rather than merely own papers that from time to time commented upon them. In his Granada lectures in 1966, published as *The Future of the Press*, he declared that 'a publisher has the right, indeed the duty, openly to exert influence through his newspaper'. But at the same time he expressed his frustration about the ineffectiveness of newspapers as a tool towards this end:

> The limitations of so-called power are painfully obvious to the publishers of all newspapers. They may speed up a movement of opinion of which they approve. They may slow down a movement of which they disapprove. What they cannot do is to reverse public opinion. It may be for example that the *Mirror* and its stable companions brought out the few extra votes which enabled Mr Wilson to win his narrow majority in 1964. But if the group had been in the opposite camp in 1966 there would still, in my opinion, have been a handsome Labour victory.

King's frustration with this ultimate lack of influence caused his downfall. When in 1968 he appeared to be part of a plot to replace the elected Labour Government with an administration of national unity, and moreover when he used the *Mirror* newspapers to publicise the idea, his fellow directors forced him to resign. Hugh Cudlipp replaced him.

*   *   *

Despite Cudlipp's unrivalled talents as an editor and editorial director, he was a failure as a chief executive. The *Mirror* group languished under his leadership. Having been manoeuvred into letting Murdoch have the *Sun* for next to nothing, he failed to devise a strategy to prevent the brisk new tabloid from eating into the *Daily Mirror*'s traditional readership. In 1969 he launched a weekly colour magazine, given away with the paper on Fridays, which proved a costly failure. In 1970 the company merged with Reed, the paper conglomerate, but continued to stagnate.

Cudlipp retired in 1973. After that, attempts to introduce new technology were successful in so far as the *Mirror* was the first Fleet Street paper to switch from hot metal to cold type, but the power of the print unions ensured that no cost savings were achieved. In 1983 Reed announced that it wanted to be rid of the troublesome subsidiary. It would be floated on the stock exchange the following year. Clive Thornton, the chief executive of the Abbey National Building Society and a man with a high reputation in the City, was appointed chairman of the *Mirror* group with a view to supervising the flotation. Reed ruled that no single shareholder would be allowed to own more than 15 per cent of the new company.

Robert Maxwell had other ideas. Since the florid Czech-born ex-Labour MP had lost the battle for the *Sun*, his fortunes had touched bottom, then risen spectacularly. An attempted merger of his Pergamon Press with Leasco, an American company, ended in acrimony and expensive legal action, culminating in a report by Board of Trade inspectors that criticised his conduct in the harshest terms. In 1975 he had another brief flirtation with the newspaper world when he gave some financial backing to a workers' co-operative in Glasgow that was launching the *Scottish Daily News* from the former headquarters of the *Scottish Daily Express*, which had been closed by Beaverbrook Newspapers the previous year. After the paper's initial failure, Maxwell was put in sole charge but resigned after a series of personality clashes and the paper soon closed.

In 1980 Maxwell won control of the British Printing Corporation and quickly turned it into a profitable base for his other activities. But he was still being thwarted in his desire to break into newspapers. He put in a bid for *The Times* and *Sunday Times* when Thomson Newspapers announced their sale in 1980, but Thomson thought him an unsuitable owner and again he was humbled by Murdoch, the eventual buyer. Four years later he made a pass at the *Observer*, whose owner, 'Tiny' Rowland, was quarrelling publicly with his editor, Donald Trelford, about a report Trelford had written concerning the activities of the security forces of Zimbabwe, a country with which Rowland wanted to foster good business relations. Rowland, feigning exasperation, opened talks with Maxwell about selling the paper to him. It was never clear how serious Rowland's intention was, but in any event he patched up his quarrel with Trelford and brusquely ended his talks with Maxwell.

Maxwell was exploring other avenues. He bought a 10 per cent stake in the *Express* group, which had been publicly floated by Lord Matthews following his acquisition of the papers from the Beaverbrook family in 1977. Then in 1983, when Reed made the announcement about the *Mirror*, he sensed that now, when he had reached the age of sixty, he was going to fulfil his ambition.

To Thornton's anger, Maxwell neutralised Reed's proviso limiting individual shareholders to 15 per cent of the equity, by the simple expedient of offering £90 million, nearly twice as much as would have been raised by the public flotation. No responsible company, obliged to act in the interest of its shareholders, could refuse, despite its earlier promises. Thus shortly before 1 a.m. on Friday 13 July 1984, Maxwell turned up at the *Mirror* headquarters in High Holborn, helped himself to a drink from the cabinet in the managing director's office and told those executives who were still there: 'This is a turn-up for the book, isn't it?'

*　　*　　*

It had taken him a long time to fulfil his ambition, so it is not surprising that, for the first few months, the excitement should have gone to his head. In the spectrum of interventionist and non-interventionist proprietors, Robert Maxwell had no doubt at all at which end he intended to place himself. The day after he took over he led the paper with a personal message to readers about the new dawn that had just broken over their newspaper. Headlined 'Forward with Britain', it was as much about Maxwell as the *Mirror*. He described how he was going to make the papers more efficient so that they would regain their rightful place as the best sellers in their market: 'The *Daily Mirror* and I already have one thing in common. We have supported the Labour Party in every election since 1945. That support will continue. But the *Mirror* has never been a slavish party paper. It will not be a Labour Party organ now. We treasure our independence.'

All independence movements need a leader. For a time there was a danger of slavish adherence not to a party but to the portly knight who had ridden in and snatched the well-used maiden from the jaws of death, bearing her to what could – who knows? – turn out to be a worse fate. For the first few weeks of his proprietorship it seemed there was scarcely a day when news or pictures of Maxwell did not appear in the paper. If he was not being photographed awash with £1 million in new notes for a bingo promotion, *Mirror* readers were being asked to interest themselves in his arcane business activities or his meetings with decrepit communist dictators.

There were, too, less apparent influences. He altered an article by

Geoffrey Goodman, the respected industrial commentator, about the miners' strike to make it less critical of the Government; then he made a futile attempt to act as peacemaker in the long coal dispute. He was clearly enjoying the realisation of his ambition, even if the old *Mirror* stalwarts were not. One evening early in his proprietorship he suggested to Mike Molloy, editor of the *Daily Mirror*, that the nickname of a habitual rapist should be changed in a front-page headline to 'The Rat' from 'The Fox' – the name by which he had been known to the tabloids and the police for weeks. The incident helped convince at least two long-serving executives, Tony Miles and Terence Lancaster, that it was time to get out.

A few months later the *Mirror* papers devoted pages of space to Maxwell's personal effort to relieve the famine in Ethiopia. Rescue bids of all kinds, with Maxwell as the rescuer-in-chief, were the subject of frequent *Mirror* stories in the early years of his proprietorship. The inventor Sir Clive Sinclair (1985) and the Commonwealth Games (1986) were among people and events dramatically rescued, at least temporarily, by the unstoppable 'Cap'n Bob'.

In an interview with Hugo Young in the *Guardian* in March 1990, Maxwell defended himself against charges of self-promotion: 'I happen to be a notorious person whom people come to see from all over the world. If the editors think that what I do is of interest to our readers, it's up to them.'

But he added that he now banned stories about himself unless they had 'genuine news value'. He claimed credit for the revival of Neil Kinnock's moderate Labour Party – then well ahead of the Conservatives in the opinion polls – because he had helped marginalise left-wing extremists. He added that his papers had been influential in the defeat of the militant miners in 1984 and in what he claimed as a victory for moderate ambulance-workers in their strike in 1989/90.

At the beginning Maxwell made few editorial changes except to bring back Hugh (now Lord) Cudlipp as a consultant. Cudlipp, who had been out of full-time journalism for more than a decade, was unable to wield any decisive influence – or to stop circulation falling by 350,000 in Maxwell's first year – but he did help forestall some of the proprietor's more blatant excesses.

Although Maxwell's direct editorial interfering did nothing to increase the appeal of his papers, his commercial influence was beneficial in tackling the excessive costs of the production processes. The old *Mirror* management had been among the most craven in failing to resist the increasingly extravagant demands of the print workers. Maxwell, with a mixture of threats and charm (both equally convincing to their victims among union leaders), was able to achieve cost savings which were overshadowed by Murdoch's dramatic move to Wapping, but which were scarcely less significant in the long term.

After he had been in control for just over a year, there began a series of disputes with the print unions in London and Manchester, resulting in wildcat stoppages and losses of production. Maxwell made numerous threats to close the papers and on 25 November 1985 signed an editorial in the *Daily Mirror* declaring that 'the gravy train has hit the buffers'. Just before Christmas he completed a settlement with the unions involving job cuts of 1,600 – and this was a month before Wapping.

*　　*　　*

There were other ways in which the new proprietor's impetuousness and commitment worked to the benefit of the *Mirror* papers. By ordering £68 million worth of modern presses in 1985, and phasing in full colour production over 1988 and 1989, he gained a start of more than two years on Rupert Murdoch's *Sun*, which was not able to print in colour until the end of 1990. But those same qualities worked against him when it came to planning his first launch of a new title, the ill-conceived *London Daily News*.

In the winter of 1985/6 newspaper proprietors, their eyes opened by Eddy Shah, came to recognise that, after years of stagnation, new technology made it possible to start newspapers on a cost basis that would, assuming reasonable editorial appeal, give them a good chance of survival. Many schemes did not go further than the planning stage, foundering when it became necessary to commit real money to them. Maxwell cleared that hurdle; but by the time the disaster of the *London Daily News* had run its course, he was profoundly regretting that he had ever set it in motion.

When pundits looked for gaps in the newspaper market, the London evening field seemed an obvious one. Since the *Evening News* had been merged into the *Evening Standard* in 1980, the *Standard*'s circulation, despite its monopoly position, had declined to around half a million, not far above its level at the merger. The lack of competition had made it lazy and flabby. Strong rumours came from the Murdoch camp that he was thinking of starting a London evening paper – although it emerged later that much of the talk had been orchestrated as a cover for his plans for the move of his daily titles to Wapping.

Taking advice from Charles Wintour, the former editor of the *Evening Standard*, Maxwell decided to launch a paper competing directly with the *Standard* in the middle market rather than, as Murdoch would have done, aiming for the mass market that had been largely unserved since the *News* closed. Maxwell believed that he needed to develop a business readership to support the classified advertising that was the commercial backbone of a metropolitan evening newspaper, even if it meant going head-to-head with a powerfully entrenched competitor.

The new paper would be printed at a number of plants on the perimeter of London. His choice of editor, again on Wintour's advice, was a curious one. He lighted on Magnus Linklater, a distinctly up-market old Etonian who had spent most of his career on the *Sunday Times* and the *Observer*. It was the same mistake that Eddy Shah had made – again partly on Wintour's advice – with Brian MacArthur on *Today*. Wintour saw both his nominees as having his own qualities: a serious, almost intellectual bent coupled with a flair for popular papers. In fact Wintour had spent most of his career in tabloid journalism whereas MacArthur and Linklater had dipped into it only briefly. Linklater's task was the more formidable because he was trying to breathe life into a product probably aimed at the wrong market, with a proprietor whose interest in the project was intermittent and whose actions were unpredictable.

Maxwell's original plan was to launch the new paper in the autumn of 1986 but he was diverted first by his rescue efforts on the Commonwealth Games in Edinburgh and then by a libel action he was pursuing against *Private Eye*. These delayed vital negotiations and decisions about manning levels, printing sites and distribution. To compensate for the dispiriting effect of the delay he decided to make it into a twenty-four-hour paper, with editions first thing in the morning and throughout the day. He believed the extra staff and increased distribution cost would be balanced by extra circulation. Only later was he to discover the essential fallacy behind this thinking: that nobody is going to buy the same paper twice a day. Although the morning edition was competing against a powerful group of rivals, including his own *Daily Mirror*, there was a time when it sold more than the afternoon editions, because their distribution was so patchy.

Nothing went right. Maxwell had hired Bill Gillespie, an Ulsterman from News International, as managing director of the new paper, but he resigned well before launch because of a dispute over the paper's name and because of the difficulties he found in working with Maxwell. Even when the third projected launch date was met, Maxwell did not sign the final printing contract (with the *Daily Telegraph*'s new West Ferry Road plant) until the eve of the launch on 24 February 1987.

This allowed insufficient time for machines to be prepared properly, or printers trained, and the paper was plagued from the outset by printing and distribution delays – far more serious for an afternoon paper than a morning one, and especially serious for one that appears round the clock.

It never really had a chance. To head it off, Rothermere cleverly revived the old *Evening News*, which he was able to distribute in the same vans as the *Standard*. It was relaunched on the same day as the *London Daily News*: the word 'News' in both the titles led to confusion and dissipated much of Maxwell's advance publicity. When Rothermere halved the price of the *Evening News* Maxwell obediently fell into the trap by following suit, instead of staying at the same price as the *Standard*. This not only harmed his revenue but compromised the image of his paper as a quality product that could compete with the incumbent on level terms. There was nothing wrong with the journalism in the *London Daily News* except that it was too similar to the fare offered by the *Evening Standard*. An established paper with an assured distribution system has incalculable advantages over a newcomer that appears on the streets erratically.

The general election in June 1987 meant that a decision had to be taken whether to endorse a political party. There was clearly no question of a paper owned by Maxwell supporting the Conservatives, but Linklater was not keen on toeing the *Mirror*'s Labour line slavishly. In that same election campaign the *Independent* was to show that it was not essential for a paper's credibility to come down firmly for one side or the other and Linklater, too, would have preferred to steer a middle course. But Maxwell saw all his papers as an integral part of Labour's campaign machinery. Although unable to resist Maxwell's pressure on the basic issue, Linklater did stand up to him on details of the coverage. He would not, for instance, despite Maxwell's cajoling and veiled threats, republish a rousing pro-Labour editorial, written by Joe Haines, that had already appeared in the *Daily Mirror*.

Although Maxwell appeared not to harbour grudges against people who stood up to him, the cumulative effect of such arguments was debilitating both for him and for Linklater. Thus when the time came to decide whether to cut losses on the paper, he could not help taking the quarrels into account. A feisty and independent editor who runs a successful paper is one thing: if he is not attracting readers his bargaining position is mortally weakened. On 24 July 1987, Maxwell called the staff together to announce that the *London Daily News* was to close forthwith. Its circulation was down to below 100,000 – a fifth that of the *Standard*.

A few weeks later Rothermere closed the relaunched *Evening News*: its spoiling job was done.

Maxwell was ungracious in defeat. Most of the paper's troubles had been caused by his misjudgments – his unsuitable choice of editor, his insistence on a twenty-four-hour paper, his failure to initiate proper printing and distribution arrangements, his misjudgment over cutting the cover price. Yet Joe Haines, in his authorised biography of Maxwell, managed to divert blame elsewhere, to 'those responsible for the *LDN*'s operation', characterising them as spendthrift and unwilling to take advice.

If Maxwell felt deflated, it was not for long. He soon produced plans for a giveaway London evening, the *Londoner*, and for a daily English-language paper circulating in Europe, the *European*. The first was abandoned and the second, after many changes of plan, became a weekly rather than a daily and was launched in May 1990. Interviewed in the *Independent on Sunday* just after the launch, Maxwell again denied responsibility for the failure of the *London Daily News*, and indeed did not accept that it had failed at all: 'It is grossly unfair to say it failed. It shut down because the printing arrangements were not working. In no sense was it a failure.' And he told the *Independent* that the lessons of the debacle had been learned:

> If we had owned the printing presses we would still have been in business. It was well edited but I made the mistake, stupidly, of leaving it to the professionals. I've not done that here. *The European* has all my attention . . . I'm in charge. I will be like Lord Hartwell at the *Sunday Telegraph*. I will set the editorial policy line. Absolutely . . . I am the editor-in-chief. I am *The European*.

He was expanding his business in other directions as well, constantly buying and selling blocks of shares in companies, most of them concerned with printing and publishing. He even had a 5 per cent stake in the *Independent* – acquired without the knowledge of Andreas Whittam Smith and his colleagues. He owned the Oxford United football club and in 1988 made one of his most ambitious acquisitions, paying $2.7 billion for the American publisher Macmillan (no longer connected with its British namesake). He appointed his 29-year-old son Kevin to run Macmillan, suggesting that, despite the poor past record of the children of press magnates, Maxwell was bent on founding a dynasty.

Before long, though, it was all to turn sour in the most extraordinary and melodramatic fashion. On 5 November 1991 Mr Maxwell disappeared from his yacht the *Lady Ghislaine* – named after one of his daughters – off the Canary Islands in the early hours of the morning. His body was discovered floating in the sea later that day.

Suicide has not been proved but soon after his death came grim revelations about the parlous financial state of his empire and, worse, about the fraudulent means he had employed in an attempt to rescue it. He must have realised before he died that the position was irretrievable. The price of shares in Mirror Group Newspapers, on which the value of most of his global assets largely depended, had fallen precipitately from 240p the previous April to just 77.5p. His creditors were beginning to call in what he owed them, and he could not pay.

In fruitless attempts to shore up the position he had siphoned £97 million from the newspaper group and a massive £350 million from its pension fund, leaving long-serving *Mirror* employees without provision for their retirement. Many people with whom he had dealt now fervently wished that they had taken more account of the 1971 Board of Trade report into the Leasco affair, which concluded that Maxwell was 'not in our opinion a person who can be relied on to exercise proper stewardship of a publicly quoted company'. His sons Ian and Kevin, inheritors of the horrendous consequences of their father's actions, refused to answer questions about the missing pension money before a House of Commons Select Committee for fear that they might be subject to legal action.

The *Mirror* newspapers, like the rest of the Maxwell assets, were taken over by the official receiver, and a buyer was sought. Richard Stott, the paper's editor, announced that he was trying to organise a management buyout, and he recruited Sir Peter Parker, the former chairman of British Rail, to try to raise money for it. Several likely publishers expressed interest, among them Pearsons, owners of the *Financial Times*, and the Manchester Guardian and Evening News Group. Both drew back, though, when they discovered the extent of the liabilities that Maxwell had bequeathed to the *Mirror*. Even the Canadian Conrad Black, proprietor of the *Daily Telegraph*, was said to be interested, but his firm Conservative views made him an unlikely proprietor for Britain's only Labour tabloid. By June 1992, seven months after Maxwell's death, the paper's destiny was still uncertain.

*   *   *

When he finally achieved the apogee of his ambition and became a national newspaper proprietor, seven years before his posthumous disgrace, Robert Maxwell inspired the same emotions among his subordi-

DAILY Mirror

nesday, November 6, 1991. **NEWSPAPER FOR THE NINETIES** Last month's daily sale 3,684,098 INCORPORATING THE DAILY RECORD 25p

MAXWELL DIES AT SEA

THE MAN WHO SAVED THE

DAILY Mirror

DEAD: Mirror Group publisher Robert Maxwell, whose body was recovered off Tenerife

By THE EDITOR

BOB MAXWELL is dead. His body was taken from the sea off Tenerife last night after he disappeared overboard from Lady Ghislaine, the yacht he loved.

In one of our many late-night conversations I asked him what he would like to be remembered for when he died.

"As the man who saved the Mirror," he said without hesitation. It's true. He did. If he hadn't taken over the Mirror group in 1984, the papers would have slid gently into terminal decline.

None of us here will ever forget the fact.

And that is why our front page headline this morning remembers just that.

LUXURIOUS: Lady Ghislaine, the yacht Robert Maxwell loved

Publisher in yacht tragedy

A GREAT BIG EXTRAORDINARY MAN Pages 2 to 11, 18, 19, 34 to 36

The *Daily Mirror* front page on 6 November 1991, the day after Maxwell died.

nates as had his predecessors and contemporaries with that exclusive job description. He was feared, envied and regarded with grudging awe. Only rarely have press magnates attracted that much more elusive feeling, affection: certainly Maxwell did not, even before the full truth about him came out. One who did was the first Lord Beaverbrook, born Max Aitken, who died at the age of eighty-five in 1964, some time after his particular brand of proprietorial intervention had become outdated and unviable. Yet in the two decades following World War Two, it worked well enough for Beaverbrook's *Daily Express* to be vying for market leadership with the *Daily Mirror*.

Nearly all journalists' memoirs covering the period 1920–60 contain fond, fawning or at least respectful recollections of Beaverbrook – some first hand, some just feeding on the legend that dominated Fleet Street for four decades. Unusually for a newspaper owner Beaverbrook, a zestful and highly political Canadian, liked journalists and enjoyed their company, even those who did not share his political opinions. The fact that he employed socialists such as Michael Foot and Tom Driberg suggested that his instinctive priority was good journalism rather than political soundness.

He would invite promising young men (and occasionally, in later years, a woman or two) to his Park Lane apartment or even his villa in the South of France. More often than not there was an ulterior motive, in that he would be trying to plant an idea for an article that he wanted to see in print. Yet he loved to think of himself as a man with a respect for talent and promise in writers and he obviously enjoyed the encounters for their own sake. The journalists found them immensely flattering and encouraging: in the paper's heyday, not many quit the *Daily Express* voluntarily.

Paradoxically, Beaverbrook's success in creating three exemplary popular newspapers – the *Daily* and *Sunday Express* and the *Evening Standard* – proved only that his ultimate *political* aim was unattainable. He was elected to Parliament before he bought the *Daily Express* and sought to show that a proprietor could wield influence on the nation's ideas by creating a successful mass-circulation paper and promoting his policies in it. In a speech in 1926 he said of the power of the press: 'When skilfully employed at the psychological moment no politician of any party can resist it.' Yet politicians are influenced by newspapers only if they are convinced that newspapers are influencing their readers. It was clear that this was not the case with Beaverbrook's *Express*, the bulk of whose readership were not overwhelmingly interested in politics, and especially not in a concept as romantic, intangible and distant from their experience as the waning British Empire, which was at the heart of most causes he promoted.

He failed to get the Conservatives elected in 1945, despite a smear campaign suggesting that Labour had dictatorial tendencies akin to those of Hitler. He failed to thwart the creation of the United Nations and he failed to prevent Britain's joining Europe (although it did not happen until after his death). He told the Royal Commission on the Press that he ran his papers to make propaganda but, as Piers Brendon wrote in *The Life and Death of the Press Barons*: 'Beaverbrook showed that in an engine of propaganda the engine matters more than the propaganda. His steamed ahead despite its cumbersome freight.'

If people did not buy the *Express* for its politics, what then did they buy it for? Most of its virtues derived from Arthur Christiansen, editor from 1933 to 1956, and they were of the most basic kind. His approach to news coverage, as I described in Chapter 3, was to get the paper's own reporters to the scene of important events and to persuade them to write vividly (first) and accurately (second, but a close second) about what they saw and what it meant. Before the arrival of the jet age, actually getting a reporter to a trouble spot was an achievement that needed initiative and organisation. The *Daily Express* foreign desk was the best organised in Fleet Street. Beaverbrook was prepared to spend whatever it took to get good reporters to the location of good stories, and to get their words back to London – and thence to the readers – in the shortest possible time.

To make up for this apparent extravagance he was, in some other respects, extraordinarily mean. Ann Leslie, who went to Fleet Street at the age of twenty-two as a *Daily Express* columnist ('she's young, she's provocative'), recalls that Beaverbrook would send her letters about her work – as he did to all his key writers and editors – mixing praise with criticism. His one outburst of real anger was provoked when she used a new envelope for one of her replies. Yet he paid way above the going rates for really first-class people.

He understood above all the importance of motivation. His executives were sometimes irritated by his persistent notes and telephone calls but more often they were flattered. They called him their 'principal reader' and, almost up to his death, the desire to win his praise injected a sense of purpose and *élan* into their efforts.

*   *   *

Max Aitken, Beaverbrook's son, lacked his father's ability to run the business efficiently. By 1974, ten years after he took over, the circulation of the *Daily Express* had dropped by a quarter to around three million, apparently losing readers to the burgeoning *Sun*, and to the *Daily Mail*, which had switched from a broadsheet to a tabloid format in 1971. In 1974 an increasingly desperate Aitken made a bizarre choice of editor: he appointed Alastair Burnet, who had been editor of *The Economist* and a television news reader.

The appointment would have been comprehensible as part of some grand strategy to take the paper up-market to compete with the *Daily Telegraph* – a move which would inevitably have meant losing well over half the circulation – but Burnet's brief was to keep it going as a mid-market tabloid, for which he had no obvious qualification. When he quit by mutual agreement in 1976, and rejoined Independent Television News, he had left scarcely a footprint in Fleet Street, and the *Express*'s circulation was still sliding. It was suffering from a characteristic ailment of ageing newspapers: the old readers were dying and young ones were not coming along to replace them. New production equipment was badly needed but the papers were not generating enough profit to fund the necessary borrowing.

Burnet was replaced by Roy Wright, a Fleet Street professional who had the background and technical skills that Burnet lacked. A change to tabloid format the following year effected only a temporary halt in the paper's decline. By that time, in any case, Aitken was already in negotiation with several media and city figures about disposing of the papers. His health was poor and the empire that his father bequeathed him had become a burden, not a joy.

Most of the familiar cast of Fleet Street's ambulance-chasing proprietors and prospective proprietors, always ready with a deal to acquire an ailing title, entered the lists: indeed at one point Max Aitken had in his hands a cheque for £1.4 million from Rupert Murdoch. (He did not bank it.) In their book, *The Fall of the House of Beaverbrook*, Lewis Chester and Jonathan Fenby give a lively and convincing account of the tortuous negotiations that ended with the group passing for £15 million to Trafalgar House, a conglomerate that included the building firm Bridge Walker. Victor Matthews, who formerly ran Bridge Walker, was managing director of Trafalgar House and the key figure in the *Express* acquisition. He became chairman of Beaverbrook Newspapers when the deal was completed. One of his first acts was to fire Wright and replace him with Derek Jameson, a flamboyant Cockney who later became a radio personality.

Matthews, though inexperienced in newspapers, was an energetic proprietor. In 1978 he decided that he wanted to use spare printing capacity in Manchester to launch a new paper in the mass market, competing against the *Sun* and *Daily Mirror*. For purely commercial reasons he ruled that the new paper, the *Daily Star*, would support the Labour Party. Research showed that a majority of *Sun* readers voted Labour, although their paper was now staunchly Conservative. The *Star* would provide a more palatable political diet for *Sun* readers who found the *Mirror* a little stodgy and old-fashioned. The *Mirror*, for instance, did not print pictures of topless women. The *Star*, like the *Sun*, did, every morning. Because of the tradition that newspapers normally reflect the views of their owners, some saw the support for Labour as the height of cynicism. Matthews made no secret of his Conservative views and the *Express* newspapers were enthusiastic supporters of the Conservative Party. How could a paper that was part of the same stable carry any conviction in advocating the return of a Labour government?

Jameson was moved from the *Express* to edit the new paper. It started well, but it could not get its sales consistently higher than a million – a quarter of that of its two rivals. It has remained in a distant third place in its market despite a flirtation with soft porn during its ill-fated 1987 liaison with *Sunday Sport* (see Chapter 10). But because so many of the overheads are shared with the *Express* newspapers it has never lost enough money to justify closing it down.

Matthews tried several editors for the *Daily Express* after Jameson, each with his own formula for adjusting the paper marginally up- or down-market and appealing to the young and female readers it had always found elusive. None succeeded in reversing the slow but remorseless downward trend in circulation, down below the psychologically important two million mark and getting perilously close to losing its slender lead over its arch-rival the *Daily Mail* – an indignity that finally occurred in 1986. Even Sir Larry Lamb, the gifted launch editor of the *Sun*, could not repeat his success here.

Matthews controlled the *Express* group for only eight years. In 1982 he persuaded Trafalgar House to agree to float the papers, as well as the Morgan Grampian magazine group that the conglomerate also owned, to form a separate new company, Fleet Holdings, with Matthews as chairman. Although this proved a smart move financially it made the papers vulnerable to takeover. This duly came in 1985 when United Newspapers, a group of magazines and regional papers, mounted a successful bid. Although Matthews was disappointed to lose control he took away a profit of some £8 million: the Fleet share price had rocketed because of the market flotation of the news agency Reuters, which had been jointly owned by the national newspapers.

The chairman of United was David Stevens, soon to become Lord Stevens, just as Matthews had become Lord Matthews. Stevens resembled Matthews in other ways. He had never really expected to be a national newspaper proprietor and was determined to enjoy this surprising turn of events, revelling in the influence that went with the position. He did not believe in editorial independence and certainly did not believe that any of his titles should be free to take a non-Conservative stance: he quickly made the *Star* toe the same political line as the *Express* papers.

Stevens is not a compulsive interferer in the editorial side but has no scruples about intervening if he sees fit. In an interview published in the *Independent* on 8 March 1989 he said that he had told his editors to stop criticising the royal family and had injected positive ideas, such as an anti-litter campaign: 'I do interfere, and say enough is enough. I don't ram my views in but I'm quite far out to the right . . . I suppose the papers echo my political views.'

A year later, when Margaret Thatcher was doing badly in the opinion polls and there were suggestions of a plot by Conservative MPs to replace her as leader, Lord Stevens wrote an angry article in her defence in the *Daily Express*, spread across two pages and headlined 'We Can't Let Maggie Go'. Criticising 'backbench fainthearts' and vigorously lay- ing into Michael Heseltine, Mrs Thatcher's potential challenger for the leadership, Lord Stevens concluded: 'There is only one person fit and able to lead the party and the country at this juncture and that is the Prime Minister. While she is in 10 Downing Street, Britain is in safe hands and has an assured future. But if the Tory party does not stop its shenanigans now, all this could be put at risk.'

Below this was an article by two *Express* reporters, questioning the credibility of opinion surveys suggesting that many Conservative MPs wanted Mrs Thatcher to step down, and attacking the papers that pub- lished them. To no avail, though. The MPs, convinced that they were bound to lose the next election without a change of leadership, forced Mrs Thatcher to resign in November 1990. But the opposition of the *Express* and the other Conservative papers to Michael Heseltine helped ensure that he did not succeed her. The post went to her own favoured nominee, John Major, and the *Express* papers lost no time in rallying to his support in preparation for the 1992 election.

Yet although Stevens had the trappings of a proprietor, including the semi-automatic peerage, and enjoyed *droit de seigneur* over the comment pages when he wanted it, he was conscious that he was not in the literal sense a proprietor at all, and thus did not enjoy the total freedom of action of most of his predecessors and contemporaries. As chairman of United Newspapers, he could be dismissed by the board (as Cecil King was) and, because it was a public company, he had always to be on his guard against potential takeovers. The most worrying threat came from a man who had much in common with Beaverbrook, including his nationality. We shall meet Conrad Black in the next chapter.

7

The New Tycoons

A great many of them are irresponsible. They have huge power and many of them are extremely reckless.

Conrad Black on journalists

A cursory reading of the editorial columns of most national newspapers, for just a few days, will leave no doubt as to where their political loyalties rest. With rare exceptions, support for one of the political parties is as consistent – and as immune to change through argument – as a football fan's support for the local team. Yet nowadays proprietors are loth to have such loyalties defined precisely, preferring to claim an independence of judgment which just happens to lead them invariably to the same conclusions as those reached by the party they support. As Stephen Koss noted, in recent years 'newspapers substituted what may be called political dispositions for what had been formal party allegiances.' In the 1970s Lord Hartwell, proprietor of the *Daily Telegraph*, engaged in a long and ultimately successful battle with the BBC World Service, persuading it to cease characterising his paper as 'Conservative' in its review of editorial comment in the London press.

Yet the political line of the *Telegraph* is as unmistakable as when it – and more particularly the *Morning Post*, with which it merged in 1937 – owed formal allegiance to the Conservatives. In 1855, after Joseph Levy had taken it over from Colonel Sleigh, it was a Liberal paper, but it switched sides twenty years later under Levy's son, Edward Levy Lawson, later the first Lord Burnham. It remained Conservative when the second Lord Burnham sold it in 1927 to William and Gomer Berry, two acquisitive and businesslike Welsh brothers who already owned the *Sunday Times*, the *Financial Times*, the *Daily Graphic*, the *Daily Sketch* and many regional newspapers and magazines. Today's legislation against monopolies would not allow a single company to amass such a large collection of titles.

William Berry was created Lord Camrose in 1929 and his brother

Gomer became Lord Kemsley in 1936. In 1937 the two brothers split the group between them, Camrose taking the *Telegraph* and *Financial Times* (later sold to Brendan Bracken) and Kemsley getting the *Sunday Times* and most of the provincial papers. In 1959 Kemsley sold his entire group to the Canadian Roy Thomson but Camrose's sons had inherited the *Telegraph* on their father's death in 1954. The elder son and heir became chairman and his younger brother, Michael Berry, editor-in-chief, exercising the greater influence. A reserved and hesitant man with none of his father's flair, Michael Berry was given a life peerage in 1968 and became Lord Hartwell.

The first Lord Camrose was a gifted proprietor who launched the *Telegraph* on its path to success in December 1930 by cutting the price from twopence to a penny, instantly doubling the circulation to 200,000. It was he, too, who insisted on maintaining the primacy of news and not being seduced by the allure of features. By keeping its cover price well below that of *The Times* he ensured a steady circulation growth, until it had reached some 750,000 by 1939 and over a million by the time of his death. Under Lord Hartwell, equally committed to hard news, circulation continued to grow but profits failed to keep pace, in part because Hartwell insisted on sticking to his father's policy of a low cover price and in part because of the lack of aggressive selling by the advertising department. The *Sunday Telegraph*, established in 1961 but still with only half the circulation of the daily paper, contributed to the crisis by being a consistent loss-maker. Hartwell was anxious to prove that the sons of press barons do not always make a hash of their father's inheritance and he nearly succeeded: he was over seventy when things began to go irreversibly wrong and seventy-five when he finally had to cede control and go the way of the Aitkens, the Astors and the rest.

In a speech to a *Financial Times* seminar in April 1988 Andrew Knight, who was managing director of the *Telegraph* group from 1986 to 1989, made some harsh criticism of Hartwell's record as proprietor, although he was careful to insert a honeyed tribute or two ('the considerable vision of a true newspaperman') to ease the pain. Circulation of the *Daily Telegraph* had peaked at 1.5 million in 1979, when *The Times* was off the streets due to an industrial dispute. Since then it had fallen, slowly but remorselessly, to 1.16 million in 1986. In that period, *The Times* and *Guardian* had increased by more than 300,000 between them.

The *Telegraph*'s circulation decline was accompanied by a consequent drop in advertising volume, especially classified. For a time, said Knight, this did not show up in the balance sheet because Hartwell increased the cost per thousand readers to advertisers, which had until then been well below the prices quoted by his competitors. He also raised the cover price, which further depressed sales. Knight circulated his speech to all *Telegraph* directors including Lord Hartwell. In a memorandum responding to it, Hartwell laid some of the blame on the rise in unemployment in 1979, which cut job advertising, the paper's main commercial strength.

By the time of this petulant exchange, Hartwell, though still on the board, had ceded control of the group, following a traumatic liquidity crisis in 1985. Some years earlier he had recognised the need to expand and modernise his printing operation, particularly so that he could fatten up the lean *Sunday Telegraph* which, unable to expand beyond forty pages, looked puny against its rivals. This would necessarily mean printing away from the paper's cramped Fleet Street headquarters and Hartwell had entered into contracts worth £105 million for new printing plants in Manchester and on the Isle of Dogs, in London's former dockland.

In addition to the cost of the new printing facilities, which were to prove much bigger than necessary, the company would have to find the money for as many redundancies among production staff as it could negotiate with the unions. These costs patently could not be financed from the paper's uncertain profits nor, as it turned out, from the company's bankers, who were distinctly unimpressed by the paper's performance in the 1980s. They would lend Hartwell £80 million on the condition that he increased capital investment in the company by making a £30 million rights issue.

Not everyone thought that was his only option. Andreas Whittam Smith, the *Daily Telegraph*'s ambitious young city editor, went to him with an innovative plan to raise the capital from readers under a Business Expansion Scheme – a device by which small investors gain tax advantages through investing in private companies. The minimum individual investment under such a scheme was £500. Whittam Smith was confident that at least 120,000 people, or 10 per cent of the *Telegraph*'s buyers, would invest that minimum amount, raising £60 million – double what was then thought to be needed. He believed the actual figure would be closer to £100 million. Hartwell sought the advice of David Montagu, an investment banker on the *Telegraph* board, who opposed going to readers, in effect the paper's customers, for finance.

Although he could not have known it, Hartwell's rejection of Whittam Smith's scheme was among the most far-reaching decisions taken in Fleet Street in the 1980s. By opting for a more conventional rescue plan he set in motion the process that would culminate in his losing control of the *Telegraph* group within a year. Equally important, it helped clarify Whittam Smith's thoughts. In great secrecy, he, Stephen Glover and Matthew Symonds had already been discussing their plans to start a new broadsheet newspaper. Had Hartwell accepted his refinancing proposal, Whittam Smith might have felt constrained to stay with the *Daily Telegraph*, where there was a chance that he might be appointed editor. As it was, the rejection of his plan was an extra incentive to risk launching his own paper.

The *Telegraph*'s refinancing went badly. Some potential investors were worried by the refusal of the paper's bankers to come up with the required sum, and by the group's anticipated loss of £5 million for that year, with redundancy costs to come. It was also unusual to be seeking finance for projects already under way, as the new printing plants were. As the deadline approached, there was still a shortfall of £10.5 million. This is where Andrew Knight, the cool and soigné editor of *The Economist*, entered the picture.

In 1980, at a luncheon in Toronto with Henry Kissinger among the guests, Knight had met Conrad Black, a rising and outspokenly conservative Canadian businessman whose holdings included a chain of small newspapers. (In 1980 he went after the Toronto *Globe and Mail* but was outbid by Thomson Newspapers.) During their talk, Knight asked Black whether he would be interested in investing in the British press. An ambitious man, Black had pondered that possibility before but had formulated no firm plan, nor even a definite intention. He replied yes, he might be interested, and Knight undertook to keep his eyes open for opportunities.

The two met on a number of occasions following the conference, and became friends. Hearing of the trouble the *Telegraph* was having with its rights issue, Knight phoned Evelyn de Rothschild, the banker handling the sale and, as it happens, chairman of *The Economist*. Knight asked whether money would be accepted from Black's Canadian company, Hollinger.

When Rothschild phoned Hartwell to tell him that a new investor had been found, the 73-year-old proprietor's first question was: 'It's not Goldsmith, is it?' His one dread was that the financier James Goldsmith, who had been sniffing round other newspapers, notably the *Observer*, would make a move towards the *Telegraph*. The two men did not get on. Goldsmith thought he was the victim of hostile coverage in the *Telegraph* newspapers, and Hartwell still resented an article about his wife, Lady Pamela Berry, that had appeared in Goldsmith's short-lived *Now* magazine a few years earlier. Told that the *Telegraph*'s potential saviour was not Goldsmith but Black he breathed a sigh of relief, even though he had scarcely heard of the 41-year-old Canadian. The investment was agreed in June 1985 and the stock issue thus met its target.

At first it was hard to see what was in it for Black. He would gain a minority interest in a group viewed by City professionals as a high risk. But he had insisted on a vital condition for his investment: if any further money had to be raised, he would have pre-emption rights on the majority interest held by Hartwell and his family. This made the deal virtually hazard-free. If the funding proved adequate, Black would eventually have a profitable investment. If it did not – and Black believed that the forward projections in the prospectus were over-optimistic – then he could exercise his option and buy the papers, either to keep or to sell on: as Thomson had found with *The Times*, there is seldom a dearth of buyers for famous national newspapers, however unprofitable.

Confident that the initial £30 million would prove adequate, Hartwell acceded to the condition with dispatch and equanimity. He said that Black planned to be a passive investor and 'does not want to be any sort of newspaper tycoon'. Yet by November it was clear that this was just what he was about to become. The money raised from the banks and by the rights issue was nowhere near enough. Several things had gone wrong. The imposition of VAT on advertising had cut revenue to all newspapers; and Hartwell's managers had failed to negotiate sufficient concessions from the print unions about manning the new plant in Manchester. The prospectus had allowed for the whole cost of the Manchester plant to be met from savings in manpower, but this was obviously not going to happen. Moreover, retraining compositors to work the new technology was costing £5.5 million, more than five times the original estimate. The banks, alarmed, threatened to foreclose. To ward them off, Hartwell found himself having to raise over £1 million from his family finances in one twenty-four hour period. The end seemed near.

Hartwell made a final attempt to cling on to his inheritance. He approached the Australian newspaper publishers Fairfax, proprietors of the *Sydney Morning Herald* (themselves to be the victims of a comparable financial crisis a few years later). He suggested that Fairfax should buy out Black's initial investment and put in some more money of their own, but leave Hartwell and his heirs in control of the business. The Fairfax board found the proposal too expensive, so Hartwell, with immense sadness, had to accept the inevitable.

Before exercising his option, Black made two prudent and highly confidential enquiries. First he commissioned a detailed report on recent changes in British labour legislation and how ready the Government and the judiciary were to enforce them against the unions. His second move was to enquire of Rupert Murdoch, through a mutual acquaintance in New York acting as emissary, what he planned to do about his plant in Wapping, which had been idle for the four years since its completion.

The results of both enquiries were encouraging. The study showed the employers could now get the backing of the Government and the police to prevent secondary picketing: Eddy Shah had taken advantage of that during the Warrington dispute. Indeed in the last few months Robert Maxwell had breached the unions' previously uncompromising position by negotiating significant labour reductions among production staff. As for Murdoch, he told the emissary that, while he could not be explicit about what he planned to do, he was not going to put up much longer with having his papers' growth crippled by the print unions: he would be taking drastic action.

Satisfied that there was a real chance of the British press escaping from its union straitjacket, Conrad Black exercised his option over the family holding and, with an additional investment of £23.3 million, became the third Canadian, following Beaverbrook and Thomson, to own a major British newspaper.

*   *   *

After taking over as chairman of the *Telegraph* Black bought a house in Highgate, north London, but continued to base himself in Canada. He hired Andrew Knight – the man who had alerted him to the opportunity – as the group's managing director. Black's absence from Britain in the early days of his proprietorship, when the crucial manning cuts were made, was tactical. He and Knight had seen how, in the past, leaders of production unions had been granted access to proprietors almost as of right, and were often able to cajole them into making concessions that professional managers would have resisted.

Black could give the impression that he was not totally committed to the ownership of the papers, that they were a hobby which he would readily abandon if it became too onerous or expensive. He believed that other proprietors – for instance his compatriot the first Lord Thomson – had badly weakened their position by letting it be known how much store they set by owning a prestige British newspaper, implying that they were prepared to invest virtually unlimited chunks of their personal fortune in the venture. This made them cherry-ripe for plucking by industrial blackmailers.

The choice of Knight as chief executive was risky, for his experience of management was limited to his editorship of *The Economist*. To balance that, Black appointed a man of enormous experience as deputy chairman. Sir Frank Rogers had been a close associate of Cecil King at the *Mirror* and was now chairman of EMAP (East Midland Allied Press), the regional newspaper and national magazine group. When Black made his initial investment in the *Telegraph* he had been invited to nominate two directors to the board: one was himself and for the other he took Knight's advice and approached Sir Frank. It was Sir Frank who in turn recommended the man soon to become managing director: Joe Cooke, a veteran labour consultant for the newspaper industry. Cooke advised Knight and Black on the kind of savings on manning that they should be looking for, and bore the brunt of the difficult negotiations with the unions.

One of Knight's priorities was to slow the drain on funds represented by the two new printing plants. He achieved this by selling half shares in them to other newspaper groups: in the London plant to *Express* newspapers and to News International in Manchester. He proved not just an adept manager but a willing public relations representative for his chairman. He told anyone who would listen about Black's talents in business and his cultural achievements, chief among which was a keen interest in the career of Napoleon and the authorship of a 700-page biography of Maurice Duplessis, Premier of Quebec for eighteen years between 1936 and 1959.

When praising his absent chairman, Knight would routinely express his hope that Black would soon see fit to base himself in London, closer to the action. His speech to the *Financial Times* seminar in April 1988 was typical of what Knight was saying in public and private at the time. Describing Black as 'extraordinarily quick and decisive – and invariably proved right', he added: 'I believe proprietors should ideally live near their newspapers, which need them.' In the summer of 1989 Black took the hint and declared that he would henceforth live for most of the time in Highgate. Not long afterwards he assumed Knight's title of chief executive, leaving Knight as joint deputy chairman with Frank Rogers.

Although it meant uprooting his family from Toronto, Black had powerful incentives to make the move. One was purely social. He had noted the status afforded to national newspaper owners in Britain – much higher than across the Atlantic. Still in their forties, he and his wife Shirley liked the idea of mixing at a high social level and felt that in later life they would regret it if they did not take the opportunities now offered.

The second motive was commercial. The *Telegraph* was now Black's single biggest holding. Moreover, it was making money which needed channelling into new investments, preferably in Britain. Black had acquired through the markets a sizeable minority shareholding in United Newspapers, owners of the *Daily Express* group – the *Telegraph*'s partners in the new Docklands printing plant. Lord Stevens, United's chairman, was suspicious of Black's motives and rejected out of hand the Canadian's cheeky plan that United should acquire the *Telegraph* in a manner that would leave Black effectively in control of both. If Black was contemplating a serious move on United in the future, he could do it more effectively from a London base.

At first, the switch of responsibilities between Knight and Black appeared to have been effected without rancour. Black had every reason to be grateful to Knight, not just for introducing him to the investment but for turning the company's financial position around so quickly. A loss of £11.2 million in 1986 became a marginal profit of £580,000 in 1987, rising to £29.2 million in 1988 and £41.5 million in 1989.

Yet one of Knight's last major initiatives as managing director had turned sour. Ever since he had taken over the group he had been frustrated by his inability to take the circulation of the *Sunday Telegraph*, now below 700,000 again, to anything approaching the *Daily Telegraph*'s 1,200,000. He thought that by merging the identity of the two papers he might persuade more readers of the daily to take the Sunday, as well as making savings on staffing. To the anger of Peregrine Worsthorne, editor of the Sunday, Knight announced the merger of the two into a seven-day paper under the overall editorial supervision of Max Hastings.

To his precise mind it may have seemed a logical move but, in terms of staff morale, it was a disastrous one. Before going ahead, maybe he should have pondered why it had never succeeded in Britain before. Although the seven-day concept works in the United States, with papers such as the *New York Times* and *Washington Post*, the tradition in Britain is of Sunday paper journalists working on their own stories at their own pace, developing their own angles. The concept of a unified news team is unfamiliar and unwelcome. The staff were upset, especially since the change was accompanied by a bid to alter their working rosters. Sub-editors had for some years been accustomed to working a four-night week but this was to be increased to five. There was industrial action and many journalists left the Sunday paper. In the end, the level of integration was less than Knight had envisaged: the proposed five-night week, for instance, became a nine-night fortnight.

Although Black did not wholly blame Knight for this fiasco, his decision to move to London was revealed soon afterwards. He had in fact made up his mind some months before, waiting only until he had cleared up some outstanding business matters in Canada. Many were surprised that Knight had agreed to switch to a position where he held far less power than hitherto. Few people – except, apparently, Conrad Black – were surprised when on 3 January 1990 it was announced that Knight was to become executive chairman of Rupert Murdoch's News International, with effect from 12 March. Murdoch had been trying to lure him for more than a year, but only now did Knight feel able to accept. When he told Black, the Canadian wrote him an irate letter, leaked widely to the press:

> It seems to be a universal view, among people whose friendship we both value in Britain, Canada and the United States, that your pro-longed (if sporadic) courtship with our principal competitor while continuing as the ostensible chief executive of the *Daily Telegraph*, leading to a consummation just 80 days after retiring (awkwardly) as a director of ours, and with your pockets loaded with a net £14m of free *Telegraph* stock, raises substantial ethical questions.

Towards the end of the long letter, he added ironically: 'Max Hastings has asked me to commend to you the merits of combining *The Times* and the *Sunday Times*.'

The £14 million of *Telegraph* stock was what Knight had acquired with the options he was granted when joining the company. Shortly before announcing his resignation as chief executive he had sold £2 million worth of them. Knight insisted that he had not acted unethically. In his reply, he described Black's tirade as 'emotional and inaccurate', defended himself against the charges and concluded: 'You have pro-vided a very jolly story for the newspapers but your letter says more about you than about me.'

Black's public roasting of his former colleague proved, if nothing else, that the days of strong-willed and outspoken newspaper proprietors were by no means over. Like many of them, he is also sensitive to criticism. When a reviewer dared find fault with his book, Black called him a 'supercilious little twit'. When a critical article appeared about him in the *Spectator* (which he later bought), he wrote a letter to the editor inveighing against the writer's 'sniggering, puerile, defamatory and cruelly limited talents'.

Reviewers are not the only writers who fall victim to Black's venom. In November 1989 he told the *Financial Times* that some journalists are 'temperamental, tiresome and nauseatingly eccentric'. In an interview with the *Telegraph* staff magazine two months earlier he had said: 'A great many of them [journalists] are irresponsible. They have huge power and many of them are extremely reckless.'

Black was always careful to exempt his own staff from these strictures, believing that British serious journalism was less prone to such excesses than American and Canadian: yet he did once write that the British press was 'habitually snobbish, envious and simplistic'.

Editors of his newspapers could be forgiven for finding such observations chilling. He has, though, seldom taken too proprietorial an attitude over the views expressed in the *Telegraph* papers. He will offer his opinion on an issue without insisting that it becomes the paper's policy. He made known his disagreement with editorials written by Max Hastings – the young editor he had appointed on Knight's advice – criticising the United States bombing of Libya and the shooting of three IRA activists in Gibraltar, but made no direct suggestion that the policy should change. During an early phase of the United States presidential election in 1988, when opinion polls predicted victory for the Democrat Michael Dukakis, he sent a forceful note to Hastings warning him not to take a Dukakis victory for granted. Within weeks the wisdom of that advice had become apparent.

Black requires only that his editors maintain a broadly conservative policy, although since basing himself in London he has acquired the habit of firing off private notes to express his disagreement with articles, even on topics that might be thought beneath his attention. When the entertainment magazine *7 Days*, distributed with the *Sunday Telegraph*, ran an article saying how much better British television was than American television (hardly an original notion), he sent a memo to the editor, Sue Summers, saying that he was tired of reading such views, which he believed to be mistaken. For good measure he tore into another article in the same issue criticising the ITN news reader Julia Somerville – the granddaughter of Admiral Somerville, a man he much admired. Black maintains that these letters do not amount to instructions to alter editorial policy, although it is hard to believe he does not appreciate how intimidating they are. Summers left the *Telegraph* soon afterwards.

Occasionally, when Black wants to dissociate himself from a view expressed in his papers, he will write a letter for publication. In August 1989, after the *Daily Telegraph* had published an editorial supporting the British Government's decision to repatriate Vietnamese boat people from Hong Kong, he wrote a letter ending: 'Britain must do better than compel the return of these wretched people to the source of their misery, while relying on the *Daily Telegraph* to cover such a retreat with a barrage of transparent sanctimony.'

The letter led the correspondence column but did not make Hastings fear for his job. When Black was criticised in the weekly journal the *Spectator* – which the *Telegraph* had acquired in 1988 – by its editor Charles Moore he wrote a pained letter for publication, ending:

> Must Mr Moore react to every subject involving the *Daily Telegraph* like a bantam rooster who feels his independence is threatened? He would do better to congratulate himself on having sought and found for *The Spectator* a proprietor who responds so equably to the minor irritations, such as this one, that *The Spectator* inflicts on that person who ultimately, and more or less uncomplainingly, pays *The Spectator*'s losses and endures Mr Moore's occasional condescensions.

Less than two months later Moore stepped down from the editorship, although both men insisted that this had nothing to do with their public argument, and he now writes regularly again for the *Telegraph*.

Black, meanwhile, had lifted his sights well above those 'minor irritations' and was actively expanding his global empire. In 1989 he outbid Robert Maxwell for the *Jerusalem Post*. He nibbled at television with a 5 per cent stake in Carlton, the company that, in 1991, won the weekday Independent Television franchise for the London area. In December 1991 he was at the head of a consortium that won a long battle for control of the former Fairfax group in Australia after the Fairfax family, saddled with debt due to over-ambitious expansion, had been forced to cede control. The group, for which the consortium paid £660 million, included two of Australia's most prestigious papers, the *Sydney Morning Herald* and the *Age* in Melbourne – both similar in nature to the London *Daily Telegraph* and offering scope for shared editorial services.

In February 1992 Black confirmed that he had made approaches to buy part of the troubled *Mirror* group, actively seeking a buyer after the death of Robert Maxwell. There would certainly have been a political outcry, though, had a man of his views emerged as owner of the traditionally Labour *Mirror* papers. Later that year he joined a consortium bidding for the new Channel 5 television franchise.

*   *   *

Like a comet's, Roy Thomson's path across the constellation of British national press proprietors was brilliant if brief; lasting from 1959, when he bought the *Sunday Times* from Lord Kemsley, until his death in 1976.

It took his son Kenneth only five years from then to secure the group's withdrawal from Fleet Street and its industrial anarchy. Yet the first Lord Thomson's role was a pivotal one, as the link between the Berry family's sixty-year domination of much of the national press and Rupert Murdoch's broadly comparable regime (comparable in terms of its scope if not of its nature) that became fully established when he acquired *The Times* and *Sunday Times* from Thomson in 1981.

Of all the proprietors who paid lip service to the notion of editorial independence – meaning independence from the owner as well as from outside political and commercial pressures – Thomson was the only one who practised it without qualification. In his memoirs, *Editor-in-Chief*, Sir Denis Hamilton, who oversaw the editorial side of *The Times* and *Sunday Times* throughout the Thomson ownership, wrote that although Thomson would sometimes comment on the political line taken by one of the papers he would never dream of suggesting that it might be altered. When he ran (unsuccessfully) for the Canadian Federal Parliament in 1953 he did not even instruct his Canadian papers to support him.

He used to carry a card with him, bearing what he called his creed, which he would show to anyone trying to persuade him to induce his papers to take a particular view on a particular issue: 'No person or group can buy or influence editorial support from any newspaper in the Thomson group ... I do not believe that a newspaper can be run properly unless its editorial columns are run freely and independently by a highly skilled and dedicated professional journalist.'

In his engaging little book *After I Was Sixty*, Thomson tells how in 1963 he was worried about editorials in the *Sunday Times* criticising Harold Macmillan's Conservative Government. He wrote:

I suspected that I was being considered for an honour by the Prime Minister's committee. I had made no secret of the fact that I aspired to a title one day ... Yet, as he took issue with the Conservative Government on several occasions, the editor of the *Sunday Times* never heard a word of reproach from me; I would have bitten my tongue first.

Harold Evans, who edited the *Sunday Times* through most of Thomson's ownership, reveals another such incident in his book *Good Times, Bad Times*. In 1974, Hamilton told him that Thomson would be unhappy if the *Sunday Times* came out for Labour. Evans had already decided to do so and told Thomson as much in a telephone conversation: 'He took it in his stride, made some shrewd comments on the characters of Heath and Wilson and concluded: "Well, Harold, it's up to you . . ." Thomson would bet his business judgement against anyone, but he did not expect any great weight to be attached to his political views.'

It pleased Thomson to cultivate a reputation as a man interested only in commerce. 'I buy newspapers to make money to buy more newspapers to make more money,' he was quoted as saying in the *Columbia Journalism Review*. Yet his purchase of *The Times* in 1966 gave the lie to that. He might have thought he saw a way of reducing its losses but he cannot realistically have hoped that it would make him any significant profit in the short or even the medium term.

Why, then, did he buy it, if not for political influence? He analysed his reasons frankly in his book. He wanted the paper, he confessed, for its 'supreme reputation, and the tremendous boost it would give to our reputation – and our ego'. He observed: '*The Times* was not just another newspaper; it was a bastion of empire and a pillar of the establishment, and so on.'

Despite the hint of scepticism in 'and so on', he was, as I reported in Chapter 3, willing to undergo all sorts of humiliating conditions for the privilege of propping up this pillar with his bankroll. The main opposition to his ownership, as he had recognised, was the perception of him as 'a rough-neck Canadian'. Describing the Monopolies Commission's enquiry into the sale, Thomson wrote: 'Not once but many times I told them that I was only taking on *The Times* because I reckoned its rescue and restoration to health would be a worthy object and perhaps a fitting object for a man who had made a fortune out of newspapers . . . This was the way my life had come to a final purpose; it was my destiny.'

Born in 1894, the son of a Toronto barber, Roy Thomson stumbled into the communications business accidentally in 1928. Having unsuccessfully tried a number of ways of making money, he moved to northern Ontario to sell radios. In the early days of radio there were not enough stations to ensure decent reception in every settlement in that remote area, so he started two of his own, one in North Bay and another at Timmins, where he bought his first newspaper, the *Citizen* (he renamed it the *Press*), at the age of forty. He acquired more papers and radio stations in Canada and in 1952 bought his first American title in Florida. The following year he came to Britain to buy the *Scotsman* and, when commercial television was introduced in 1955, he took a controlling interest in Scottish Television. With some of the money he made from that, he bought the Kemsley newspaper empire, including the *Sunday Times*, in 1959.

It is hard now to appreciate precisely why the establishment was so reluctant to hand *The Times* over to someone willing to inject desperately needed capital and fresh management. In the event, although nobody could have foreseen this, the conditions imposed on the sale were among the factors that forced Roy Thomson's son Kenneth to give up Times Newspapers in 1981 – well before the end of the twenty-one-year 'guarantee' that he and his father had agreed to in 1966.

The much-vaunted Thomson management turned out far less capable in practice than they were by reputation. For instance, the move of *The Times* in 1975 from Printing House Square, near Blackfriars Bridge, to Gray's Inn Road, alongside the *Sunday Times*, was bungled. A day's production was lost because of unforeseen production difficulties. Relations with the print unions had generally been better on *The Times* than on the *Sunday Times* but with the move *The Times* printers became caught up in the combative atmosphere of Gray's Inn Road. And when the old building was sold, the negotiators inadvertently included in the sale the valuable sundial commissioned for *The Times* from Henry Moore only a few years earlier. The paper had to make do with a small model in a glass case in the entrance hall of its new building, while the original was sold by the old building's delighted purchasers.

Had Roy Thomson involved himself more directly in managing the papers – as by the agreement he was not allowed to do – he might have taken a tougher line with the print unions at an early stage and avoided the necessity of the feeble attempt at a showdown that 'Duke' Hussey and Gordon Brunton muffed so badly three years after Thomson's death. It is easy to see why Hussey and Brunton, along with Hamilton and the two editors, were so fond of Thomson and grateful that he was meticulous about fulfilling his pledge of non-intervention. Executives find it liberating to operate without the restraining hand of a meddlesome proprietor. Yet successful newspaper groups have invariably had just such a proprietor at their head. Thomson's failure to provide leadership for his management team was a weakness. The role he was forced into was that of a first-class surgeon who, although technically capable of saving the patient's life, chose instead to ensure that she approached death in the utmost comfort and dignity. The alternative would have been to undertake the operation, defying the restraints placed on him in 1966, which were almost certainly unenforceable. Had the surgery been successful and the infected parts removed, the conditions would not have existed that allowed Rupert Murdoch – with far fewer of the traditional qualities of the English gentleman even than Thomson – to revive the much-abused patient, bear her away and comprehensively ravish her.

*   *   *

The final exhibit in my tycoons' gallery is in many respects the most unlikely and most puzzling. To nearly everyone's surprise Roland 'Tiny' Rowland, chief executive of the international conglomerate Lonrho, emerged in 1981 as the proprietor of the venerable Sunday paper the *Observer*, despite the best efforts to thwart him by a group that included the paper's editor, Donald Trelford. Lonrho's only other important media interests were the *Glasgow Herald* and its sister *Evening Times*, although Rowland's name usually figured in the lists of those lining up to bid for national papers as they came on the market. He was a contender for both the *Times* and *Express* groups but in neither case was there a serious prospect of his emerging the victor.

Seeking explanations as to why Rowland should want to run the *Observer*, a bastion of liberal opinion, pundits pointed to the fact that many of Lonrho's most important holdings were in Africa, of whose affairs the *Observer* had long enjoyed a reputation for comprehensive coverage. It soon became apparent, though, that Rowland saw his control of the paper as an unmissable opportunity to promote his company's interests – and to conduct its feuds – not just in Africa but anywhere he liked. Non-intervention was a concept he neither embraced nor understood.

For the *Observer*, the 1970s had been stormy. The paper entered the decade in the precarious ownership of a single family. David Astor, proprietor and editor since 1948, had inherited the paper from his father, Lord Astor, who in turn had inherited it from *his* father, who bought it in 1911. (David's mother, Nancy Astor, was Britain's first woman MP to take her seat in Parliament.) The Astors were a wealthy Anglo-American family highly influential in British society in the first half of the twentieth century. David's cousin, Gavin Astor, had been the principal proprietor of *The Times* until Lord Thomson bought it in 1966.

The *Observer* was an independent conservative paper under J. L. Garvin, who edited it from 1908 to 1942. David Astor had, during the 1950s, pointed it further to the left, directing its appeal to the liberal-minded middle-class intelligentsia. Its opposition to the British military action at Suez in 1956 lost it some older readers and a handful of advertisers but gave it a clearer identity as one of the few serious papers that was not committed to the Conservatives: the *Guardian* was the only other in the quality field, with the *News Chronicle* and *Daily Herald*, both ailing, in the middle market.

The launch of the *Sunday Telegraph* in 1961, and the steady expansion of the *Sunday Times* throughout the 1960s, put pressure on the *Observer*. For some years it had been printing on *The Times* presses at Printing House Square and occupied office space at the east end of the building. When *The Times* decamped to Gray's Inn Road in 1975, the *Observer* was left to print in economically unviable conditions on presses that were now used only one day a week. Circulation was declining too: at 670,000, it had been overtaken by the *Sunday Telegraph*.

Astor negotiated some reductions in manning and costs with the print unions, and stepped down as editor in 1975 in favour of Donald Trelford, a young *apparatchik* who had been groomed for the post. But the paper's financial position remained parlous, and Astor had no capital resources to give it the boost it badly needed. He saw no option but to find a buyer with the means to put the paper back on a profitable course.

Lord Goodman, one of the *Observer*'s trustees, spearheaded the attempt to find a buyer. Many tycoons nibbled at the bait and by mid-November 1976 the clear front runner was Rupert Murdoch, whose national newspaper holdings were then restricted to the *Sun* and *News of the World*. The prospect of being owned by Murdoch horrified Trelford and most of his colleagues, who managed to generate sufficient opposition at least to delay any deal. Then a chance encounter led to a near-miraculous rescue – or so it seemed at the time – by the American oil company Atlantic-Richfield (Arco).

The company appeared at first to see its investment in the *Observer*, and funding its continuing losses, as an unconventional kind of sponsorship, a contribution to international understanding and the free flow of ideas. For a while it seemed an ideal arrangement, at least as far as Trelford and the journalists were concerned, with no proprietor on the spot to exert any influence over editorial policy. In his shrewd book *My Life with Tiny* Richard Hall, a senior *Observer* executive at the time, observed that many of the staff seemed to imagine that they were on a paper with some supernatural exemption from normal economic laws: 'They could make a loss, year in and year out (as they did), yet grandly assume that the unique qualities of *The Observer* – its liberal intellectualism – could never perish.'

The experience with Arco seemed to disprove the maxim that there is no such thing as a free lunch – until the brandy and cigars ran out. Robert Anderson, chairman of Arco, was a right-wing supporter of President Reagan and found it hard to accept the *Observer*'s liberal line, especially its opposition to Margaret Thatcher, who began her long reign as Prime Minister in 1979 and was much admired by Reagan. There seemed no early prospect of the paper making a profit and there was a debilitating union dispute in 1980. The final straw was the rejection by the *Observer* board of Anderson's proposal to make his friend Kenneth Harris vice-chairman. Harris, a senior journalist, had been an important conduit during Arco's purchase of the paper but he was not a popular choice among the staff. That was when Anderson decided to sell. Rather than set a general auction in motion, he accepted an offer of £6 million from Rowland, with whom he already had a business acquaintance.

For Rowland, it was the fulfilment of an ambition. He was not a member of the British establishment. Born in India of a German father and a Dutch mother, he had not attended the same schools, nor did he belong to the same clubs, as those he perceived to control access to real power and influence. His sense of grievance was heightened when, in 1972, Edward Heath described Lonrho, the company he had built from small beginnings, as 'the unacceptable face of capitalism'.

His tussles with authority began as far back as 1942, when, at the age of twenty-four, he was detained in the Isle of Man as a possible war risk, because of his parentage. He had been born Roland Fuhrop. His parents moved to England in the 1930s and sent him to Churcher's College in Hampshire, a fee-paying school without the social cachet of the large public schools. Already a British subject, in 1939 he changed his name by deed poll to Rowland.

When World War Two began he joined the Royal Army Medical Corps. His elder brother was in the army and his parents interned in the Isle of Man. He campaigned for their freedom so fervently that he was discharged from the army and detained near them. On his release in 1944 he worked briefly as a porter at Euston Station. After the war he and two others established an import/export company in London but in 1948 he decided to uproot himself from the country that had, by his perception, so abused him and his family. He emigrated to what was then known as Southern Rhodesia.

It took time for him to establish himself there. He acquired interests in a farm, in mining enterprises and a car dealership and gradually gained a reputation as an entrepreneur. In 1961 he was invited by Angus Ogilvy (later to marry Princess Alexandra) to become joint managing director of a company of which Ogilvy was a director, the 52-year-old London and Rhodesia Mining and Land Company, or Lonrho. The firm seemed past its heyday and in need of a drastic transformation: declared profits in 1961 were £65,000.

Under Rowland, Lonrho diversified into many fields in Central and East Africa, including brewing and newspapers: he learned early that the ownership of a newspaper can be an invaluable weapon in a tycoon's armoury. He also learned how to deploy charm, courting people of influence, such as the leaders of black African states, and flattering them by swapping confidences and dropping names. He found it useful to have powerful people and their relatives on the payroll. While Jomo Kenyatta led Kenya his son-in-law Udi Gecaga ran Lonrho's operations in East Africa, only to be removed soon after Kenyatta's death.

During the 1960s Lonrho expanded but by 1972 it was facing financial problems. A firm of chartered accountants recommended restructuring the board and Rowland and Ogilvy invited Duncan Sandys, a former Commonwealth Secretary, to be non-executive chairman. His fee of £130,000 was paid through banks in the Cayman Islands and provoked a boardroom row and Ogilvy's resignation. A government enquiry was held and Heath made the remark that rankled with Rowland for so long. Among the directors to join the board at this time was one Mohamed al-Fayed.

When they learned of the sale of their paper to Lonrho, Trelford and other senior *Observer* journalists began a campaign to have the deal referred to the Monopolies Commission. In March 1981 John Biffen, Secretary of State for Trade and Industry, asked the commission to look into it and now the anti-Rowland campaign had a new focus. Trelford presented the commission with a 10,000-word document arguing that it would be impossible for a Lonrho-owned paper to report Africa objectively and colleagues made the same point – notably Colin Legum, the paper's veteran writer on African matters.

In the end the commission gave more weight to the evidence of Richard Hall, who had once edited the Lonrho-owned *Times of Zambia* and testified that the company had never interfered with his editing of that paper. The commission gave the go-ahead to the Lonrho purchase. David Astor, who had campaigned vigorously against Rowland, resigned from the board (he had stayed on it during Arco's ownership), Legum resigned from the paper but Trelford remained as editor, protected by five new 'independent directors' – an arrangement modelled on that at *The Times*.

*   *   *

In *My Life With Tiny*, Hall tells of a banquet at Claridge's some time later, where he sat next to Rowland. The conversation turned to the editor. 'I get along well with Donald Trelford,' Rowland declared. 'He is very weak.'

The relationship was certainly a unique one between a newspaper proprietor and his editor. Rowland's demands on Trelford were never political in the sense of being fuelled by a coherent philosophy of how the nation or the world should be run. His politics were personal and commercial; indeed it was impossible with him to disentangle the two. He wanted his papers to gratify his friends and wound – even destroy, if that were feasible – his enemies, and he wanted them to recommend policies that would make it easier for him to do profitable business.

Rowland is not unique among newspaper proprietors in seeking to use his paper to further his other interests. Robert Maxwell serialised his own biography in the *Daily Mirror* – at some cost in terms of circulation – and Rupert Murdoch's venture into satellite television was covered at length, and mostly uncritically, in his papers. Freedom of the press includes the freedom of those who own it to use it for their purposes. The reason that the compromising of the *Observer* so saddened its staff and former admirers was because of a sentimental folk memory of the nice, upright, liberal paper that it used to be.

Trelford made two initial concessions to his new owner. He appointed as City editor Melvyn Marckus, whose work on the *Sunday Telegraph* had been well regarded by Rowland. Soon Marckus took over the editorship of the whole business section from William Keegan, whose opposition to the Government's economic policy was not to Rowland's taste. Later Keegan's weekly column was relegated from the front of the section to a less prominent page. Trelford also agreed to the departure of his weekly columnist Conor Cruise O'Brien, who had denounced Rowland to the Monopolies Commission even more ferociously than Trelford had.

For a while the editor defended the paper, more or less successfully, against attempts by Rowland to exert undue influence on its coverage of matters that had a bearing on the company's interests, especially in Africa. Then some eighteen months into his proprietorship, Rowland began to behave as the doubters had feared. While visiting Zimbabwe early in 1983 Richard Hall, who had been appointed Commonwealth correspondent after the Lonrho takeover, learned that Godwin Matatu, the nephew of the country's Minister of Legal Affairs, had been made Africa correspondent. The move was clearly aimed at improving Lonrho's relations with Zimbabwe's Government, and Trelford had agreed to it in the belief that it was a relatively unimportant concession. He was developing a strategy of giving way to Rowland on minor issues while still, as he hoped, retaining his autonomy on broader matters of principle. Then in 1984 the two men had a public row – again, coincidentally, over Zimbabwe – when Trelford himself wrote a report on atrocities in Matabeleland that angered the Zimbabwe Government, whose goodwill Lonrho was trying to foster.

Trelford had in fact gone to Zimbabwe to interview Robert Mugabe, the Prime Minister. The encounter had been arranged by Rowland, who was trying to make up to Mugabe for Lonrho's earlier support of his rival, Joshua Nkomo. When Trelford heard of unrest in Matabeleland his reporter's instinct took over. He hurried there and wrote a vivid account of atrocities by Government soldiers on tribesmen opposed to Mugabe, and he gave instructions that it should be published on the front page. He appeared not to have recognised at first how much Mugabe and Rowland would object that he had used his visit to blacken the name of the country's armed forces.

Rowland denounced Trelford in extreme terms and invited Robert Maxwell to a well-publicised breakfast to discuss selling the paper to him. It seemed that Trelford's resignation or dismissal was inevitable – but they patched up the quarrel. Rowland held on to the paper and his editor kept his job. Only the two men know the exact terms of the settlement but from then on Rowland's influence became more and more apparent in the news pages, most notably in the hostile coverage of the al-Fayed brothers, who had succeeded in taking over the House of Fraser store group while Rowland had been barred from bidding.

For several years Rowland had been anxious to acquire control of House of Fraser, whose flagship was Harrods in Knightsbridge. Amateur psychologists speculated that Rowland wanted to establish his social position by owning the most famous luxury emporium in the land. Whatever his motive, he pursued with passion the object of his desire, building a shareholding of 29.9 per cent and making a full takeover bid for House of Fraser in 1981, when the Monopolies Commission made a puzzling ruling that such a takeover would be against the public interest. Rowland was made to pledge not to renew his bid, but the Department of Trade and Industry had the power to release him from that promise should the position change.

Rowland is a determined man and this initial setback did not divert him from his long-term aim. He maintained a substantial minority stake in House of Fraser and was a member of the board, along with another Lonrho director, Lord Duncan-Sandys. The Monopolies Commission looked into the matter again but by the summer of 1984 the DTI had still not released him from his promise not to bid.

Losing patience, in November Rowland sold the Lonrho shareholding to Mohamed al-Fayed and his brothers Ali and Salah. He regarded them as friends and allies and believed that they had neither the resources nor the inclination to mount a full takeover bid themselves. He soon discovered he was wrong. By March 1985 the al-Fayeds had secured 51 per cent of the shares. Norman Tebbit, the Secretary of State for Trade and Industry, decided not to refer the al-Fayed bid to the Monopolies Commission and, with a touch of irony, said the way was now clear for Lonrho to make a rival bid. But it was too late: Rowland had been defeated, and he was enraged.

The al-Fayeds were already familiar to staff of the *Observer* and were to become more so to its readers. Trelford first met Mohamed al-Fayed, at Rowland's suggestion, in 1983. A favourable profile of the al-Fayed family was published in the *Observer* assessing their worth at some £500 million. Relations between al-Fayed and *Observer* journalists remained amicable until al-Fayed won control of House of Fraser in 1985. That was when the *Observer*'s Melvyn Marckus first raised questions about the source of the al-Fayeds' money. They claimed it came from their family businesses in the Middle East and the Ritz Hotel in Paris, which they also owned. Marckus reported suspicions that some of it had been put up by the Sultan of Brunei. Mohamed al-Fayed issued a writ for libel but it was not proceeded with. The business section of the *Observer* ran numerous stories criticising the al-Fayeds and casting doubt on their veracity. Marckus campaigned for the DTI to investigate the source of the brothers' funds.

In January 1986 the *Observer* stepped up the pressure with a front-page story, written by Trelford himself, that brought up the name of Mark Thatcher, alleging that he had visited Brunei in al-Fayed's private jet. Again, Lonrho was a prime source of the information. Rowland believed that the alleged involvement of the Prime Minister's son explained why the Government seemed to be resisting his demands for the takeover to be investigated. The Mark Thatcher story was denied from all sides and it transpired later that some documents on which it was based had been forged.

The *Observer*'s campaign was criticised by many of its senior journalists, who argued in vain for fewer Lonrho-inspired stories. Others, too, felt that, however just the cause, it was wrong for a newspaper so vigorously and blatantly to promote the interests of its proprietor. Conor Cruise O'Brien wrote in *The Times* (12 April 1989): 'Readers like to feel that the paper they take regularly is designed to meet their particular needs. They don't like to feel that it is being adulterated for some ulterior motive.'

Rowland did not see it in that way, appearing to reason that if he could not pursue his company's interests in its own newspaper, there was little point in owning it. Numerous stories discrediting the al-Fayeds appeared in the *Observer*. When Trelford was criticised by his colleagues for failing to resist Lonrho's pressure, he would tell them that they had to be realistic and recognise that the company owned the paper and paid its bills. The campaign did have one positive result: in April 1987 Paul Channon, Secretary of State for Trade and Industry, appointed inspectors to look into the House of Fraser takeover.

Their report was completed by July 1988 but Lord Young, who had replaced Channon at the DTI, decided not to publish it pending the results of investigations of the al-Fayeds by the Serious Fraud Office. The following month the *Observer*'s business section printed a full page personal account of the feud and the DTI investigation by Rowland himself. In January 1989 Marckus published an open letter to Lord Young urging action against the al-Fayeds.

On Thursday 30 March, their patience exhausted, Rowland and Trelford took matters into their own hands and published a special midweek edition of the *Observer*, its sixteen pages devoted entirely to long extracts from the report (leaked to Lonrho), especially its conclusion that the al-Fayeds had lied about their background and possibly about the source of their funds. 'Exposed: The Phoney Pharaoh' was the main headline. Thousands of copies of the special edition were distributed, many outside a meeting of Lonrho shareholders in the City. The DTI immediately issued an injunction forcing the *Observer* to withdraw the special edition and to prevent other papers from quoting from the report, although an attempt to convict the paper of contempt of court was thrown out by the Law Lords. The DTI report was not officially published until March 1990, by which time the Fraud Squad, although accepting that the al-Fayeds had lied, had decided to take no action.

Earlier, in March 1989, the *Observer* had run yet another front-page story that Trelford admitted later (*Sunday Times*, 21 May 1989) had been inspired by Lonrho. It was about alleged overcharging by British Aerospace for jet fighters ordered by Middle East countries. There were two reasons for Lonrho's interest. One was that the chairman of British Aerospace was Prof. Roland Smith, the former chairman of House of Fraser who had opposed Rowland's takeover attempts. Moreover, Lonrho had sometimes represented Dassault, the French manufacturer of a rival plane to the Tornado. Four days after the story appeared,

Jordan cancelled its Tornado order and ordered Dassault planes instead
– a series of events that provoked adverse comment in the House of
Commons and a complaint by *Observer* journalists to the paper's independent directors.

The directors found no specific wrongdoing over the Tornado story
but did comment that the excessive coverage of the House of Fraser
affair had 'tarnished the image of the paper'. They said that no proprietor with wide commercial interests and determined views, whose
vigorous actions attracted much publicity, could be expected to stand
back totally from a newspaper owned by his company; but 'given the
public perception of *The Observer* at this moment, the proprietor and the
editor need to take especial care over their mutual relationships'. After
the report was published David Leigh, the paper's best-known investigative journalist, resigned.

That admonition and resignation appeared to have no effect on Trelford, for the very next week the paper ran a front-page story asserting
that a secret £50 million deal over unpaid tax was being negotiated
between the al-Fayeds and the Inland Revenue. In March 1990, when
yet another Trade Secretary, Nicholas Ridley, finally announced that
the inspectors' report would be published, the *Observer* led its City
pages that week with a preview ('Harrods: Lies and Deception') and the
following week devoted three more pages to a digest of the report ('The
Lies of Mohamed Fayed'). Editorially, the paper raged against Ridley's
decision to take no action against the al-Fayeds based on the report,
and on this occasion many other papers shared its view.

Although the report had vindicated Rowland and the *Observer* by
justifying their allegations against the Egyptian brothers, their long campaign had been counter-productive in two respects. First, because it was
conducted in a paper whose owner had a clear interest in its outcome,
rival papers had, until the publication of the report, been reluctant to
look too closely into the affair. As Lord Rees-Mogg wrote in the *Independent* (12 March 1990):

> The *Observer* told the truth, even though it made some errors. What-
> ever allowance may be made for the fact that its proprietor, Tiny
> Rowland, was an interested party, with an obsessive concern to show
> up the Fayeds, there is a sharp contrast between the pertinacity of
> the *Observer*'s editor, Donald Trelford, and the silence of the rest of
> the Press.

Yet – and this is the second item on the debit balance – the report's publication did nothing to clear away the tarnish on the paper's image that had been remarked upon by the independent directors and which had been reflected in the paper's sagging circulation. In the last six months of 1986 the average weekly sale had been 769,290. In the last six months of 1989 that had fallen to 639,294 – down 17 per cent – and it dropped to below 600,000 with the launch of the *Independent on Sunday* in January 1990. Two years later it was down to 560,000. No doubt other factors played their part in the decline, but the odour of tawdry self-interest emanating from the al-Fayed coverage was certainly an important element.

OBSERVER

Chelsea Bridge House, Queenstown Road, London SW8 4NN. 01-627 0700

Harrods and the public interest

READERS will not be surprised that *The Observer* ...

All the fun of the Fayeds

Tall tales told to the press

OBSERVER BUSINESS

Harrods: Lies and deception

Mohamed Fayed: May seek to suppress publication of the report.

'An odour of tawdry self-interest': examples of the *Observer*'s coverage of the House of Fraser affair, March 1990.

8
Take Me to Your Leader

The editor of a newspaper, ultimately, has no more freedom than the owner chooses to accord.
Conor Cruise O'Brien, *The Times*, 12 April 1989

Editors of national newspapers are fond of saying that theirs is the best job in the world. No doubt they believe it and, although there are no agreed criteria for 'best', they may be right. Less easy to sustain is the widely accepted belief that theirs is the most *influential* job in the world. Even when the leader columns express their own views rather than those of their proprietors, they seldom have any detectable direct influence on the actions of governments and are more likely to reflect public opinion than to be decisive in its formation. Academic studies, notably Colin Seymour-Ure's *The Political Impact of the Mass Media*, suggest that people's opinions are not often influenced by the editorial policies of newspapers they buy. A MORI poll taken in the spring of 1991 showed that more readers of the fervently Tory *Sun* voted Labour (43 per cent) than Conservative (42 per cent). In the case of the *Star* the contradiction was even more marked – 59 per cent of its readers vote Labour and only 24 per cent Conservative.

In some cases, though, political perceptions can be affected by the range and style of news coverage. An example is the spate of reports in Conservative tabloids in the 1980s of what they dubbed 'loony left' local councils, whose cumulative effect was to persuade the Labour Party leader Neil Kinnock to take a tougher line against his extremists.

There is generally little correlation between the circulation of papers that support major political parties and the number of votes those parties attract in elections, as Jeremy Tunstall shows in *The Media in Britain*. Such influence as the press has is more cultural than political. The tabloids, and among them notably the *Sun*, influence the tone and context of public discourse and help determine what is fashionable and acceptable. Only to the extent that editors play a role in this process can they justly claim to be figures of influence.

Nor are editors usually well known. I would guess that the number of people who can name the editor of the daily paper they read regularly is negligible, especially in the case of the tabloids. The name of the editor of the *Sun* is indeed better known to readers of the broadsheet papers, where he figures often on media pages, than to readers of the paper he edits. Tabloid readers are more likely to be familiar with editors of broadsheet papers, because of their appearances on television and radio discussion programmes – or more rarely, as in 1989/90, because of their involvement in a titillating and ludicrous scandal.

For Donald Trelford, 1989 was an eventful year. While the al-Fayed dispute was reaching its climax and his paper's circulation was tumbling, his name cropped up in one of the more diverting scandals of recent years. Pamella Bordes, a former Miss India, had been lured into offering sex for money to a *News of the World* reporter. In reporting this, the paper revealed that she had a pass to the House of Commons as a researcher ('investigating the net book agreement') and had been photographed in the company of a number of public figures including the Minister of Sport, Colin Moynihan, and the editors of the *Observer* and the *Sunday Times*. Trelford denied that his relationship with Miss Bordes involved more than casual visits to night clubs, but that did not protect him and Andrew Neil, the *Sunday Times* editor, from attack in print by Peregrine Worsthorne, editor of the *Sunday Telegraph*. In an editorial headlined 'Playboys as Editors' (19 March 1989) that was later to become the subject of litigation between Worsthorne and Neil, Worsthorne wrote:

> The great quality paper editors of the past, like Garvin and David Astor – to name only two of Mr Donald Trelford's immediate predecessors – had better things to do with their spare time than hold hands with ladies of easy virtue in public. 'All I did,' says Mr Trelford, 'was to go with Miss Bordes to the opening of a night club,' as if going to a night club with Miss Bordes was the most natural thing for an editor of *The Observer* to do: as natural and proper as attending – or even addressing – a meeting of the Fabian Society or of the Royal Commonwealth Society or taking a Nobel prizewinner to lunch at the Athenaeum. But it isn't, or at any rate wasn't. Editors of quality newspapers used to be *hommes sérieux*.

Trelford would not claim to be that but he did possess (to a greater extent than Worsthorne) some other qualities needed by occupants of editors' chairs in the last quarter of the twentieth century. Principally, he was an accomplished practitioner in the art of survival. Not only was he the sole national newspaper editor in recent years to have lasted more than a few months after a change of ownership, but he did it twice. It meant the occasional compromise but he believed that only by keeping his job could he ensure that at least part of the paper's liberal tradition was preserved. The argument was that any successor appointed by Rowland would be certain to sell the pass completely. Compared with that catastrophe, his small betrayals could be tolerated.

In 1975, aged only thirty-eight, Donald Trelford inherited the editor's chair from David Astor. The young man had come to Astor's attention in the mid-1960s, when he edited a newspaper in Malawi, obtaining a sound grounding in the diplomatic skills needed to run a reasonably independent paper under a dictatorial regime. A small man with a taste for physical action, Trelford had been among the last of the National Service pilot officers in the RAF, and at Cambridge had excelled at rugby and cricket. One of his early jobs in journalism was on the *Sheffield Telegraph*, where Oxbridge graduates were unusual. He learned there how to accept being teased. In 1986, when the Sheffield paper closed, some of those who had patronised him were still on its staff, while Trelford had been editor of the *Observer* for more than ten years.

Nobody disputes his stamina, tenacity and technical skills. Those were the qualities that recommended him to the staff when they were consulted about Astor's successor in 1975. He had been deputy editor for six years. Three-quarters of the journalists preferred him to his main rival, the better-known Anthony Sampson. Although the trustees were not obliged to accept the staff choice, they did.

Trelford's initial moves as editor were widely approved. He hired Alan Watkins to write his discursive political column and Adam Raphael from the *Guardian* to do hard political news. The controversial Nora Beloff, who had dominated the paper's political coverage for years, was persuaded against her strong will to switch to European affairs. But before he had time to make many other appointments he became embroiled in the machinations over the paper's change of ownership.

Astor had decided to sell and Rupert Murdoch had expressed interest. Not only that, but Murdoch had let it be known that he would bring in two of his own men to oversee the editorial side of the paper. Trelford would be kept on as editorial director, with undefined duties. Trelford flew to New York to see Murdoch and a few days later news of the bid was leaked to the press – by Trelford, some suspected, although he denied it. In any event, the publicity enabled him to orchestrate an outcry against the proposed deal and Murdoch backed off, leaving Trelford as one of the few people able to claim a victory over the redoubtable Australian.

The paper was sold instead to Arco, who promised a more benevolent regime, although Trelford was surprised when the Irish politician Conor Cruise O'Brien was appointed editor-in-chief, his nominal superior. O'Brien wrote a thoughtful weekly column and was a useful figurehead for the paper, but Trelford ensured that he never exerted any executive control.

These manoeuvrings preoccupied the young editor for a while but even after they were over his staff looked in vain for a revival of the paper's fortunes. Trelford had by now developed a taste for moving in high social circles. He enjoyed making speeches, even if they involved travelling to distant parts, and he accepted many invitations to join panels and committees, listed in his constantly expanding entry in *Who's Who*. One of his regrets at the paper's move from Blackfriars to Battersea, as he confided, was that he could no longer stroll back from the Garrick Club to the office after lunch.

One Saturday he and some colleagues had been to a wedding reception at the Garrick. They returned in a relaxed mood to find the printers threatening to stop work because of a cartoon in the paper that they thought racist. Trelford, who has a stronger head for drink than he sometimes pretends, took a grip on the crisis. He met the dissidents and argued persuasively against their proposed action. They left mollified: the paper and the cartoon duly appeared.

He was a skilled editorial technician and a first-rate negotiator, a smoother of ruffled feathers. Yet some of his journalists complained that he did not trouble to motivate them. Not for him the congratulatory memos or praise in the corridor that are part of the stock-in-trade of many successful editors. 'I worked there for two years,' said a former staff writer, 'and he never addressed a word to me.' Nor was he in any sense a political editor. He admitted to being a party political agnostic with no passionate views on many topics.

One issue on which he did speak out consistently over the years was press freedom. He fought court battles over the right to publish, against a Government instinctively suspicious of any such thing. He penned leaders and made speeches on the subject in several continents. Some of the *Observer*'s best scoops under his editorship related to questions of individual liberty – blacklisting and political vetting. Yet on other burning topics the paper failed to stake out a distinctive position, as it had done in the twenty years after World War Two. Then it stood firm on three liberal policy planks – decolonisation, détente between East and West and a voluntarily planned economy for Britain. By the end of the 1960s those causes had been effectively won, and nothing replaced them in the newspaper's canon.

If Trelford had resigned after his row with Rowland over Matabeleland he would have been a hero for a while around the dinner tables of Islington, but what else would he have achieved? He was, in any event, decidedly not the resigning type. Rumours of his imminent demise appeared regularly in *Private Eye* yet he seemed safe from dismissal by Rowland, whose purposes he served with such apparent good cheer. It is probable that he would like to move on to something else but if you become a national newspaper editor at thirty-eight, options for advancement become ever narrower. The more Trelford was seen to compromise the *Observer* with Lonrho, the less likely he was to be invited to take on another national newspaper editorship or one of the big public patronage jobs – Director-General of the BBC, for instance. As long as Lonrho continues to own the *Observer*, Trelford looks safe, but it would be remarkable if even such a doughty survivor could keep his job through a third change of ownership.

*   *   *

Andrew Neil shares Trelford's taste for the occasional bout of night-clubbing – and thus shared the redoubtable wrath of Worsthorne – but otherwise the two men could scarcely be less alike. While Trelford is a political agnostic, Neil's editorship of the *Sunday Times* has been notable for his vigorous espousal of what is broadly defined as Thatcherism: support of individual initiative and freedom of choice and opposition to all forms of syndicalism and cartels. On questions of press freedom, however, Neil generally finds himself in the opposite camp from the Government and on the side of most of his fellow broadsheet editors.

Neil's running-in period as editor of the *Sunday Times* lasted longer than that of most editors because of the timing and circumstances of his appointment. Frank Giles, the immediate successor to Harold Evans, had been an interim editor who did little to alter the paper's essential power structure apart from losing Ron Hall, Evans's former chief lieutenant, and bringing in Brian MacArthur as heir apparent. Giles's two-year term was notable chiefly for an incident he would prefer to forget: starting to serialise the faked Adolf Hitler diaries. Murdoch and MacArthur played more significant roles in the fiasco than Giles, but he was after all the editor.

When Neil was surprisingly appointed to succeed Giles, he was faced not just with MacArthur's disappointment but with the resentment of most of the members of Evans's former 'magic circle', who now felt that they had been affronted twice. Nearly all of them had opposed Murdoch's acquisition of the paper and would have supported legal action to force the Monopolies Commission to enquire into it. Some now left: notably Hugo Young, who had at one time entertained hopes of becoming editor himself, and the photographer Don McCullin, a symbol of the paper's leftish past, concerned as he was with the suffering brought about by war and poverty. Others stayed and fed poisonous tales about the new editor to *Private Eye*, in the vain hope that their cumulative effect might be to force Murdoch to recognise what they saw as the error of his ways.

Neil did not try to ingratiate himself with the old guard. One of his first assaults was directed against the prestigious Insight unit, then led by Christopher Hird, a left-wing journalist who had worked for the *New Statesman*. Neil maintained that the unit had become too political, that it had done no worthwhile investigations for some time and had none in the offing. He did not disband it but moved new people in to alter its direction. Under Neil the unit has uncovered some major stories, notably that Israel was developing an atomic bomb – a report the Israelis viewed with such gravity that they kidnapped and jailed the man who leaked it – and the gift of Libyan money to the National Union of Mineworkers during the miners' strike.

Neil was just beginning to win over some of his dissidents when the storm broke over Wapping, introducing a fresh element of division. Most of the refuseniks who finally decided to sleep through the new dawn of proprietorial freedom were members of the old guard. Those who did go to Wapping were upset by having to pass howling pickets to get to work every day. Nothing could more vividly have pointed up the contrast with the companionable comforts of the Evans days at Gray's Inn Road, filled with the psychological reinforcement of mutual praise. They, too, began to drift elsewhere.

For Neil, the departures and the resultant destabilisation were a mixed blessing. The physical difficulties of actually bringing out the paper in new premises and using new equipment would have been a little less traumatic had there been more stability among the staff. Those that left kept in informal association with one another, creating what Neil called 'the great tribe of the dispossessed', complaining to all who would listen about the terrible things the new editor was doing to their former paper. Hugo Young wrote: '*The Sunday Times* used to be a force in the land, a lamp in the darkness. For reasons which are capricious and unnecessary, these it has ceased to be.'

On the other hand, the upside of the exodus of the dispossessed was that Neil could more quickly build up a staff that fitted his own conception of how the *Sunday Times* should look. He believed that Evans's paper, a creation of the 1960s and 1970s, was becalmed in the values of those now despised decades, still espousing the left-liberalism and collectivism that had then been the fashion.

Neil was born in 1949 in Paisley, in west Scotland, where he attended the local grammar school. After coming down from Glasgow University in 1971, he had worked in the Research Department of the Conservative Party, where he had been involved in the early arguments about privatisation, competition policy and deregulation – policies that were to become the hallmark of the Thatcher era. He had cultivated his interest in these issues when he joined *The Economist* in 1973; and when he became that paper's correspondent in the United States in 1979 he enjoyed working in a country where he could see in action something approaching his political philosophy. Deregulation of television was one of his main concerns and it was at a conference on the topic that he first met and impressed Murdoch, who was beginning to think of establishing satellite television stations, first in the United States and then in Britain.

In an essentially unfriendly profile in the *Listener* (15 December 1988, p. 14), a former *Sunday Times* staffer, John Sweeney, wrote:

> Long before he met Murdoch, Neil was a man of fluently articulated hates. The Old Establishment hypocrisies, trade union megalomania, kowtowing (for example, to the monarchy), environmental moaners, lah-de-dah artsy-fartsy types and bleeding-heart journalism all turn him off. The United States, the Big Apple and 'thrivers' all turn him on.

Sweeney added: 'Like it or hate it, *The Sunday Times* each week runs articles that repay reading. It has captured the flavour of our times.'

It was also now beginning to recapture its former undisputed dominance in the Sunday market. From the beginning of 1987, when the pickets left Wapping, circulation began to climb. Neil added new sections until it became the nearest British equivalent to the monster Sunday papers in the United States. From a low of 1,147,405 in the last six months of 1986, when the pickets were still outside Wapping, the circulation climbed in two years to 1,314,504, although it fell back slightly the following year because of the impact of plumper Saturday papers, then the launch of the *Sunday Correspondent* and, in 1990, the *Independent on Sunday*.

Neil naturally felt that his paper's success between 1986 and 1988 vindicated his assault on the values he had inherited from the Evans *Sunday Times* and the constituency it served. He had a somewhat romantic notion of himself as journalism's new man, the feisty youngster from Scotland coming down to rattle the shutters of a profession that was dozing off and had not noticed that its world was changing. He did not expect the old Fleet Street establishment to concede the point without resistance and, when it did snap back, he felt it important to carry on the assault. That explained why, when criticised by Peregrine Worsthorne over the Pamella Bordes affair, he was determined to fight the matter to a conclusion in the courts, despite advice from more cautious colleagues that it would make him look foolish.

As Neil saw it, Worsthorne, by declaring that people who went to night clubs did not make suitable editors of serious papers, was reinforcing the antiquated establishment image of an editor who dined with bishops at the Athenaeum and was part of the magic circle of influence that had guided (or misguided, as Neil would have it) the nation's destinies through the ages. The specific allegation of libel was over the suggestion that Neil had known that Ms Bordes was a prostitute at the time of their brief relationship.

Defending his editorial when the case came to court in January 1990, Worsthorne said that going to 'sleazy nightspots' indicated membership of café society, 'a social circle where strict and even conventional moral strictures don't apply'. He added: 'Consorting with a gold-digging adventuress can aptly be described as frivolous ... I think he would have been prudent not to have touched her with a barge pole.'

Neil, who is unmarried, responded that the implication of all this was that 'I should stay at home every night and do my knitting'. He said that, far from showering expensive gifts on her as Worsthorne implied, the only present he had given Bordes was a Magimix food processor. When an article about the affair by the journalist Paul Johnson was quoted to him, Neil said that Johnson, and by implication Worsthorne, was 'part of the Garrick Club mafia who think they should be running everything'. The result was generally regarded as a draw: Neil received damages of £1,000 – paltry by recent standards – and his co-defendants News International were awarded a mere 60p, the price then of a copy of the *Sunday Times*. Neil maintained that it represented 'a victory for the new Britain against the old Britain'.

*   *   *

By that assessment, then, Peregrine Worsthorne is a representative of the old Britain. The former editor of the *Sunday Telegraph*, lean and elegant with a startling shock of white hair and a scarlet silk handkerchief overflowing from his well-tailored breast pocket, would be the last to deny the aptness of that attribution. On the contrary, he is certainly proud of being a figure from a disappearing world. In a revealing personal article in the *Daily Telegraph* on the day following the trial, he mused on his sense of bewilderment at being subjected to a 'verbal mugging' by advocates, urbane people of the kind he meets at the Garrick:

> The demoralisation had nothing to do with shame or guilt. It came, I think, rather from the surprise and dismay at finding oneself faced by a professional man, the very kind of man to whom one normally turns for help and succour – doctors, surgeons, accountants, and lawyers, too – ranged against one; and ranged against one, not over some trifling argument, but in a matter involving one's very reputation. Surely he must be joking, teasing, only pretending to want to do one down? Would he not break into a smile any minute, or at least give a friendly wink? ... The safe world of middle-class cordiality was turned upside-down ... It was a mugging by a highly well-spoken gentleman who looked and sounded just the type who could be relied on to defend rather than attack.

In other words, it was a kind of class betrayal. For thirty years, writing mainly in the *Sunday Telegraph*, 'Perry' Worsthorne has promulgated his idiosyncratic brand of conservatism based on aristocratic values. His philosophy is rooted in his belief in the class system as the bedrock of the British way of life that must be protected against assault from collectivism.

His *curriculum vitae* affords a clue to his preoccupation with the concept of privilege; for Peregrine Gerard Worsthorne was brought up in the English upper class but not born to it. His father was a Belgian Catholic who settled in Britain, served in the Irish Guards and changed his name from Koch de Gooreynd to Worsthorne in 1921, two years before Perry was born. His parents were divorced when he was five and he spent his formative years chiefly in the care of the family butler. In the 1920s servants knew their place even better than their masters, and an instinctive perception of what was fitting rubbed off on to the lad. It was reinforced by his years at Stowe, a fee-paying boarding school then run on rigidly traditional lines. His university career took him both to

Cambridge and Oxford. He joined the *Glasgow Herald* in 1946 and moved via *The Times* to the *Daily Telegraph* and then its Sunday sister.

One reason why Worsthorne felt so strongly in March 1989 about the role of Sunday paper editors is that he had only recently, and somewhat unexpectedly, joined their ranks, at the late age of sixty-two. For years he had been the star columnist on the *Sunday Telegraph*, famous for stretching High Tory philosophy to the very edges of logic and for contesting the liberal assumptions that dominated political debate in the 1960s and 1970s. He had, however, been passed over for the editorship, due to a lapse from standards that were still being upheld in the Athenaeum, if in few other places. In a television discussion programme in 1973, commenting on the sex scandal involving Lord Lambton, he had used an earthy four-letter word.

Lord Hartwell, then the proprietor of the *Telegraph* newspapers, decided that this outburst showed a lack of judgment and dignity that disqualified Worsthorne from the responsibility of editorship. The contrite offender had to wait until Hartwell ceded control of the papers to Conrad Black in 1986 before he received what he believed to be his due and ascended to the editorial chair. He was Andrew Knight's choice and a surprising one: Knight's taste is for vigorous youngsters such as Max Hastings, whom he appointed to the *Daily Telegraph* at the same time, Felicity Lawrence, whom he hired to revive the *Telegraph Magazine*, and Simon Jenkins, whom he would later bring to *The Times*.

Although he had longed for the editorship, Worsthorne was as surprised as anyone else when it was granted him. He discovered quickly that he loved the job and for the first year did it with great success, significantly increasing the paper's circulation. He wrote opinionated leading articles and put his name at their foot – an innovation in the contemporary British press that set the paper apart from the rest. But by 1988 things were beginning to go wrong and the sales figures started slipping. Edward Pearce, a former *Telegraph* columnist, believes that part of the trouble was over-confidence. At the beginning, as Pearce wrote in *New Statesman and Society*, Worsthorne was diffident, careful to do nothing extreme, allowing experienced subordinates to get on with the job unhindered. As he grew in confidence he let his individuality be overlaid with quirkishness, not just in his editorials but on the news pages as well.

The most notorious case was the Kingsley Amis letter. The novelist Amis, a fellow member of the Garrick Club, had been asked by a magazine to pose for a photograph with his son Martin Amis, also a novelist. He declined the request in crusty and dismissive terms and showed Perry the letter. At best, it should have made no more than a whimsical item in a gossip column but Perry put the story on the front page, just below the masthead, claiming that the letter was a supreme example of coruscating wit – which it patently was not.

His 'Playboys as Editors' editorial showed comparable misjudgment, making too much out of a trivial incident. Three months after it appeared – though not as a direct consequence of it – Worsthorne's term as editor came to an abrupt and cruel end with Andrew Knight's decision to merge the daily and Sunday papers under Max Hastings. Worsthorne's role was reduced to editing three pages of comment in the middle of the Sunday paper. From his own pen we know how grievously hurt he was by this demotion. In the *Spectator* he described how Knight had broken the news to him over breakfast at Claridge's, the expensive London hotel:

> I remember well when the thunderbolt, coming out of a blue sky, hit me. It was when the waiter had just served two perfectly poached eggs on buttered toast – a dish of which I am inordinately and insatiably fond. In my mind I knew that the information just imparted was a paralysingly painful blow: pretty much a professional death sentence. But for some reason this sense of acute shock did not get through ... and I continued eating the eggs with as much pleasure as usual; and also, a bit later, the rolls and marmalade.

After breakfast, as he admitted, he wept.

Over the years, Worsthorne disclosed a lot about himself in intimate personal anecdotes of this kind, exposing his vulnerabilities. In 1977 he revealed that, while at Stowe, he had been seduced by George Melly, now a jazz singer. (Melly said he did not recall it.) In the 1960s, when most of London's rented apartments were vanishing as a result of a property boom, he wrote a self-pitying account of how he had been made homeless through not having had the foresight to buy a place of his own: traditionally, aristocrats do not have to worry about such matters.

To colleagues and friends Worsthorne is, in the words of Edward Pearce, 'humorous, kind, stylish and the best of company'. Yet he can also be spiteful, as he showed in January 1990 when he published a hostile and unfair profile of Andrew Knight, 'the constant smiler with the knife', who was about to join Rupert Murdoch's News International. The profile began with an attack on Knight's record as editor of *The Economist*, where he achieved an increased circulation by exploiting the United States market:

Knight's enemies would say that his bland *Economist* was a reflection of his personality, except that he does not have enemies in the way strong personalities – certainly those of them who are newspaper executives – do. His life has been devoted to smoothing paths, and not only his own. He has a gift not so much (or merely) for buttering up the great and the good, the rich and the powerful, but for making them feel secure. He has long been an assiduous attender at those staging posts of the conventionally ambitious – international conferences. His contemporaries on the same circuit still talk of his technique, perhaps enviously: to wait for the most powerful people present to speak, then to agree with them, then to reinforce that agreement over cocktails afterwards ... He seems to assume that power and wealth imply virtue.

The article went on to report Black's belief that Knight had behaved improperly by moving to be chief executive of Murdoch's British group so soon after leaving the *Telegraph* papers. In publishing the anonymous profile, Worsthorne was seeking revenge for the trauma over the poached eggs at Claridge's. As with the Bordes leader, the Amis letter and the four-letter word, restraint would have been more seemly and more admirable.

After Knight left the *Telegraph* his plan for bringing together the daily and Sunday papers was allowed to wither, largely because of Max Hastings's lack of enthusiasm for it, and the Sunday regained most of its autonomy under Trevor Grove, a former editor of the *Observer Magazine*. Worsthorne stayed in charge of his Comment section for a while, before stepping down in September 1991.

*　　*　　*

Knight's first executive act on arriving at News International was to fire the editor of *The Times*, Charles Wilson, and replace him with Simon Jenkins, an Oxford man far closer to Knight's image both of himself and of *The Times* – and a former colleague of his at *The Economist* to boot. Wilson was moved into a newly created post overseeing the company's European developments. It would have been out of character for Rupert Murdoch entirely to abandon the rough diamond who had effectively carried out the paper's tricky move to Wapping and who, earlier, had helped establish the house style at the Chicago *Sun-Times* immediately after Murdoch acquired it. But he did not stay in the executive suite long, being recruited by Robert Maxwell to run the *Sporting Life*, his horse-racing daily, and then to be editor-in-chief of all the *Mirror* papers.

Andrew Knight was the prime mover behind Jenkins's appointment but it had to be approved by Murdoch and represented a substantial alteration of his philosophy about *The Times*. The idea of going down-market to compete for *Telegraph* readers had been Murdoch's, as had the notion that a broadsheet paper was just a tabloid paper with longer words. He deplored the intellectual elitism that, to him, the old *Times* appeared to represent. He derided 'fancy writing' of the kind that, by some judgments, Jenkins indulged in as a columnist for the *Sunday Times*. All three men who had previously edited the paper under Murdoch's ownership had been attempting, in their differing ways, to prove the correctness of his central idea, which he now had tacitly to admit was flawed. The popularisers had had their chance but had blown it.

Although the paper's circulation, around 440,000, was some 50 per cent higher than when Murdoch bought it, it was still little more than a third of the *Telegraph*'s. More gravely, the *Independent* had been allowed to seize the high ground, to become the paper of first choice among a significant proportion of the intellectual elite. Knight's initial achievement at News International had been to persuade Murdoch that *The Times* had to go head-to-head with the *Independent* and that this strategy required a more cultivated editor than Wilson.

Jenkins, a 46-year-old Oxford graduate, was certainly that. His *Sunday Times* columns, for which he won a *What the Papers Say* award in 1989, were models of urbanity. Although his views are broadly conservative, they are distant from the dogmatism that had until then been a feature of Murdoch's *Times*. His previous experience as a Fleet Street editor, with the London *Evening Standard* shortly before it merged with the *Evening News*, had lasted only two years and had not been notably successful. He had made his name on the *Standard* as a writer about London, especially its buildings, in the period just before the protection of the environment had become a fashionable cause.

The reaction of other newspapers to the change at *The Times* was an indication of the peculiar regard in which it was still held, despite nine years of Murdoch's ownership. It was also a further manifestation of journalists' obsession with class, that had emerged with such force in the Neil/Worsthorne case. If the London *Evening Standard*'s headline, 'Dallas Star's Husband to Edit The Times', was tongue-in-cheek (Jenkins is married to the American actress Gayle Hunnicutt), the *Independent*'s 'Exit a Rough Man, Enter a Smooth One' was not. It was indicative of a widespread impression that *The Times*, under Murdoch, had got into the hands of the wrong set. Maggie Brown, the media editor of the *Independent*, wrote that 'the key problem with *The Times* has been that it has lacked a serious intellectual base and become more vulgar without becoming noticeably more popular.' She added: 'In choosing Simon Jenkins, Rupert Murdoch is returning to a more traditional and clubbable editor for *The Times*.'

Wilson's offence, apart from his broad Glasgow accent, was that he had spent much of his career working for the *Daily Mail*. Richard Donkin wrote in the *Financial Times*: 'While Mr Wilson sharpened its news content, his more hard-hitting style and appetite for what colleagues call "diseases and disasters" alienated some readers in the establishment and among the intelligentsia.' A profile of Jenkins in the *Observer* drove home the point: 'Jenkins's pugnacity in defending quality journalism from the Visigoths is a good reason for welcoming his appointment to *The Times*. His predecessor, Charles Wilson, has demonstrated that you can't conduct a serious newspaper as a series of Royal Marine Commando beach assaults.'

David Walker, a home affairs specialist on *The Times*, wrote an article in the *Listener* posing the question whether Jenkins would reverse the hard-line Conservative policies introduced by Wilson's predecessor, Charles Douglas-Home, and continued under Wilson. For his pains, and for naming the names of 'guilty' right-wing leader-writers, Walker was asked to resign – the new editor's first firing.

The *Guardian* staged a fascinating debate between two men with opposing views on the Wilson legacy and the prospects for the new regime. On one side was Edward Pearce from the *Sunday Express*, an admirer of the Wilson *Times*:

The recent *Times*, Charlie Wilson's paper, was, for all the snob-carping, a working newspaper which fork-lifted its circulation by noticing the readers. The fact that a flock of columnar contraltos took off from Wapping with a screech of horror, as if Charlie had planned to run Page Three girls, reflected only prim, cliquish self-esteem.

The other view was expressed by Geoffrey Wheatcroft, a member of the Garrick, a friend of Peregrine Worsthorne and, like him, a man who deplored many manifestations of modernity: '*The Times* today is produced on the general cultural and intellectual level of the *Daily Mail* 25 years ago ... we could use a serious newspaper of record once more.'

Wheatcroft recalled a conversation in which Jenkins had expressed a wish to see classified advertisements return to *The Times* front page, and dared him to carry it out. When Jenkins gave his introductory address to the paper's staff a few days later, almost the only positive pledge he gave was that he would keep the classified ads where they were. Apart from that, he offered only a general outline of his views on the paper's strategy and where he saw its place in the market, coupled with a rousing call to arms:

> There has been some unease over the great question: which way is *The Times* going? I have to say that I think the paper has suffered from fighting on two fronts at one go, which is always bad generalship. On the one hand we've been fighting the *Daily Telegraph* and on the other we've been fighting first *The Guardian* and then *The Independent* and I don't think it's easy to edit the paper when you're looking over both shoulders at the same time. Now when people have asked me: 'All right, then, which are you fighting?' I have finally come to the conclusion that there is only one answer. I never want to be upstaged by the *Daily Telegraph* on news ... *The Guardian* on the arts or comment or criticism. But there is only one paper which, five years ago, put its tanks on our lawn and that is *The Independent*. *The Independent* came along and quite deliberately tried to occupy *The Times*'s territory. I have no doubt at all that we have got to try to re-occupy it ... *The Independent* is our prime target.

Jenkins stressed his commitment to stylish writing: 'Time was when I think the newspaper could survive simply on its ability to gather very large quantities of news. I just don't think readers will take that as being sufficient any more. It's the calibre of our writers and the calibre of our writing that *The Independent* went for when they launched and we have got to be sure they never do it better than us.'

While sales went down in the first two years of his editorship – to 387,000 in the second half of 1991 – he achieved his aim of staying ahead of the *Independent*, which had gone down to 372,000. In April 1992 the *Independent* inched ahead, but the following month *The Times* regained the lead.

*   *   *

The success of the *Independent*, described in Chapter 5, was the most significant development in the quality newspaper field in the last quarter of the 1980s. Its air of sobriety was what made *Private Eye* dub it, almost from its birth, as the *Indescribablyboring* but it was this very impression of solid respectability that initially persuaded readers of longer-established titles that here was a proper alternative paper in whose hands they were safe. In fact its attitudes on many important issues, as they emerged over the first months, turned out to be, like those of Andreas Whittam Smith, far from predictable and conformist.

Whittam Smith's image of an ideal newspaper was *The Times* in the mid-nineteenth century when, as Stephen Koss noted, it 'gave offence on every side' (*Rise and Fall of the Political Press*, p. 113). The debutant editor believed that for a paper to be influential it had to make a nuisance of itself. Though he and his co-founders were alumni of the *Telegraph* school of Conservatism, they were far from uncritical supporters of Mrs Thatcher's Government. They shared her enthusiasm for the economics of the free market and for the retention of an independent nuclear deterrent but on social issues they were often to her left.

In the 1987 general election Whittam Smith, after an earnest internal discussion and disregarding much advice, decided not to advocate the support of a particular party. The danger that such a self-denying stand would be seen as pusillanimous was outweighed by the meaning that such a show of independence gave to the paper's masthead. People had been attracted by the *Independent* as a name and this refusal to take sides – repeated in 1992 – reinforced its appeal, as did the decisions not to take part in the formalised system of Parliamentary Lobby briefings (see Chapter 13) and not to allow staff to accept free travel or other gifts from people seeking publicity. Not just independent but incorruptible: that was the signal the paper sent out.

Its reporting was very much in the radical, inquiring tradition. It slowly won a reputation for determination and persistence in its coverage of such major and difficult stories as the Guinness financial scandal, the *Spycatcher* affair (see Chapter 14) and, in 1990, the initially bewildering tale of the export to Iraq of giant pipes, apparently part of a super-gun. Its foreign reporting, too, was comprehensive and lively. Before 1986, newspapers had, for reasons of cost, gradually been cutting back on overseas coverage by reducing the number of their foreign bureaux and relying more on non-staff reporters. The *Independent* decided that the young and essentially serious-minded readers it wanted to reach would respond to a paper with an international outlook, despite the difficulty of making the case in terms of pure cost-effectiveness for a multiplicity of expensive foreign bureaux.

The strength and iconoclasm of its domestic and overseas reporting was the factor that recommended the *Independent* to some readers of the *Guardian*, despite its right-wing editorial stance on economic issues. In

September 1988, when the *Independent* was two years old, the *Sunday Telegraph* ran a curious profile of what it called *Independent* Man, head-lined 'How *Guardian* Man lost his soul and was reincarnated'. Identifying the traditional *Guardian* reader as 'the high-minded, the Fabian, the Wet, the liberal with both a small and a big "l"', the profile-writer said that the old paper now seemed to have given up the fight to keep them: 'They have gone to *The Independent*. We are witnessing the Death of *Guardian* Man and the Birth of *Independent* Man.'

The argument was that under Peter Preston, editor since 1975, the paper's soul had been sacrificed to Marxists and feminists, that *Guardian* Man had given way to *Guardian* Woman. But because he had nowhere else to go, the disoriented traditional reader stayed with the *Guardian* until the *Independent* came along and provided him with an alternative.

This partial and partisan view of contemporary newspaper history ignored the inconvenient fact that Simon Jenkins was to point out eighteen months later – that *The Times* had lost as many readers to the new paper as the *Guardian*. While its news coverage and its lack of formal commitment to a political party were both important elements of the *Independent*'s appeal, a third factor was rather more pragmatic: its listing service of theatre, films and musical performances of all kinds. One role of a good newspaper is as a guide to current fashions and happenings; it has to establish itself as a tool that readers can use to enrich their lives and to discover how others are disporting themselves. Harold Evans recognised this: one of his first innovations as editor of *The Times* was an Information Service listing events in a broad variety of fields – too broad to be really useful, some felt. The *Independent* devoted space every day to thorough arts and leisure listings, which again proved a magnet for young readers. All its rival papers were soon forced to copy it.

9

The Vanishing Middle

> We know what happens to people who stay in the middle of the
> road. They get run down.
>
> Aneurin Bevan, 1953

Peter Preston, *Guardian* Man personified, is a low-profile editor. In very few books about the contemporary press does he even rate an entry in the index. A sardonic and somewhat unpredictable man, whose unsettling manner is accentuated by a paralysed arm, Preston was appointed to the editorship in 1975, aged only thirty-seven, after a thoroughly *Guardian*esque exercise in staff consultation in which he edged out the then deputy editor John Cole (later to gain wider renown as the BBC's political editor).

Preston's has been a mostly successful editorship, judged both by sales figures and by his achievement in sustaining the newspaper's essential political and social character while introducing radical changes in production methods and design. When he took over, circulation was fairly stagnant at 320,000. After an initial dip it climbed steadily, with a pronounced leap in 1979, when *The Times* was closed because of its industrial troubles. The climb continued after *The Times* returned and by 1986 the half million barrier was broken. The surge came to a halt at that point, however, and went into reverse as the *Independent* claimed readers from all the quality dailies. An unpopular redesign at the beginning of 1988 made matters worse and by mid-1990 the figure was down to 425,000.

There may, too, have been political reasons for the paper's decline. In the mid-1980s, Mrs Thatcher's style of Conservatism was riding high. She had won the second of her three elections, fought the Falklands War, launched a share-owning spree by privatising nationalised industries and inflicted a serious defeat on the National Union of Mineworkers and, by extension, on the trade union movement as a whole – a triumph confirmed by Rupert Murdoch's cavalier treatment of the print unions in 1986. The liberal consensus that had been a dominant influence on much of British public life for some forty years, until Mrs Thatcher won the 1979 election, was in headlong retreat.

As the *Sunday Telegraph* had noted, the *Guardian* had long been the natural voice of that consensus, as well as a sympathiser with the electoral alliance of the Liberal and Social Democratic parties. That alliance collapsed in the wake of the 1987 election, leaving the *Guardian*, once seemingly the repository of received rational opinion, suddenly exposed as a maverick, expounding 'wet' views that were no longer endorsed by any significant political party.

The *Independent*, launched in Mrs Thatcher's middle period, had no such historical baggage to carry. It evolved a line that, while never slow to challenge the Government, shared many of its philosophical assumptions – the failure of collectivism, the importance of the free market, the need for change in decaying institutions such as the trade unions, local councils and the BBC. By comparison, the *Guardian*'s attitudes seemed trapped in the 1960s, as it moaned about the social consequences of Thatcherism in action.

Preston saw this but, in trying to make adjustments to the *Guardian*'s traditional postures, he alienated some of his staff, who thought he was compromising the paper's values for commercial reasons. In 1989 he circulated a controversial memorandum containing the findings of a market research survey among readers, potential readers and lapsed readers. He wrote: 'Readers don't automatically want to be told every five seconds how awful the Government is. They don't want personalization of every issue into Thatcher this and Thatcher that. They don't want slanted headlines. They don't want slanted intros. And they want a broader range of views.'

The staff had already been angered by a long-running pay dispute and by Preston's elevation to be chairman of the company as well as editor, which left him with less time to devote to editing. They were displeased, too, when, unusually, a non-*Guardian* man, Jonathan Fenby from the *Independent*, was appointed deputy editor to run the news side of the paper, after Peter Cole had left to edit the new *Sunday Correspondent*. They saw the memorandum as a third body blow, a sign that Preston was, for commercial motives, trying to shift the paper from its traditional political commitment. Members of the National Union of Journalists voted to strike in the spring of 1989, but the pay dispute was settled, Preston was able to still their worst political fears and the action was called off.

Things improved from that point. Fenby introduced notable and needed verve into the news coverage, while the political mood began to swing in the *Guardian*'s favour. With the economy moving into recession the appeal of Thatcherism waned and the Prime Minister herself was ejected in November 1990 in a palace coup. At the same time the fortunes of the Liberal Democrats revived under a new leader, Paddy Ashdown. While circulation figures for all papers remained fairly stagnant in 1990/1, the *Guardian* remained ahead of its two main rivals, the declining *Times* and the *Independent*. In February 1991 it was named Newspaper of the Year in Granada TV's *What the Papers Say* awards, cited for its 'all-round recovery of confidence and sheer exuberance'. That year it suffered a lot less than its two main rivals from the general decline in newspaper sales. Its July–December figure, at 409,660, was only 3.4 per cent down on the previous year's, while *The Times* was down 7.8 per cent and the *Independent* 9.5 per cent.

*   *   *

The *Daily Telegraph* was another paper that had been diverted from its political course by the philosophical change at the top of the Conservative Party. Bill Deedes, a former MP appointed editor by Lord Hartwell in 1974, was a Conservative of the old school, having served in the Cabinets of Harold Macmillan and Sir Alec Douglas-Home as Minister of Information before moving back to his former trade as a journalist. The harsh radicalism of the new Conservatives made no appeal either to him or to Hartwell.

In the first half of the 1980s, though, the group's increasing labour difficulties and financial problems seemed of greater moment than the political differences with the Government of the day. Conrad Black, who took over in 1985, is a natural Thatcherite, but was persuaded by Andrew Knight to appoint as editor Max Hastings, a young man of somewhat erratic political views, that, although right of centre, were in most cases well to the left of Black's. A lover of field sports, Hastings, like Deedes, was more at home with the Conservatism of weekend house parties than with the slick City operators who surrounded Mrs Thatcher. This meant that Hastings's relationship with his proprietor was never warm, and deteriorated further when Black moved to London full-time in 1989 to take a more direct role in running his papers.

Hastings certainly would not have been offered the job in 1985 had Black then been as active a proprietor as he was to become later, and as aware of the nuances of British political life. Andrew Knight believed that youth was the quality the paper needed above all if it was to shake off the cobwebs it had accrued during a decade of being run by elderly men, and to protect its circulation base from attrition as old readers died and were not replaced. Knight was much less interested than Black in the paper's political line.

Before his appointment Hastings, who had made his name as an intrepid reporter for the London *Evening Standard* during the Falklands War, wrote to Knight stating his view on the *Daily Telegraph*'s future direction. His chief point was that the paper should be conservative-slanted but independent, rather than merely a house magazine for the Conservative Party. He added that on the big moral issues, which he thought especially important to *Telegraph* readers, he would generally be at one with the paper's readership, although he might differ on specific political questions with them and with the proprietor.

The first important shift in the *Telegraph*'s policy under Hastings came over South Africa, perhaps the biggest moral issue of all. Under Deedes the paper had been supportive of President Botha's gradualist approach to ending apartheid and had, like Mrs Thatcher's Government, opposed the imposition of trade sanctions. Hastings believed that the South African Government would eventually be forced to make concessions to enfranchise non-whites and he felt that sanctions could encourage the process and reduce the chance of bloodshed. By 1991 he would be proved right but this was 1985 and he hoped fervently that he would not have to write a leader on it during the first weeks of his editorship. As luck would have it, the subject cropped up almost immediately.

With deep misgivings, Hastings wrote a leader that changed the paper's historic policy, and followed it with others denouncing Botha and supporting sanctions. He waited for a hostile reaction but, apart from one reader who wrote that it was obvious that the *Telegraph* was now run by the KGB, the response was muted, as it was when he wrote a leader opposing capital punishment – a cause that *Telegraph* readers are traditionally supposed to hold dear. It was clearly wrong, though, to make sweeping assumptions about his readers' views. One piece of market research found that many of them were concerned that the paper supported the Government too slavishly.

Hastings's approach was to make clear to readers that his was a Conservative paper that broadly supported the Government but did not feel obliged to agree with it about everything. The Gibraltar incident in March 1988, in which three members of the IRA were summarily shot dead by the SAS, was a case in point. The two men and a woman were suspected – rightly, as it turned out – of planning to plant a bomb in the colony and there was a view, especially on the right, that, although the niceties of the law had not been observed, they deserved no better.

The most loyal Conservative papers, especially the tabloids, canvassed that view forcibly and berated critics of the action. Hastings, though, had misgivings, and expressed them in a leader. Again there were protests from readers, but not many.

Conrad Black, the proprietor, made known his disagreement with that and other of Hastings's leaders, especially when they were critical of the United States (as over the bombing of Libya). However, he grew to admire Hastings as a journalist, despite his failure to capitalise, in circulation terms, on his initial success in preventing any significant loss of readers to the *Independent*. The *Telegraph*'s circulation declined slowly from the 1,150,000 when he took over to around 1,050,000 by the end of 1990. Yet Hastings was appointed a board member and in July 1990 was made editor-in-chief of the group, a title held by Andrew Knight until he defected to News International. In 1991 the paper survived the recession better than most of its rivals, with a year-on-year loss of only 1.7 per cent for the July–December period.

*　　*　　*

The *Telegraph* maintains its position as Britain's largest-selling broadsheet newspaper by aiming down-market of *The Times*, the *Guardian* and the *Independent*. It sells more than twice as many copies as any of them. No other paper competes in its precise market segment. That is true of only two other national papers, the *Financial Times* and *Today*.

The *FT* has a lucrative monopoly as a specialist business paper, although its fortunes tend to fluctuate with the economy. In the boom of the mid-Thatcher years, with numerous new jobs being created in buying and selling securities, its circulation rose to nearly 300,000. The market crash of October 1987 knocked more than 10 per cent from that figure almost overnight and recovery, like the economy's, was slow. Although strong in industrial and overseas news its lack of sports and leisure coverage (except on Saturdays) means it does not compete head-to-head with the other broadsheets. By the end of 1991, under its new editor Richard Lambert, it had almost halted its circulation slump and in 1992 was named Newspaper of the Year by *What the Papers Say*.

When *Today* was launched in 1986 it was as a middle-market tabloid competing directly with the *Daily Express* and *Daily Mail*. It was never a viable competitor for them and when Rupert Murdoch bought it the following year his editor, David Montgomery, aimed it at a slightly different audience. Montgomery, a cool Ulsterman, had edited the *News of the World*. On *Today* he used the techniques of mass-market tabloids to reach down and try to cream readers from the top end of the *Sun* and *Mirror* markets. Two days after he took over, he abolished the former headline typeface, identical to the *Daily Mail*'s, and replaced it with a bold sans-serif face resembling the *Sun*'s, with the specific purpose of attracting readers accustomed to the mass-market tabloids.

Montgomery, who was managing director of *Today* as well as its editor, had a vivid image of his target reader. He told his first editorial conference: 'We are going to appeal to greedy people.' He elaborated on this in an interview with *Business* magazine in 1989:

> We're absolutely not a paper for the middle-aged Surrey housewife who's always been middle-class and is probably a *Daily Mail* reader. We're more interested in people from pretty ordinary backgrounds who are asserting themselves, the children of the Thatcherite social and industrial revolutions . . . People are much more mobile. They no longer depend on the nanny state or the nanny trade union as they might have been inclined to do in the sixties or seventies. There's much more incentive for people to get on, win rewards and enjoy spending those rewards. Our philosophy is one of hard work and decent and honest family life.

To emphasise the paper's contemporary relevance, Montgomery paid close attention to 'green' issues about the environment and advocated support for the Green Party in the European elections. Among other topics that he believed to be of special interest to his greedy readers were television (especially television commercials), money, travel and holidays:

> It's an attempt to relate the news to people's ordinary lives and what they spend their money on. They work hard for the money and shouldn't be ripped off by big business and government . . . We have our two holidays a year and our new car every so often, but what do you look for next? You look for the life your children will be leading in 20 years time and the prospects are fairly bleak in many respects. The country is overcrowded and the world is getting overcrowded and we have to conserve what we've got. You don't have to be an intellectual or a sophisticated person to appreciate that.

In an interview just after he took over as editor, Montgomery used a television image to give as succinct a definition as any of the middle market: 'With a choice between *Newsnight* and football on TV, we've got to face the fact that most of our readers will watch football, but they will switch over to *Newsnight* at half time and take in a few minutes of a debate on child abuse.'

He hoped that the strategy that had worked for the *Independent* would work for him – that he could locate an audience for a paper not committed to a political party, unlike the two existing, staunchly Conservative mid-market tabloids. This formula seemed to be working when, two years after taking over, he had more than doubled the circulation to 600,000; but it stalled there as the 1980s spending spree petered out.

Today's support for the Green Party did have at least one definite result: it provoked a vicious attack from Lord Stevens's *Daily Express*, still trying to halt a long-term slide in its circulation. For months Montgomery had been irritating Nicholas Lloyd, editor of the *Express*, and Sir David English of the *Daily Mail* by shamelessly copying their special promotions: when the *Express* had a dieting series, *Today* would match it; if the *Mail* had bought the memoirs of a celebrity, *Today* would run a series of articles about the same person, written in-house. Lloyd, an old rival of Montgomery from the days when they both worked for Murdoch, called the *Today* editor 'the jackdaw of Fleet Street'. Montgomery responded cheekily by introducing a fictional byline, 'Jack Daw', on stories aimed at spiking the guns of his rivals.

Eventually the full weight of the law was brought to bear on these petty tiffs. In April 1989 the *Daily Express* sued *Today* for breach of copyright after *Today* had reproduced verbatim some quotes that the *Express* had obtained from Pamella Bordes, the young woman named in the Neil/Worsthorne case (see Chapter 8). The *Express* won its action but in October *Today* initiated a counter-claim against the *Daily Star*, also part of the *Express* group, for copying quotes from Marina Ogilvy critical of her mother, Princess Alexandra, and other members of the royal family. *Today* won that case, so honours were even and editors grew a little – but not much – more careful when lifting stories and quotes from their rivals.

When Montgomery decided to support the Greens, Lloyd, almost certainly with Stevens's support, wrote an angry editorial denouncing *Today* for backing a party that advocated, among other things, unilateral nuclear disarmament, as well as one that opposed cutting down trees for newsprint. The *Express* called on Murdoch, who owed quite a lot to the Conservative Party, to bring Montgomery to heel. Montgomery says that Murdoch did not raise the matter with him. His brief was to produce a paper that reflected the views of contemporary readers, and he believed that supporting the Greens was consistent with this.

Yet he succeeded only in demonstrating again that clutching the coattails of political fads can be treacherous in the long term. Although the environment remained an important issue for many young people, support for the Green Party as such faded as fast as it had appeared. As for greed, it is always with us, but the capacity for fulfilling it grew less as the recession deepened in 1990 and 1991. *Today*'s circulation resolutely refused to grow and in January 1991, when it had fallen below half a million, forty-five journalists – about a third of the editorial staff – were made redundant. Three months later, just after the paper's editorial office moved to Wapping from its original base in Pimlico, Montgomery stood down as editor and was replaced by Martin Dunn, deputy editor of the *Sun*, whose first act was to replace Montgomery's bold, black headlines with those in the style of the *Daily Mail*, very similar to what had been used before Montgomery took over. Dunn hired Roy Greenslade, former editor of the *Daily Mirror*, as a short-term associate editor, provoking speculation that he may be planning to shift the paper's political line to the left, setting it apart from the *Mail* and *Express* and helping sales, which had sunk to 450,000 by the end of 1991.

*　　*　　*

The middle market had been the trickiest section of the newspaper landscape for some thirty years. Hugh Cudlipp tried unsuccessfully to break into it with his ill-starred *Sun* in 1964. Sir Larry Lamb, looking back twenty years after he became Murdoch's first editor of the *Sun*, told the *Guardian* in November 1989: 'The middle market that Abrams' [Mark Abrams, the sociologist] research pointed to never really existed. The IPC *Sun* wasn't new enough or fresh enough to persuade people away from the *Express* and the *Mail* and I don't think the market was there to be significantly widened.'

He was right. Even the punchy *Today* had failed to enlarge the market, mainly because of the downward pressure resulting from the expansion of the quality papers. Between 1985 and 1991, total sales in the middle market went down from 3,726,000 to 3,666,000, despite the arrival of *Today* in 1986, while those of the quality dailies increased from 2,414,000 to 2,514,000. During that time total national daily newspaper sales fell from 14,834,000 to 14,324,000. Yet both the established mid-market tabloids were earning profits. Lord Rothermere's *Daily Mail* and the *Daily Express*, under its chairman Lord Stevens, had benefited like everyone else from being able to introduce modern production methods.

The one middle-ground paper that contrived at least to maintain its share of the market, though not its total circulation, was the *Daily Mail*. Since 1971 it had been edited with a great deal of craft and insight by

Sir David English – one of several tabloid editors ennobled by Mrs Thatcher. He went to the *Mail* when Associated Newspapers merged it with the tabloid *Daily Sketch*, of which he had been editor. Soon after he arrived at the *Mail*, then a broadsheet paper like the rival *Daily Express* and selling about 1.8 million copies a day, he switched it to a tabloid format. The move produced no sudden increase in demand but at least the *Mail* was not shedding circulation as quickly as the *Express*, which lost nearly a million sales a day between 1971 and 1976, down from 3.5 million to 2.6 million, before it too turned tabloid in 1977.

The *Mail* had overtaken the *Express* by 1990 but both papers then began to register small increases in circulation, at a time when sales of other titles were declining. In part this was to do with the continuing loss of readers by *Today*, but it may also have been a signal that people were at last starting to find the mass-market tabloids too trivial. In May 1991 the *Mail* and *Express*, alone among the national dailies, were registering small year-on-year increases in circulation, although by the end of the year their figures, like everyone else's, had begun to decline.

English's success with the *Mail* was centred on his recognition that the generation of readers who had relied on the solid virtues of the mid-market papers during World War Two, and in the two decades that followed it, were passing on, and their children were either moving up-market to the more serious broadsheets or being drawn by the increasingly strident appeal of the mass-market tabloids.

'The country is divided into two classes of people,' English said in an interview in 1987, 'one who just want pop and thoughtless stuff – not real newspapers but entertainment magazine sheets – and the other market which is the upper and middle market together. Today we have to regard the *Times* and the *Telegraph* as our opposition. What has gone is the old post-war middle ground with a lot of respectable papers in it. That was the biggest chunk of the market, with the posh papers and the tabloids as the two polarised fringes.'

The most serious encroachments on the middle market were coming from above, from the broadsheets, which already in the 1970s were increasing their range of features on domestic and consumer issues – cookery, fashion, home furnishings – so as to broaden their appeal. This harmed the *Mail* and *Express* by luring some of their wealthiest readers. They became less attractive to advertisers as their style and their readership grew closer to those of the mass-market tabloids. Who would want to advertise in a paper with a sale of two million if the readership was not pronouncedly different from that of the *Mirror*, which sold four million?

The trick, then, was to define a new market among younger readers. English concluded that the young adults least adequately catered for in the serious press were women. This was not an original notion: since the beginning of the century editors had known that women, with their growing purchasing power, represented a potentially profitable market, but their attempts to reach them generally lacked the required mix of determination and panache. Hugh Cudlipp had been the last to make a big pitch at young women when he launched the *Sun* in 1964, but in the event he produced a paper without much appeal to either sex.

English managed it partly by engaging some of the best women reporters and feature writers and partly by placing emphasis on the paper's design, believing that stylish women wanted the look of their newspaper to say something about them and their tastes, just as their gloves, handbags and other accessories did. A middle-market tabloid had until then not been attempted in Britain: Cudlipp's *Sun* was a bit smaller than a conventional broadsheet but a broadsheet nonetheless. Inevitably the reduction in size meant devoting more space to pictures and, overall, running shorter stories, but English ensured there was still room for epics of 2,000 words and more from his star writers such as Ann Leslie and John Edwards. A tabloid, he reasoned, did not automatically have to be brash, competing for attention by using ever bigger, blacker and more excitable headlines. It could be elegant, stylish and sometimes understated: the *Daily Mail* was.

So successful was he at carving out the paper's market niche, and defending it from encroachment by rivals, that *Daily Mail* staff were often poached by papers seeking to attack the market he had located. When Charles Douglas-Home was made editor of *The Times* in 1982, he and Murdoch agreed that hiring a few people who had worked for the *Daily Mail* would help instil a tabloid sense of urgency. Among key people recruited from that background were the political correspondent Anthony Bevins and Charles Wilson, who became editor when Douglas-Home died in 1985. Wilson in turn hired some of his former colleagues, notably John Bryant, who rose to become deputy editor.

Wilson's strategy was to lure readers – and advertisers – from the *Mail* and *Express* in a bid to take the circulation of *The Times* up towards that of the *Daily Telegraph*'s million plus. English recognised this. 'The *Times* in my view is moving towards the middle market,' he said in the 1987 interview. 'It is no longer an up-market paper. A lot of the material in it could have gone into a middle market paper of 25 years ago.'

His response to the challenge was to hit back with a still greater emphasis on appealing design and with better written features on entertainment and consumer topics, especially on Saturdays, when competition from the expanded broadsheets was at its greatest. Readers did not seem to mind that the paper's political coverage was over-simplistic, with its knee-jerk support of the Conservative right reaching its zenith in the run-up to the 1992 election. The *Daily Mail* and its editor remained highly respected among his peers, not least because he had occupied his editorial chair longer than any of them. He survived not only because of his matchless editorial instinct, but also because over the years he built up a relationship of mutual confidence with his proprietor, Lord Rothermere – a relationship that was strengthened by Rothermere's preference for living in Paris, where he had to stand largely aloof from the day-to-day running of the paper.

English was also largely responsible for the ultimate success of the *Mail on Sunday*, launched by Rothermere in 1982 as a direct challenge to the *Sunday Express*, whose circulation had already declined from over four million to under three million in a decade, despite having the Sunday middle market to itself. Under its first editor, Bernard Shrimsley (formerly of the *Sun* and *News of the World*), the *Mail on Sunday* failed to jell quickly enough into an appealing commodity, partly because Shrimsley, oddly for a man of his background, was aiming it too high in the market. For example, he engaged the playwright John Osborne to write television reviews and the humorist William Donaldson to do the gossip column. Admirers of Osborne's plays were probably *Guardian* and *Times* rather than *Mail* readers, and Donaldson's rarefied humour found a more appropriate place some years later in the *Independent*.

After a few weeks, when sales slid down to little more than a million, Lord Rothermere, taking advice from English, dismissed Shrimsley and replaced him with Stewart Steven, one of English's senior associates at the *Daily Mail*. Steven had been an admirer of English since they worked together in the foreign department of the *Daily Express* in the 1960s. With English as his editor-in-chief, he changed the *Mail on Sunday* into a much closer copy of the daily paper, hoping to draw in more of its readers. The management also invested in a colour magazine which quickly established itself as one of the best on the market, appealing powerfully to advertisers because it reached a different – though scarcely less affluent – set of readers from the magazines of the up-market Sunday broadsheets. It took a while for Steven to establish the kind of paper he and English wanted but by 1989, only seven years after its launch, it had overtaken the increasingly anachronistic *Sunday Express*, and it continued to buck the trend of declining circulations into the 1990s. In the six-monthly figures for the second half of 1991 it was the only national paper, apart from the comparatively new *Independent on Sunday*, to register a year-on-year increase.

*   *   *

No paper more poignantly illustrated the decline of the middle market through the 1980s than the *Sunday Express*. It was the misfortune of the *Express* group that its two principal newspapers were firmly rooted in that dwindling sector. While the *Daily Express*, after becoming a tabloid in 1977, tried hard to escape from the straitjacket of its post-war image, its Sunday partner appeared, until well into the 1980s, to revel in the time warp in which it had become wrapped too cosily for its own good.

It was not a question of carelessness, of failing to notice that the world had passed by while the *Sunday Express* stood still. To keep the paper virtually changeless was the deliberate policy of John Junor, its editor from 1954 to 1986. He thought that people wanted above all to be comfortable with their Sunday paper, to see the same things in it week after week – the Giles cartoons, the Crossbencher political column, the pictures of starlets 'jetting for the sun' and above all Junor's own curmudgeonly column, in which he roared in defence of common sense, conservatism and the eternal verities. All these were features he had inherited from his almost equally long-serving (and equally Scottish) predecessor, John Gordon, editor from 1928 to 1954.

Junor denied that he preserved the paper in aspic. In an interview marking his seventieth birthday in January 1989, he said: 'I believe that newspapers should constantly change, but in the same way as a mirror changes when you look into it. You don't look in a mirror one morning and find you have lost all your teeth or have gone bald. It's a gradual change reflecting the society in which the newspaper operates.'

This philosophy proved no defence against his paper's sharp circulation decline that began in the 1970s and accelerated after the arrival of the *Mail on Sunday* in 1982. Some months after United Newspapers acquired control of the *Express* group in 1985 Lord Stevens, its chairman, summoned the courage to ask the irascible Junor to hand over the editorship to Robin Esser, a *Daily Express* veteran, although Junor's column was retained.

Esser lasted three years until, with the circulation showing no sign of recovery, he was replaced by Robin Morgan, a 35-year-old executive from the *Sunday Times*. It was a surprising appointment but one that at least suggested that the management had been engaged in some constructive thinking about a change in the paper's market positioning, exploiting its broadsheet format to move decidedly up-market of the

Mail on Sunday. Interviewed at the time of his appointment, Morgan spoke of making the *Sunday Express* 'required reading in Westminster and the City' and mentioned the *Sunday Times*, *Observer* and *Sunday Telegraph* as his competitors.

Despite his hiring of several former *Sunday Times* colleagues, the re-positioning, if such it was ever intended to be, was scarcely discernible. The political coverage certainly improved, but the change in the paper's second section, concentrating on sport and leisure instead of on business, was a move in the opposite direction, aimed at catering to existing readers rather than attracting new ones.

The furthest-reaching effect of Morgan's arrival was negative. Sir John Junor, who felt slighted by not having been consulted about the appointment, decided that 'an ersatz *Sunday Times*' was not the kind of paper he wanted to work for and resigned, to be snapped up eagerly by the rival *Mail on Sunday*. The *MoS* spent heavily on promoting their new columnist in television commercials. By the time Morgan was dismissed as editor in February 1991, circulation of the *Sunday Express* had dropped by 200,000 to 1,650,000, while that of the *MoS* had gone up in a shrinking market. His successor, Eve Pollard, changed the second section into a leisure-oriented tabloid and the promotion that accompanied the change assured at least a temporary halt in the circulation slide, but the paper's long-term image problem remained.

It is impossible to match accurately one paper's circulation loss with another's gain. There is no mechanism for determining whether readers have in fact moved directly from one title to the other or whether the change is part of a more complex shift involving other papers. It is, however, fair to assume that many of the lost *Sunday Express* readers followed Junor to the *MoS*. He is one of only a handful of journalists who could persuade a substantial number of readers to switch loyalty. In Stewart Steven's *MoS* the new readers found a paper comparable to the *Express* in the level of its appeal, but one which did most things better and with more conviction: Nigel Dempster's Sunday gossip column, for instance, was a lot sharper than Lady Olga Maitland's in the *Express* (after Morgan left she was replaced by Peter Tory); and the *Mail*'s magazine, *You*, was plumper and better written than the *Express*'s.

Morgan complained that his editorial changes had not been backed by adequate investment in promotion or extra paging. Andrew Cameron, the managing director, responded that before spending money on promotion it was necessary to have a saleable product to promote. After Morgan's departure the management remained undecided whether to turn the paper into a tabloid – a move that had failed for the daily paper but had worked with, for example, Murdoch's *News of the World* – or to persevere with a broadsheet and make a more determined effort to secure a position up-market of the *MoS*. Without any such firm decision, the downward drift in circulation seemed bound to continue.

Even an expensive promotion campaign and a welcome watering-down of the paper's over-riding masculinity could not prevent sales dropping below 1,500,000 before the end of 1991. Pollard's main experience as an editor had been with magazines and the paper seemed to lack a sharp news sense. Stories passed maliciously to *Private Eye*, presumably from disgruntled colleagues, suggested that she was not always easy to work for. Her job seemed secure, though, in part because she was married to Sir Nicholas Lloyd, the editor of the *Daily Express* and a powerful figure in the group. He and Pollard – Lady Lloyd – were the first husband and wife to edit two Fleet Street papers at the same time, which at least cut the cost of their daily commuting.

* * *

The *Sunday Express* has for years been the most profitable paper in the stable, a circumstance that almost inevitably led to rivalry between its editor and that of its higher-profile sister, the *Daily Express*. When the era of long-serving editors on the *Sunday Express* came to an end with Junor's departure, it switched to the rapid hire-and-fire pattern that the daily paper had adopted since Arthur Christiansen bowed out in 1956.

In the twelve years between 1974 and 1986 the *Daily Express* went through six editors – an average of two years each, nowhere near long enough to build a secure defence against a consistently declining circulation. In 1986 the chalice was passed from Sir Larry Lamb to Lloyd, another Murdoch protégé, an Oxford graduate who had begun his career in national newspapers on the *Daily Mail* before moving to the *Sunday Times*, then joining the *Sun* in 1970, just after Rupert Murdoch bought it. Murdoch sent him to Harvard Business School for a year to learn something about management, but soon afterwards he left the group for the *Sunday Mirror*, then the *People*, where he enjoyed his first editorship.

In 1984 Murdoch brought him back to edit the *News of the World*, although he lacked the essential nastiness needed to oversee the kind of paper that it had become by then. At the *Daily Express*, he managed to slow down the decline in circulation by improving the writing and sharpening up most aspects of the paper: for instance the gossip columnist, Ross Benson, became the first to mount a seriously effective challenge to Nigel Dempster's long domination of the field in the *Daily Mail*.

Lloyd's loyal support for Margaret Thatcher – echoing the voice of his master Lord Stevens – was most apparent during the challenges to her leadership of the Conservative Party in November 1989 and 1990. The 1989 contest was with a little-known MP, Sir Anthony Meyer, who was assumed to be acting as a stalking horse for a more serious contender, Michael Heseltine. There was no realistic chance of Sir Anthony winning, yet Lloyd still felt obliged to smear him in a front-page story with the headline: 'Sir Nobody in KGB Sex Plot'. This turned out to relate to an incident of attempted blackmail in Moscow in 1958, when police stopped a taxi just after Sir Anthony had been invited into it by a young woman. It had been reported in the *Sun* in 1970.

Mrs Thatcher was re-elected as leader with ease that year but faced more serious opposition from Heseltine in 1990. Here again the *Daily Express* was her most vociferous supporter and its front-page headlines were put at the disposal of her campaign: 'Maggie to Win, Says MPs' Poll', the paper shouted just before the first ballot. She did indeed win a majority but it was not large enough to prevent a second ballot. The next day, before she announced her decision to stand down, Lloyd was still urging her to fight on and seeking to persuade Heseltine to end his campaign: 'The only way out of the hole is to stop digging and give Mrs Thatcher now the loyalty she so richly deserves.'

When she announced she would quit, the tears of the *Express* were copious:

> By her deeds she created a world for our children . . . The electorate may not always have loved her but they respected her strength of character and her remarkable intellectual abilities . . . Tragically, in the end, her supporters at Westminster allowed adverse opinion polls to rob them of their nerve. Now they have robbed the nation of our greatest peacetime Prime Minister. History will be infinitely kinder to her than the MPs she served so long. Britain and the world is a much better place than when she embarked on her remarkable crusade. While Margaret Thatcher may have gone, Thatcherism must not be allowed to die.

When John Major beat Heseltine and Douglas Hurd in the second ballot, Lloyd was convinced that his hopes for the survival of the creed had been fulfilled. Describing Mrs Thatcher embracing her successor, he wrote in his editorial: 'And well she might. She knows she is passing the torch of Thatcherism into safe hands.' His reward for such loyalty was not long in coming: a knighthood in her resignation honours list. The political payoff was still more ferocious support for the Conservatives in the 1992 election.

Another *Express* group editor honoured in the same list was the *Daily Star*'s Brian Hitchen, who was awarded the CBE. He expressed the house line in terms appropriate to a newspaper vying with the *Sun* for position at the lower end of the mass market, trying to match and exceed it in all things, including jingoism:

> How our enemies must be gloating today. Britain's greatest ever Prime Minister has been forced out by pygmy politicians who put their own job security before the good of their country ... With their Judas kisses, they have shamefully tarnished our reputation in the world ... Maggie wasn't perfect. But she was the best we have had in living memory. We are unlikely to see anyone of her calibre again.

Worth a CBE in anyone's language.

*   *   *

As for the *Sun*, it did not let Mrs Thatcher down either. Its loyalty to her stretched back to her first election victory in 1979 when, on polling day, the paper's two main front-page headlines were 'Vote Tory This Time' and 'The First Day of the Rest of our Lives'. The newly elected Prime Minister wrote a thank-you letter to Larry Lamb, the first editor under Murdoch's proprietorship, and two years later made her gratitude more concrete by proposing him for a knighthood.

The paper's enthusiastic support for 'Maggie' reached a crescendo under Kelvin MacKenzie's editorship during the Falklands War and in the subsequent 1983 election. It was revived in full measure in the next election, in 1987, with the *Sun*'s vociferous denunciation of the Labour Party as being under the control of the 'Loony Left', concerned chiefly about gay and lesbian rights. In the run-up to the Conservative leadership ballot in November 1990 the *Sun* devoted nearly all its front page to posing the question: 'If you judge a man by the company he keeps, is Heseltine really fit for No 10?' The company Mr Heseltine kept was summed up in the splash headline: 'The Adulterer, the Bungler and the Joker'. The story pointed out that one of Heseltine's lieutenants once had an affair with an actress, another had been criticised by a Commons committee for failing to disclose business interests, while a third had been acquitted of 'groping a plain-clothes policeman in a gay club' which he said he had gone to out of 'devilment'. The story additionally dragged in two other Heseltine supporters omitted from the headline: the ditherer, who had once almost joined a new centre party, and the love cheat, who had five children by his wife and four by his House of Commons secretary – a story that had been picked up from the previous day's *Daily Express*.

The conviction with which the Heseltine smear was presented was certainly the work of the editor. Kelvin MacKenzie maintained the confidence of his proprietor through all the public controversies in which he became involved. In an article in the *Sunday Correspondent* in November 1989, Charles Wintour quoted Murdoch as saying: 'MacKenzie is what he is. He's out there screaming, and he's good. Somehow it works.'

Wintour was one of the few of the 1950s and 1960s generation of editors and executives to have a good word to say for MacKenzie. For the most part they deplored the depths to which popular journalism had sunk under his influence. This was especially true of former executives of the *Mirror* group, which had suffered most from failing to keep up with the *Sun*'s excesses. Lord Cudlipp's rousing 1988 assault on the current state of popular journalism was detailed in Chapter 1, but others of his generation at the *Mirror*, such as Robert Edwards and Mike Molloy, were equally scathing.

Cudlipp's stand was the most ironic, for he had himself been the object of just such attacks for his own paper's alleged excesses thirty years earlier. If you make adjustments for the mores of their respective generations, Cudlipp was the journalist whom MacKenzie most resembled, with the unerring gift for surprise, sensationalism and attracting attention. Both became adept at the traditional skills of tabloid journalism early in their careers and took them to more extreme lengths than any of their contemporaries dared. Neither would be happy to think that he has much in common with the other, but the resemblance is unmistakable.

The *Sun*'s Heseltine smear was in the same deliberately offensive vein as MacKenzie's famous 'Gotcha' headline, and the numerous chauvinistic attacks on the French, Germans and Japanese. The paper was taken to the Press Council for its 1990 classic, 'Up Yours, Delors', the front-page headline attacking the French President of the European Commission, who had dared to cross Mrs Thatcher. The headline preceded three pages of invective against the French ('Frog off! . . . Kick them in the Gauls'), which provoked fifty-four complaints to the council. In one of its last adjudications before its demise at the end of 1990 the council, ambivalent to the end, said the complaints were 'understood but not upheld'.

Other skirmishes between MacKenzie and the Press Council, as well as a few pitched battles, will be reported in the next chapter.

10

Shame and Scandal

People think that rubbish-journalism is produced by men of discrimination who are vaguely ashamed of truckling to the lowest taste. But it's not. It's produced by people doing their best work. Proud of their expertise with a limited number of cheap devices to put a shine on the shit. Sorry, I know what I'm talking about because I started off like that, admiring it, trying to be *that good*, looking up to Fleet Street stringers, London men sometimes, on big, local stories. I thought it was great. Some of the best times in my life have been spent sitting in a clapped-out Ford Consul outside a suburban house with a packet of Polos and twenty Players, waiting to grab a bereaved husband or a footballer's runaway wife who might be good for one front page between oblivion and oblivion. I felt part of a privileged group, inside society and yet outside it, with a licence to scourge it and a duty to defend it, night and day, the street of adventure, the fourth estate. And the thing is – I was dead right. That's what it was, and I *was* part of it, because it's indivisible. Junk journalism is the evidence of a society that has got at least one thing right, that there should be nobody with the power to dictate where responsible journalism begins.
Journalist Jacob Milne in Tom Stoppard, *Night and Day*, pp. 60–1

It had to be a fairly startling front page headline to surprise readers of the 1980s *Sun*. People weaned on such masterpieces of dramatic miniaturisation as 'Freddie Starr Ate My Hamster' had learned to expect almost anything. All the same, the edition of Monday 12 December 1988 was remarkable for more than one reason. The main story, headlined 'Sorry Elton', was about the *Sun* itself. The gist was that it had paid an agreed £1 million in damages for allegations it made in 1987 about the private life of Elton John, the popular singer and pianist.

It was by far the highest libel settlement ever reached in Britain – double the sum awarded by a jury to the novelist Jeffrey Archer the previous year, when the *Daily Star* had falsely accused him of picking up a prostitute in Mayfair. That the *Sun* had agreed to pay twice that amount to the wealthy singer reflected their recognition that juries were using these awards to symbolise their disgust at recent trends in the popular press, and that the paper's hounding of John had been persistent and shameless. At a seminar on press freedom in April 1989, Peter Preston, the editor of the *Guardian*, said: 'We must do something to turn round the fatal way in which the readers, the people we're there for, when they sit on libel juries or write to their MPs, see the press and broadcasters as enemies to be despised and not people who are intrinsically on their side.'

The Elton John settlement was announced the day before the court case was due to begin. The front-page apology was not in itself unique. Indeed you could make the case that 'sorry' was becoming the *Sun*'s favourite five-letter word. A few months earlier there had been a 'Sorry' banner headline, beneath which the paper apologised for having published a private photograph of the royal family without the Queen's permission. That time the payment – to four charities nominated by the Queen – was a mere £100,000.

Common to both apologies was an irrepressible chirpiness of tone that made it hard to take the words of regret at their face value. The theme of the Elton John report, perhaps with the coming Christmas season in mind, was reconciliation. The singer was quoted as saying: 'This is the best Christmas present I could wish for. Life is too short to bear grudges and I don't bear the *Sun* any malice.' A spokesman for the paper chimed in: 'We are delighted that the *Sun* and Elton have become friends again and are sorry that we were lied to by a teenager living in a world of fantasy.' To seal the pact, John granted an exclusive interview, spread across the *Sun*'s centre pages, about how he had lost twenty-eight pounds in weight by exercise and cutting down on alcohol.

Such a cosy – if pricey – deal irritated at least one of those involved in the case. Mr Justice Michael Davies, who had been scheduled to hear it that day in the Law Courts in the Strand, complained that the effect of the settlement and the coverage given it was to turn his court into 'a supine adjunct to a publicity machine for pop stars and newspapers'. He added that from reading the *Sun*'s account of the settlement, 'one would think that Elton John and the newspaper had formed a mutual admiration society'.

His diagnosis was accurate. From John's point of view, having won such a big settlement his obvious interest was to get as much publicity for it as he could, to prove to the world that he had been maligned and that the scurrilous allegations made about him were a pack of lies. This, happily, was consistent with the paper's equally transparent motive. Having been forced to pay out £1 million in damages, it wanted to recoup at least part of its money by attracting extra readers. The front-page headline got the paper talked about and the exclusive interview, despite its tameness, was something that could be promoted profitably. As the judge discerned, it had little to do with justice and a lot to do with show-business.

But how had the *Sun* managed to involve itself in such an expensive misadventure? How could such a worldly-wise newspaper fall for the inventions of 'a teenager living in a world of fantasy'? A detailed and well-researched account of how it came about, written by John Sweeney, appeared a few weeks later in the *Independent Magazine*. According to Sweeney, the *Sun* received a tip at the beginning of 1987 that a former male prostitute, or rent boy, had a story about the supply of young boys for sex and drug orgies, implicating big names in show-business. It had all the makings of a mainstream *Sun* story, so a reporter made contact with the youth. Originally John's name was mentioned only as an acquaintance of one of the men said to be involved but, because of his star status, it was his name that interested the *Sun* most. The informant, as he later confessed, obligingly invented stories about the singer to earn his fee.

The first of them appeared in the paper on 25 February 1987, headlined 'Elton in Vice Boys Scandal'. It was credited to two reporters, one of whom, Craig MacKenzie, is the brother of the paper's editor, Kelvin MacKenzie. John, then in Australia, took legal action right away, but that did not deter the paper from publishing a second instalment ('Elton's Kinky Kicks') the following day – the same day that the rival *Daily Mirror* led with John's denial, including the disclosure that he had been in the United States on the date that one of his encounters with rent boys was alleged to have taken place.

Drawing its inspiration from Kelvin MacKenzie, the *Sun* customarily takes a robust attitude to victims who challenge its stories about them. The small, volatile MacKenzie is one of the more remarkable of modern Fleet Street editors. Larry Lamb, the paper's first editor under the Murdoch ownership, had created it from virtually nothing to become the best-selling daily paper in the land. The topless pin-ups on page three were its best-known feature but they alone could not have turned it into the phenomenon it was without the expertise and flair apparent in nearly everything it did.

Any successor to Lamb was in danger of being swamped by his

shadow. Yet MacKenzie quickly established the reputation of running a paper more ruthless, more outrageous, more populist, more offensively outspoken than Lamb's. Mike Molloy, editorial director of the rival *Daily Mirror*, called him a 'barbarian'. Still fewer subjects became taboo. Few ruses were too brazen if a good story was the possible result. It was too much even for Lamb, who told the *Independent*'s Terry Coleman in November 1989 that there were things in MacKenzie's *Sun* that made him feel ashamed of his former connection with it. 'It makes me shudder and feel itchy,' he said. 'My wife and daughter have been known to hide the paper from me.' (As with Lord Cudlipp, ex-editors of tabloids can become especially sensitive about the excesses of their successors.)

MacKenzie was the architect of the *Sun*'s jingoistic coverage of the Falklands War in 1982. When the Murdoch papers moved to Wapping in 1986, he defended them against attacks from the left with verve. His response to criticism on that, or on the paper's reporting methods, became increasingly devil-may-care. The *Sun* had to be the place to turn to for the really thrilling revelations, however the stories were obtained. That, after all, was what the public demanded, if circulation figures were the guide.

Most editors, sensing that Elton John was in a fighting mood, would have counselled caution after the *Mirror* story, in a bid to avoid confrontation. Not MacKenzie. Confrontation is what he thrives on and prudence not a quality that he or his paper much value. Instead, he devoted fresh resources to the attempt to substantiate the allegations.

Elton John, though, was made of fibre just as tough as MacKenzie's. He sued repeatedly after every fresh instalment of the *Sun*'s fictional account of his sexual and other adventures. The episode reached the height of absurdity in September, when the paper printed a zany story alleging – again quite falsely – that John kept Rottweiler dogs that had been operated on so that they would not bark. John sued yet again. That case was on the point of being heard when the £1 million settlement was reached. 'We accept that he loves his pets and we are very sorry we suggested otherwise,' the paper's spokesman announced solemnly.

'The *Sun* was easy to con,' its informant boasted to the *Daily Mirror*. Anyone would be easy to con if they showed such an overwhelming desire for the false stories to be true, or at least to contain sufficient intimations of truth to warrant the risk of publication. The reporters who interviewed the phoney sources knew that if the stories were published their names would be on them, bringing them honour, at least among their superiors and colleagues. Such considerations stifle any lingering doubts, especially when the whole ethic of a newspaper and its editor is to be bold, to take chances and hang the consequences. The *Sun*'s circulation chart showed that readers love scandals, the farther-fetched the better, and the paper is, after all, primarily the servant of its readers. Such attitudes explain the persistent success of hoaxers who telephone newspapers with yarns that, however improbable, would be tremendous tales if they *were* true. Reporters and editors almost will themselves into a state of belief.

(Joe Flynn, who claims many successful press hoaxes, said on Channel 4's *Hard News* in May 1990: 'I fail to understand why journalism in Britain is regarded as a profession. I would hate to come under a surgeon who took the same interest in his profession as a British journalist does. I offer them exactly what they offer their readers – half-truths. And more often than not, they invent the rest.')

The *Sun*'s habitual response to criticism of its excesses was to ignore it. MacKenzie for a long time adhered to his rule of refusing interviews and comments. This began to change after the Elton John fiasco when Rupert Murdoch started worrying about a brace of clouds on his horizon. In Parliament, Private Members' Bills were now being introduced quite regularly, attempting to curb the freedom of the press by strengthening the law on privacy and giving aggrieved victims a statutory right of reply. The Office of Fair Trading was charged with looking into ownership of the media, with particular reference to cross-ownership between newspapers and television. Murdoch admitted in an interview with Terry Wogan on BBC1 on 8 February 1989, that sometimes the *Sun* went too far 'and if it does I stamp on it'.

'Stamp on it a bit harder,' Wogan urged.

In September 1989 a book about the *Sun*, written with the co-operation of MacKenzie and his colleagues, was published by Murdoch's Angus and Robertson. Although Roslyn Grose's *The Sun-sation* was in most respects a breathless celebration of the paper's merits, it was not entirely uncritical. The Elton John case was mentioned and MacKenzie was quoted as saying:

The truth about the whole sorry business is that the *Sun* was taken in hook, line and sinker by a very plausible young man who turned out to be an expert liar. In a way we deserved to suffer. If you pay people like rent boys or prostitutes, who live by deceit and criminality, you should be wary about believing them . . . But the idea that the *Sun* is like some rampaging army searching the sewers of life for front page stories is ridiculous.

MacKenzie concluded, however: 'The *Sun* is not clubbable. You wouldn't want the *Sun* to belong to your club and we don't want to belong to the Establishment club. Therefore every so often the paper for the working men and women of this country is going to do something a bit off the wall.'

The *Sun* often finds itself near the top of the chart of complaints made against national papers to the Press Complaints Commission and its predecessor the Press Council. Its worst year was 1987, when twenty-two cases were brought against it, fifteen upheld and one partially upheld – accounting for 40 per cent of all successful complaints against national newspapers that year. This appears to have given Murdoch and Mac-Kenzie pause for thought, for in January 1989, a month after the Elton John payout, the *Sun* announced the appointment of an in-house ombudsman to adjudicate on readers' complaints. He would have the right to order corrections to be printed and his adjudications, like those of the Press Council, would be published in full. 'If a wrong has been done we will put it right,' said Ken Donlan, the paper's managing editor and a former editor of the *News of the World*, the first holder of the new office.

It was generally assumed that this move was initiated by Murdoch in a bid to curb his editor's expensive excesses. The proprietor's public image was becoming more relevant as he entered the contentious field of satellite television and sought to avoid embarrassing enquiries into the extent of his media holdings.

Donlan was not the first national newspaper ombudsman. In 1985 the *Mirror* group had appointed Sir William Wood to the role, but he retired in 1989 having made almost no public impact. The *Sun*'s move was derided by commentators in the serious papers, but several *Sun* readers' complaints were upheld, notably one about the Hillsborough disaster in Sheffield in April 1989, where ninety-five Liverpool football supporters were crushed to death when the crowd became out of control. On the Wednesday following the incident the *Sun*, under the front-page headline 'The Truth', published allegations that the fans themselves were largely to blame because they had been drunk and rowdy – a version of events that caused deep offence on grieving Merseyside.

Donlan ruled that the paper had been wrong to publish the allegations under a headline that suggested they were the correct version of events. According to Donlan, in his first six months in office he took a hand in thirteen cases where the paper carried an apology and another thirty-eight that were settled amicably in private. Despite the scepticism of other newspapers, all national press editors agreed in November 1989 that they would appoint ombudsmen of their own, and by April they had done so.

As part of the *Sun*'s new policy of openness, the paper's deputy editor, Martin Dunn, was authorised to appear on Channel 4's *Hard News* to answer allegations that the paper disgracefully distorted stories about unhappy people. Then MacKenzie decided to come out of his shell and host a lunch for the media correspondents of five broadsheet daily papers. He said it would be wrong of them to think that the criticism of the paper had not been taken on board: 'Previously we have been a bit too high-handed. If somebody denied something we'd just march on, saying: "They would deny it, wouldn't they?" We have got to think about what our non-readers are thinking about us . . . We are a great newspaper, and I apologise for our errors, but our strengths outmatch our errors.'

In the outspoken style of a *Sun* leader, he spoke abusively of the papers whose representatives he had invited to lunch:

> All our guys could do the jobs of the more heavy newspapers. We could go and edit *The Guardian*, where none of them could possibly edit ours, they haven't got the intellectual firepower. If they have a popular thought they have to go into a darkened room and lie down until it passes. They attack popular papers because they can't under-stand that what we do touches the nerves of the nation . . . The *Sun* arouses hatred because it represents a power outside the Establish-ment. In a sense nobody likes it.

That was authentically his master's voice. Throughout his career in Britain, Murdoch and his representatives have found it useful to project him as a simple colonial boy kicking over the traces and battling for self-expression against the instruments of established power. It is not an entirely perverse argument. There have long been members of the British ruling class who feel their position threatened by a press that bypasses them and appeals directly to the mass of the people. In the 1950s Randolph Churchill accused the popular prints of 'pornography' when they were guilty of only the mildest titillation, at least by current standards. His simultaneous criticism of their new cheeky attitude towards the royal family (again different in degree from the style of royal coverage that would come later) suggested that an equal worry was the danger of provoking disrespect.

Yet although Murdoch's heroic image of himself as a bold iconoclast may have had a vestige of validity at the start of his career in Britain, it was scarcely applicable in 1989, when the first editor of the *Sun* under his ownership had already been knighted, and when he had become adept at persuading politicians that his papers' interests and the national interest often coincided. Most obviously, it was the despised establishment that had lain back and allowed him to have his way with *The Times* and the *Sunday Times* without recourse to the Monopolies and Mergers Commission in 1981.

*   *   *

Led by the *Sun* and its stablemate the *News of the World*, the tabloids in the 1980s discovered that the boundaries of the acceptable had been extended. The frankness about sex that had begun to emerge in British society in the 1960s had taken more than a decade to filter into the mainstream public prints. The satirical fortnightly *Private Eye* played a significant role in this development, showing that it was possible to be less mealy-mouthed and stay on the right side of the law, at least for much of the time.

Private Eye demonstrated that there was a market for intrusive and lubricious reporting among its own six-figure readership and the tabloids discovered that their readers, too, enjoyed it. In their millions, they put down their money for papers that wrote vividly about sex, preferably – although not exclusively – involving indiscretions by people in the public eye or in authority. Thus there grew a lucrative trade in revelations from rent boys, prostitutes, jilted lovers and occasionally cuckolded spouses. The rewards grew higher as competition among the tabloids intensified, and inevitably put pressure on informants, as in the Elton John case, to manufacture lies.

Although many of the details were sleazy the papers developed what they saw as a wholesome attitude to conventional heterosexual sex, exemplified in the merry captions to the page three nudes. The word 'bonking' burst into the tabloids' vocabulary to describe the sex act: a hearty, innocent-sounding word, redolent of saucy seaside postcards; a physical word that separates the bodily function from the complication of emotional involvement.

A few journalists on the tabloids revelled in writing such material but more of them shrugged, told themselves and their friends that it was part of the job and tried to think about something else – their mortgages or salary. 'There's no doubt ethical standards have gone down and it affects all of us,' said one seasoned tabloid practitioner. 'If you live in a swamp you get your feet wet.'

Countless scandals roared across the front pages of the tabloids during the 1980s and into the 1990s. Here is a handy alphabetical guide to the most notable of them, and some of the costlier libel cases, that are not covered elsewhere in this book:

Jeffrey Archer : Best-selling novelist, former MP, athlete and vice-chairman of the Conservative Party, victim of a pseudo-scoop in the *News of the World*, to the effect that a man acting on his behalf had paid a four-figure sum at Victoria Station in London to a prostitute, to dissuade her from alleging that he had been among her clients. Archer won £500,000 in libel damages from the *Daily Star*, which said that he had actually slept with the woman. (Lloyd Turner, editor of the *Star*, stepped down shortly afterwards.) Other papers settled out of court for smaller amounts.

Paddy Ashdown : Liberal-Democrat leader, forced to confess to an affair with his secretary that had taken place five years earlier, after documents relating to it had been stolen from his solicitor and offered to the press shortly before the 1992 election.

Frank Bough : The former presenter of BBC Television's *Grandstand*, *Breakfast Time* and *Holiday* left the BBC after admitting to a Sunday paper that he had attended parties where call girls had been present and cocaine had been taken. Later he was hired by Sky Television (owned by Rupert Murdoch, whose tabloids had played the leading role in his persecution).

Jason Connery : Son of the actor Sean Connery, awarded £35,000 in January 1992 because the *Sun* had said a year earlier that he was a coward who was 'scared to death' at the thought of being conscripted to fight in the Gulf War.

Edwina Currie : Awarded £5,000 in May 1991 against the *Observer* for a magazine article that implied indirectly that she was the kind of woman who would commit murder to further her political career.

Prince Edward : Victim of 'I'm Not Gay' front-page splash headline in the *Daily Mirror* in April 1990, after a reporter had put the question to him at a Broadway première. This afforded a pretext for the *Mirror* and other tabloids to recycle the nudges and winks about Edward that began after he decided to leave the Royal Marines and work in the theatre. Alleged ex-girlfriends were interviewed and testified how 'manly' the prince was. It provided an object lesson on how such a story is manufactured, then keeps the tabloids' pages full for days.

Major Ronald Ferguson : Polo-playing father of the Duchess of York, greatly embarrassed by revelations that he visited a West End massage parlour. Resigned as treasurer of the Guards Club.

Mike Gatting : Cricketer who lost the England captaincy after allegations by a barmaid in a Leicestershire hotel of late-night sex play after a drinking session during a test match. Later Gatting led the 1990 rebel tour to South Africa.

John Golding : Former Labour politician and general secretary of the National Communications Union. Resigned his union post after revelation that he patronised a prostitute.

Sir Ralph Halpern : Chief executive of the Burton store chain whose liaison with a young model, Fiona Wright, was the subject of detailed revelations in the *News of the World*. Ms Wright claimed they had sex five times in one night. Sir Ralph later separated from his wife but the revelations did not immediately harm his business career, although he later quit his job as Burton's met financial difficulties. Ms Wright became something of a tabloid celebrity, with her romantic liaisons thoroughly reported.

Russell Harty : Television personality, victim of rent boy allegations shortly before his premature death in 1988.

Viscount Linley : Son of Princess Margaret, sued *Today* for reporting that he had been ejected from a London pub for throwing beer. *Today* maintained that its reporter had been misinformed by a barmaid. Linley was awarded £35,000 but did not claim most of it and made a statement clearing the newspaper's reporter from blame.

Nina Myskow : Former sardonic TV critic. Subject of revelations about a one-night stand with a young 'toy boy' after a party at a hotel. Being in the business, she appeared unembarrassed by the story and was able to command high fees for articles and TV appearances as a 'toy boy' authority.

Cecil Parkinson : Member of Mrs Thatcher's Cabinet who fathered a child by his House of Commons secretary, Sarah Keays. He left the Cabinet in 1983 when the story was published in *Private Eye* but was allowed back after the 1987 election. Miss Keays later obtained damages from the *Daily Express*, the *Mail on Sunday* and the magazine *New Woman* for suggesting she had sought to exploit the case for profit. Parkinson left the Government when Mrs Thatcher lost the leadership in 1990.

Esther Rantzen : Awarded £250,000 against the *People*, which wrongly alleged that she had failed to expose on her programme a man she knew to be a child molester.

*   *   *

You did not need to be rich or famous to be exposed by the raunchy tabloids. In another case, a hitherto unknown woman who left her children with a baby-sitter to engage in what the *News of the World* characterised as a three-night 'sex romp' saw the story all over the paper. The experience was often shattering to people unused to the limelight.

Stewart Steven, editor of the *Mail on Sunday*, which publishes (among many other things) high-class but usually sex-free gossip about celebrities, sought to draw a distinction between writing about the famous and the unknown. His view that the right to privacy diminished in proportion to a person's fame earned him an unusual rebuke from his paper's proprietor, Lord Rothermere, in a letter to the *Financial Times* in May 1988. If Steven's 'Utopian socialism' was accepted, Lord Rothermere wrote, 'As citizens succeed in this material world, they would be increasingly subject to the obscene inquisition of the current hypocritical journalism of the sensational press ... Even the upright Mr Steven [who had in fact been a victim of *Private Eye* gossip some years earlier] might have, one day, the seven-year-itch and a double-page spread in the *News of the World* to look forward to.'

Steven responded: 'People who own fame, fortune or political power in a democratic society must not be surprised if the press takes a greater degree of interest in their activities ... It is not Utopian socialism but honest-to-God populism.'

The libel laws are a defence for those who can afford to resort to them and can convince a jury that the allegations made are untrue: but to go to law often involves the litigant in being questioned in court about embarrassing personal matters. With juries awarding ever higher sums to successful plaintiffs, more and more victims are prepared to risk embarrassment for the sake of the glittering rewards in prospect.

Not all the costliest libels involve allegations of sexual licence. Sonia Sutcliffe, estranged wife of the mass murderer known as the Yorkshire Ripper, was awarded £600,000 damages against *Private Eye* for suggesting that she had made money out of selling her story to the press. The magazine appealed against the size of the award and raised more than £100,000 from its readers. As a result of the appeal the damages were reduced to £60,000, plus costs and an extra £100,000 for two more libels committed after the case had been brought.

Nor did all libel cases against the press succeed. Michael Meacher, a Labour front-bench spokesman, sued the *Observer* over an article by Alan Watkins, the political columnist, who charged Meacher with misleading people about his middle-class origins. Meacher lost the case and was faced with a bill for costs of some £200,000. Even winners did not all make financial killings. Charlotte Cornwell, the actress, won damages against Nina Myskow (see above), television critic of the *People*, who had written that she had a 'big bum' and a poor singing voice. But the case just preceded the Archer affair and the consequent inflation of libel awards. After three trials, Ms Cornwell found that the costs exceeded the amount of her damages.

For all their boldness, newspapers never claim the privilege of telling untruths with impunity. However careless they are in ascertaining the accuracy of a salacious story, they recognise their responsibility at least to try to get things right and to make proper amends in the case of error. This presumption of an intent to be accurate had to be reassessed in the case of *Sunday Sport*, which arrived on the scene in 1986.

Of all the new papers launched in the second half of the 1980s, this had the most cynical prospectus. It was not based on any desire to broaden the range of opinions on offer but sought simply to exploit the new inexpensive production methods to produce a paper appealing to the very lowest instincts of tabloid readers. Its founder was David Sullivan, who ran a chain of sex shops and had an interest in the new exploitative business of premium telephone lines offering titillating chat or recorded messages. Many of these services were advertised in *Sunday Sport*, whose editorial content was dominated by pictures of naked women and stories containing much explicit sexual description. From the beginning too, there were unbelievable tales of the occult – the return to earth of Elvis Presley, aeroplanes landing on the moon – and callously offensive pictures of freaks.

Circulation quickly climbed to half a million, far more than initially attained by the other newcomers. Yet in most conventional respects it could scarcely be called a newspaper, and would not be worth considering here had it not impinged on the mainstream press in a surprising way in 1987. United Newspapers, under the chairmanship of David (now Lord) Stevens, had bought the *Express* group from Lord Matthews in 1985. None of the papers was doing especially well but the *Daily Star* was a particular worry, selling only just over a million in direct competition with the *Sun*, which sold four times as many.

Neither Stevens nor Sir Gordon Linacre, the group's editorial director, knew much about the mass tabloid market but they noted the early success of *Sunday Sport* and wondered whether that formula could somehow be transferred to the *Star*. It is easy to see how they came to make this dreadful miscalculation. To anybody not steeped in the nuances of tabloid journalism there must seem little essential difference, except one of degree, between a mainstream tabloid flaunting a pair of naked female breasts daily, together with numerous stories about sex, and one that boasts multiple nudes and stories of an even raunchier nature.

Lacking, therefore, any instinct for where the line should be drawn, Stevens and Linacre entered into an arrangement whereby United bought 25 per cent of Sullivan's company for £1.5 million and Michael Gabbert, editorial director of the *Sport*, became editor of the *Star*. An increase in naked breasts and offensive stories duly followed, but it did not bring any increase in circulation: rather the reverse. It was not what people wanted in their daily paper.

Within weeks the *Star*'s sales figure had gone down by 100,000. Advertisers fell away, too, fearing that their products would become tainted in such an environment. After less than two months Gabbert was removed from the editorship and the deal with Sullivan was unstitched. Later Stevens was to maintain that Gabbert (who died of cancer not long afterwards) was 'a lunatic' who had repeatedly ignored his instructions about crucial matters such as the 'nipple count'. Stevens said there must be no more than two pairs of nipples a day, but there were invariably more. Gabbert, in an article in *UK Press Gazette*, said that Stevens and Linacre had initially liked the revamped paper, only turning against it in the light of adverse public reaction. He was replaced as editor by Brian Hitchen, an old Fleet Street hand, but the circulation continued to decline and soon fell below a million. By December 1991 it was below 800,000.

11

The Watchdog with False Teeth

Editors who would hardly recognise the public interest if it had them pinned against the wall will be inviting support for the proposition, in the public interest, that all our freedoms are about to be shattered. That support is no longer possible for any responsible journalist, or any sensate human being, to supply ... It is time to end the professional blackmail by which it is pretended that the interests of the *Sun* have anything in common with the interests of the *Guardian* ... The very function of journalism is being defiled by the reckless transgressions of the biggest operators.

Hugo Young, *Guardian*, 1989

Neither of the two Private Members' Bills on the press survived the 1988–9 session but they received a great deal of publicity and were interpreted as reflecting a higher level of public concern at the excesses of the tabloids than ever before. The Privacy Bill was sponsored by John Browne, the Conservative MP for Winchester, himself the subject of press interest over his divorce settlement and his financial dealings and eventually deselected by his constituency. His Bill would have made it a statutory civil offence to disclose private information publicly. Topics thus protected would have included personal relationships, the home, communications (letters and telephone calls), health, behaviour and personal financial affairs. A limited public interest defence would have been allowed: in other words it would be possible in some instances to argue that the public interest in and benefit from the disclosure overrode the right to privacy.

Tony Worthington, Labour MP for Clydebank and Milngavie, introduced the Right of Reply Bill. This would have allowed automatic corrections for inaccuracies in newspapers, free of charge, given the same prominence as the material complained about. The Home Secretary would have appointed a Press Commission, with legal powers to enforce the regulation. The newspaper industry's objections to the Bills were concisely summed up by David Newell, head of government and legal affairs at the Newspaper Society, the trade association for regional newspapers. He wrote in *UK Press Gazette*:

> Both measures give more legal rights to individuals against the press, without any indication that ordinary individuals will benefit, but at the expense of jeopardising individuals' rights to be informed and to express their own views . . . They exaggerate the power of the press and undervalue the need for the press to have the freedom to inform and to investigate, particularly in a legal environment which already favours secrecy.

On privacy, Newell said the Bill's definition of private information was too broad. Unlike with libel, substantiated truth would not be a defence. Under the legislation it would be easy for people to obtain injunctions to prohibit press enquiry. The measure would hamper investigative journalism and could be used 'as a cloak to hide impropriety and wrongdoing'.

On the right of reply, Newell was worried about the lack of any tight definition of the kind of inaccuracies that would trigger the application of the right. Technically, it would often be hard to publish the correction in exactly the same place as the original article and there was scope for endless argument about its length and wording. The Bill did not cover the eventuality of a third party finding something offensive or inaccurate about the correction itself, leading to possible demands for infinite further corrections. Nor did it make any distinction between facts and opinions. Editors have always resisted giving up the ultimate right to decide what does and does not go into their newspapers. Mr Newell said the proposals 'attack the freedom to express ideas and opinions and the freedom to be biased'.

Private Members' Bills are seldom passed into law but it was apparent from the support these two received from MPs that they stood better chances than most. Nor did the press present so united an opposition as it usually does to threats to its freedom of action. The *Guardian*'s columnist Hugo Young – there is a quotation from his article at the beginning of this chapter – broke ranks with the majority of his colleagues and wrote in support of a Privacy Bill, although not the one proposed by Browne. Only through privacy legislation, Young believed, could the press reassemble public support for it to do its perceived job. In 1972 the Younger Committee had concluded that there was no need for a privacy law because the Press Council was a sufficient deterrent against excess. Young maintained that the situation had changed radically since then and that the freedom of newspapers to act in the brazen way of the tabloids could no longer be defended.

Peter Jenkins of the *Independent*, whose credentials were equally libertarian, agreed, though with less passion: 'The excesses of the gutter press have become indefensible. John Browne's Bill may be defective as drafted but it is hard to gainsay the principle it embodies, which is that privacy is in need of protection from the "heavy mobs" of Fleet Street.'

One of the public figures most victimised by the tabloids added her voice to the clamour. Koo Stark, an American actress, had enjoyed a brief romance a few years earlier with Prince Andrew, now the Duke of York. In November 1988, she had won £300,000 in damages from the *People*, which had wrongly suggested that she continued a relationship with Andrew after her marriage. In an article in the *Independent* she described how she had been hounded by photographers for as long as two years and on one occasion chased into a ladies' lavatory. After she and other users of the lavatory had confiscated the man's cameras, Stark asked him why he did it: 'He told me that three photographers over the last year had earned £1 million for their agency by syndicating pictures of me world-wide.'

When the Privacy Bill came up for its second reading on 27 January 1989, Timothy Renton, a junior minister at the Home Office, said the Government would not at that stage oppose it, despite reservations. He spoke of the growing resentment in many quarters about the excesses of the tabloids but said the Government still favoured *voluntary* regulation: 'The press at times outrages the bounds of decent behaviour, but that may be a price we have to pay for freedom of speech.'

Mr Browne, the Bill's sponsor, quoted polls showing that 70 per cent of people were disgusted and concerned about breaches of privacy. The Conservative Julian Critchley maintained that as the *Sun*'s standards dropped, its circulation rose. When it came to the division, the Bill failed by two to receive the hundred votes it needed to move automatically to a third reading but, because of the great interest it had engendered, 309 MPs signed an Early Day Motion and time was found for it. The third reading came up on 5 May 1989. A week earlier Louis Blom-Cooper, who had become chairman of the Press Council at the beginning of the year, had delivered the James Cameron Memorial Lecture and surprisingly agreed that his Press Council was no longer an adequate defence against breaches of privacy. He advocated a carefully drawn up privacy law such as applied in the United States – although there it is used infrequently because it specifically does not apply to people whose jobs, by their nature, keep them in the public eye.

Tony Worthington's Right of Reply Bill was potentially the greater threat because it challenged editorial sovereignty over a newspaper's content. It came up for debate a week after the Privacy Bill and fared better, gaining its second reading by 120 votes to 0. Timothy Renton, for the Government, took the same position as he had over the Privacy Bill – that although he had sympathy with its aims and motives, he was inclined to give self-regulation another chance. The less intervention by the courts in matters relating to press freedom, the better.

On 21 April, during the debate on the third reading, Mr Renton spoke more strongly, saying that if enacted the Bill would introduce a measure of government control over the press, 'something not seen since the time of Cromwell'. To compensate for his opposition to the Bill, he announced an inquiry into the law relating to the press, to be conducted by an independent figure. He said: 'Editors and publishers of the national press in this country are on probation. They have a year or two to clean up their act.'

The Conservative Jonathan Aitken, a former journalist, used the occasion to deliver a colourful attack on tabloid journalism: 'The reporter's profession has been infiltrated by a seedy stream of rent boys, pimps, bimbos, spurned lovers, smear artists with grudges, prostitutes and perjurers.'

This was the most powerfully expressed of many similar criticisms that indicated the low esteem in which the popular press was held at Westminster. But the Bill made no progress, as the time allotted for the debate ran out before a vote could be taken.

It happened that the debate on the third reading took place on the same day as an International Press Institute seminar at which Peter Preston, the editor of the *Guardian*, warned of the dangers of public disillusion with the press, and its implications for press freedom. Louis Blom-Cooper was one of the last speakers and was able to relay Renton's announcement to the journalists and executives in the lecture hall of the London School of Economics. He revealed that the Press Council had been in discussion with the Home Office about what could be done to repair the reputation of the newspapers: the planned review had emerged from that discussion.

Blom-Cooper hoped that the Press Council would be asked to undertake the review but it soon became clear that this was not what Douglas Hurd, the Home Secretary, had in mind. In July Hurd announced that the review would be chaired by David Calcutt, a lawyer and Master of

Magdalene College, Cambridge. The Home Secretary defined its terms of reference thus:

> In the light of recent public concern about intrusions into the private lives of individuals by certain sections of the press, to consider what measures (whether legislative or otherwise) are needed to give further protection to individual privacy from the activities of the press and improve recourse against the press for the individual citizen, taking account of existing remedies, including the law on defamation and breach of confidence.

The Labour Party said that if it came to power a law would be introduced. Neil Kinnock, the Labour leader, explained on Channel 4's *Hard News* in May 1990: 'As far as privacy is concerned, that should be a basic right of the citizen guaranteed by law. The exception made to it should only be in circumstances where a reasonable person . . . would conclude that it was fair for the privacy of that person to be reduced or invaded.'

In other words, protect the innocent while leaving scope for exposing the guilty: a difficult legislative trick to pull. Kinnock also committed Labour to act to secure 'a right to reply safeguarded in law and applicable in particular circumstances to ensure that people are not left dumb and bewildered by their treatment by the press, especially private citizens who are not in the public eye.'

*   *   *

If Blom-Cooper was disappointed that the Press Council was being sidelined in the organisation of the Calcutt review, he can scarcely have been surprised. The reputation of the council had been falling steadily for more than a decade, as it was shown to be powerless against newspapers driven, as they saw it, by the pressures of competition to extend further and further the bounds of the permissible.

The Press Council was born in 1953 out of an idea put by the National Union of Journalists (NUJ) to the first Royal Commission on the Press, which reported in 1949. Half the council's members were appointed by the Newspaper Society and the Newspaper Proprietors' Association – representing the interests of, respectively, the owners of the regional and national press – and by the two journalists' trade unions, the NUJ and the Institute of Journalists (IoJ). The NUJ returned to the fold in 1990 after falling out with the council in 1980 and withdrawing its representation. Nominees of these professional bodies were balanced by lay members, representing the reading public.

The council's stated objectives were to maintain the freedom of the press, to preserve professional standards and to adjudicate complaints about the conduct of newspapers – the duty that provided by far the bulk of its work. Three complaints committees sat monthly to consider either verbal or written evidence from both sides and pass recommendations to the full council. It had no powers to enforce its adjudication but newspapers were expected to publish any rulings on their own conduct and usually did so, although not always with enthusiasm or conviction, and sometimes with an editorial comment registering disagreement. Defenders of this 'honour' system maintained that it worked because newspaper executives feel genuinely ashamed when they are censured for misconduct. Over the years, though, the shame factor became less and less apparent.

The cases that received the most publicity were to do with intrusion into privacy, often taking the form of blatant harassment of a person who had, sometimes inadvertently, got into the news. The council deplored chequebook journalism – the purchasing of exclusive stories or interviews, especially from criminals and their associates – and frowned on the use of subterfuge by reporters. But while cases such as these got into the news, there were many more complaints of simple inaccuracy, usually in the regional rather than the national press.

The question whether the council should be able to impose sanctions on the papers was raised from time to time and always answered in the negative. The objections, apparently insuperable, were put succinctly by Sir Zelman Cowen shortly before he retired after five years as the council's chairman in 1988. A lawyer by training and a former Governor-General of Australia, Sir Zelman told the *Independent*:

> For penalties to be effective they'd have to be very severe indeed; otherwise it would just be a minor pinprick, a minor cost of doing business. So we have to contemplate pretty severe sanctions and that would change our character. If a newspaper were in jeopardy of a very large penalty, say of six figures, it must be entitled to appropriate legal protection – including representation by counsel, which we don't have – and to very regular procedures of trial and appeal. It's difficult to see how a part-time council like ours could do it ... Give us the power to lay a severe penalty on a wrong-doing newspaper and you're giving us the power to extend the range of the law over the press.

The council always avoided getting tangled with the law. When individuals pursued complaints against newspapers, it would not act until the complainant signed a declaration waiving the right to take legal action against the paper on the subject of the complaint. That was usually an unnecessary safeguard, because most complaints would not have been covered by any existing legislation: if the offending article was libellous, victims preferred to use the courts, where they could win tangible compensation. All the same, the waiver provision was seen by critics of the industry as being solely to protect the interests of newspapers. In a speech to the Fleet Street Lawyers' Society in July 1989, Louis Blom-Cooper spoke of the possibility of abolishing the waiver. Newspaper representatives warned that such a move might limit the extent to which the papers would be prepared to co-operate with the council.

The council's procedures also provoked criticism. In the autumn of 1988 two reputable journalists – Adam Raphael of the *Observer* and the freelance Francis Wheen – wrote articles poking fun at what had happened to them when they appeared before it. Wheen had been criticised for an article in *Radio Times* alleging drug abuse on United States air bases in England. In an article in the *New Statesman* on 16 September 1988 he noted that of the thirteen people who heard his oral evidence only two were women and most were over fifty: 'As became apparent the moment they opened their mouths, all were very middle-class indeed. It was like walking into a meeting of the Crawley Rotary Club.'

The panel criticised his grammar and quizzed him on such matters as how long he had lived near an air base. 'There seemed little point in wasting any more breath on these goons,' he maintained, when it was clear from their hostile questions that they would decide against him. 'Why should such an addle-brained crew be entrusted with anything?'

The following December Adam Raphael wrote an account of his experiences – only slightly more moderately phrased – in the *Observer*, headlined: 'My Day on Trial in the Kangaroo Court'. He had written an article about payments for entries in a hotel guide and the author of the guide, Elizabeth Gundrey, complained that it was 'a hatchet job' on her. After six months, the documentation in the case had swollen to a hundred pages, with detailed charges and replies.

Raphael described the hearing as 'a mock mini-trial' in which the jury of nine ranged from a former policeman to an obituaries sub-editor on *The Times*, afflicted with an 'apparent lack of understanding of journalists and journalism'. He added: 'The committee was faced by a rambling series of charges ranging from the relevant to the incoherent. Nor were the Council members aided by the chaotic procedures of the hearing, chaired in a notably relaxed style by a former provincial newspaper editor.' There was a row about the admissibility of witnesses, then mutual cross-examinations by Mr Raphael and Ms Gundrey. 'As a blood sport it was probably quite entertaining; as a way of illuminating the issues it was hopelessly counter-productive.'

These two articles appeared in the months before Blom-Cooper took over as chairman of the council on 1 January 1989. They reinforced his view that it was important to alter its procedures, and in particular to speed them up. Before taking office he held discussions with editors and influential journalists, cautiously floating some possible ideas for change.

It was by no means a simple matter, for the council was not ineffectual by accident. It was funded by newspapers unwilling to pay the bills of any organisation that would have real power to curb their competitive activities – as they showed in their reaction to the proposal to abolish the waiver of legal redress.

The Newspaper Society had been against Blom-Cooper's appointment initially: its preferred candidate had been Lord McGregor of Durris, a more conservative figure. Both the society and the Newspaper Publishers' Association were annoyed that Blom-Cooper had clearly been the inspiration behind a number of newspaper articles advocating reform, before he had put his ideas to the council members formally.

The Newspaper Society and the NPA had been talking about setting up their own review of the council's activities, partly to pre-empt any similar initiative by Blom-Cooper. The NPA chairman Lord Marsh (formerly the Labour politician Richard Marsh) can be prickly on such matters and wrote a memo to senior members of the NPA council criticising Blom-Cooper's approach. In the event the two bodies gave way to Blom-Cooper and his review committee was established, although eventually overshadowed by the Government's Calcutt inquiry.

*   *   *

In 1987 the *Sun* was taken to task by Sir Zelman Cowen in a ferocious introduction to the council's report for 1986. Singling out one case in particular, stemming from News International's move to Wapping and the subsequent industrial dispute, Sir Zelman wrote that the *Sun* 'struck at the very heart of the Press Council's role and functions'.

The complaint was made by Terrence McCabe, a lorry driver who had refused to cross the Wapping picket line. In an angry story about him, the *Sun* asserted that he was motivated not by principle but by a desire for revenge against the *News of the World*, which in 1982 had published a report alleging that, as a district councillor, he had been involved in sexual activity with two young women after promising to find them homes. He had also been convicted of dishonesty and given a conditional discharge by magistrates. The *Sun* said he had obtained a job with their distribution company, TNT, through failing to disclose his previous convictions and headlined their story: 'You Lying Trucker'.

In evidence to the Press Council, McCabe said he was not obliged to reveal spent convictions when applying for a job. The *Sun* responded that he had brought the investigation on himself by contacting other papers and giving what the *Sun* believed was a false account of his motives for refusing to drive into Wapping. The council ruled in McCabe's favour, saying that there was a particular obligation on the *Sun* to be fair in reporting a story in which it was involved.

What happened next appalled Sir Zelman. The *Sun* fulfilled its formal obligation to the council by publishing the adjudication but in doing so it repeated all its previous slurs against McCabe plus some others. He was mocked for having 'scuttled to the Press Council' and invited to sue the paper, which released him from the waiver of legal action to which he had agreed at the start of the council's proceedings.

In one of its sternest judgments ever, the council said it was 'wholly wrong' of the *Sun* to attack someone for exercising his right to complain:

> The newspaper's offence was compounded by its unfair decision after the Press Council's finding had been announced, to try to taunt the complainant into taking action in the courts. The attack on him for complaining to the Press Council and the attempt to inveigle him into reopening the matter in the courts when the Council's decision had gone against the paper were calculated to damage confidence in the British press and the procedures and standing of a voluntary Press Council.

The *Sun* persisted. It published this second adjudication in full but repeated the characterisation of McCabe as a 'lying trucker'. In an editorial it said that the council must not claim that its decisions were above criticism. In response to this Sir Zelman Cowen wrote in *The Press and the People*: 'I think it is important to bring to the attention of press and public the seriousness of such conduct. If newspapers persist in such behaviour, they will surely jeopardize what the Council characterised as "the future of self control by British newspapers". If this goes, it cannot be imagined that nothing will be put in its place.'

Another of Murdoch's papers, *Today*, was also giving the council trouble. When Murdoch bought it from Lonrho in the summer of 1987, the council issued a statement urging that the deal be referred to the Monopolies and Mergers Commission, because it represented a further concentration of press ownership. David Montgomery, the former *News of the World* editor whom Murdoch had installed as editor and managing director of *Today*, was offended by this initiative, which he believed to be outside the council's terms of reference. He said he would not co-operate in resolving any complaints against his paper until the council apologised. Sir Zelman raised this personally with Murdoch, a fellow Australian, and Montgomery eventually rescinded his boycott.

Timothy Renton was clearly being used by Douglas Hurd, the Home Secretary, as his stalking horse on these matters. In a speech to the International Press Institute seminar in February 1988, Renton applauded Sir Zelman's comments on the *Sun* affair and warned the press again about the future of self-regulation if the Press Council's rulings were flouted. He said that while public figures ought to expect criticism of their public conduct, it was another thing to 'intrude merci-lessly' into the private lives of ordinary men and women, 'or to pillory those who lack the money to seek redress through the courts'.

In the spring of 1989 Channel 4 caught the general mood of disgust at much tabloid journalism by launching *Hard News*, a television pro-gramme dedicated to exposing the murkier practices of the press and to providing a platform for those who felt they had been wronged in the public prints. One case it exposed was of Josephine Hunt, who sought publicity for her handicapped five-year-old son in order to arouse public concern over his affliction, septicaemia, which led to behaviourial disorders. The *Sun* ran the story under the headline 'Worst Brat in Britain', which upset her. Subsequent attempts at 'corrections', in the woman's view, only made things worse. Tony Worthington MP, sponsor of the Right of Reply Bill, said it was the worst case he had come across of the ill-treatment of a private citizen by a newspaper. Mrs Hunt later sued the *Sun* and won substantial undisclosed damages.

But in some other cases it chose to expose, *Hard News* seemed in danger of becoming part of the affliction it was seeking to remedy. One woman had approached the *News of the World* with the story of her affair with a judge. The paper wired her for sound and she arranged to meet him. She said the paper told her that she must engage in a sexual encounter with the judge although its reporters denied this, saying she was expected only to lead him to the point and then make an excuse. In any event the encounter occurred and was splashed on the paper's front page. The woman's next step was to approach *Hard News* with a complaint that the story had not come out the way she had expected. When, at the paper's urging, she asked for her interview not to be screened, the producer decided to go ahead.

Blom-Cooper was attracted by the idea of individual papers appointing ombudsmen, on the pattern of the *Sun*, so that some complaints could be dealt with before they reached the Press Council. The Newspaper Society proposed the appointment of one national and three regional ombudsmen to adjudicate on complaints, with the council involving itself only if adjudications were disputed. In October 1989 the council called a meeting to discuss these possibilities, with contributions from Ken Donlan and existing ombudsmen in the United States. Timothy Renton (in his last days in the Home Office before being promoted to Chief Whip) seized yet another opportunity to castigate the press. He called for sanctions against offending editors and journalists that 'should actually damage the person in the profession, be it the editor, newspaper proprietor or journalist, so that someone's future promotion is not helped but damaged by the warning rebuke given out by the Press Council'.

Later that year the whole national press, including the Murdoch papers, subscribed to a voluntary code, suggested by Andreas Whittam Smith of the *Independent*, undertaking to behave better. They would respect privacy, give a right of reply 'when reasonably called for', correct mistakes promptly, use only 'straightforward means' of getting information and not authorise payments to criminals. Irrelevant references to race, colour and religion would be avoided. Finally, they would appoint their own ombudsman, or 'readers' representative', to safeguard these standards.

Blom-Cooper was put out by this initiative, although he never criticised it in public. He felt the council was in danger of being sidelined. The newspapers, in turn, were lukewarm about the main proposal to come from the Press Council's own review of its functions. This was for a procedure to allow people who believed that their privacy was about to be invaded to alert the council in advance, on a kind of emergency help line. The council would then investigate whether any unjustified violation of privacy seemed likely and put the paper on alert. In explaining the plan to a dinner of the Royal Television Society in February 1990, Blom-Cooper stressed that it did not amount to prior restraint, because the final decision as to whether publication was justified in the public interest would remain with editors.

That, indeed, highlighted the council's weakness as a regulatory instrument: it lacked effective sanctions. Newspapers who went ahead with publication in defiance of the council's recommendation would simply be rapped on the knuckles a bit more sharply than usual. Blom-Cooper insisted, though, that it was a useful device for editors and readers alike: 'If the newspaper industry sensibly embraces this help line it will have removed the one area of justifiable public disquiet that has, not unnaturally, prompted attempts to legislate against the press. A sensible probationer seeks to placate those who put him or her on probation.'

These proposals did not cover all those press activities that the public finds reprehensible. In January 1990 a two-day-old baby was taken from its mother's bedside in St Thomas's Hospital in London. It was missing for two weeks and there was tremendous public interest in the case. When the baby was found and returned with its parents to the hospital, scores of journalists turned up for a press conference with the mother. They got a photocall but nothing else. The parents' lawyer summoned newspaper representatives one by one and eventually sold the exclusive interview to the *News of the World* for a reported £75,000. The parents were not criminals, so there was nothing in the code to prohibit such behaviour. But it still amounted to chequebook journalism which, given the continued high level of competition among the tabloids, seemed likely to prove immortal.

The circulation of the mass-market tabloids fell in the wake of the self-denying ordinance. The outspoken Wendy Henry, in a BBC2 programme about press intrusion in May 1990, attributed this slump directly to the watering-down of their staple diet. It is impossible to tell whether that was any part of the reason. No respondent to an opinion poll would confess to having stopped taking a paper because it was not raunchy enough.

Two incidents in that month suggested that the *Sun*, at least, was chafing at the new restraints. The Press Council ruled against the paper over the use of the words 'poof' and 'poofter' to describe homosexuals. The *Sun* properly published the ruling under the heading 'Rap for the Sun' but in the same issue wrote a scathing editorial criticising the council:

In *Alice in Wonderland*, the Queen of Hearts ordained that words meant what SHE SAID they meant.

The Press Council has the same lordly manner over language.

In their judgment today it [sic] seeks to tell us which words we may and may not use.

Our offence was that we spoke of homosexuals as poofs and poofters.

The Press Council researched in the *Shorter Oxford Dictionary* before reaching its conclusion.

The Council's chairman, Louis Blom-Cooper, knows a lot about the law.

But we know a great deal more about how people think, act and speak.

Readers of the *Sun* KNOW and SPEAK and WRITE words like poof and poofter.

What is good enough for them is good enough for us.

Blom-Cooper, like Sir Zelman Cowen before him, was angered by this show of defiance. Interviewed on Sky Television he said that attacks by newspapers on the council made it more likely that they would be subject to statutory control. As well as the *Sun*, he criticised the *Daily Mail* and *Mail on Sunday*, which have often objected to council rulings on reporting the racial origins of people accused of crimes.

Blom-Cooper said the *Sun* had dismissed the council as 'a bunch of loonies' and commented: 'There is no attempt to sustain the valued prize – press freedom. They are destroying the very thing they wish to keep.'

*   *   *

The Committee on Privacy and Related Matters, better known as the Calcutt Committee, published its report on 21 June 1990. Some critics found the document more responsive to the political impetus behind the committee's formation than to any cool look at the facts. It suggested stronger curbs on the press, while admitting that suggestions that newspaper standards had deteriorated were unproven.

'We have found no reliable evidence to show whether unwarranted intrusion into individual privacy has or has not risen over the last 20 years,' the report said. Even without reliable evidence, most people were in little doubt that such an increase had occurred.

Although the committee did not endorse a statutory right of reply or the creation of a broad new offence of infringing privacy, as the two most recent Private Members' Bills had sought to impose, it recommended that certain forms of intrusion by reporters and photographers should become criminal offences. These included entering private property to obtain information, installing secret surveillance devices and taking pictures or making recordings without permission. Victims could apply for an injunction against publication of material obtained by those means, or seek damages if it had already been published. New restrictions on the naming of minors in court cases were also advocated.

The most controversial recommendation was for the abolition of the Press Council and its replacement by a Press Complaints Commission, funded by the industry. The new commission would operate at first on a voluntary basis, but if newspapers ignored its rulings and continued to behave recklessly, then it should be given statutory powers. Criticising the council, the report said that 'its impact has been limited in part by its nature and in part by the lack of full commitment by the industry to its aims and objectives'.

Yet the commission's terms of reference did not seem much different from those of the Press Council, except for one omission: it would not be part of its brief to defend press freedom. A smaller body than the top-heavy council, it would have only twelve members, who would 'concentrate on providing an effective means of redress for complaints', both of unfair treatment and unwarranted infringements of privacy. Newspapers would be expected to accept the commission's advice on what kind of apology or other redress would be appropriate. Complaints should be handled with the minimum of delay, and there should be a '24-hour hot line' for instant action on abuses or threatened abuses.

Most editors and commentators criticised the report for the vagueness of the new commission's powers and for dangling the threat of statutory controls over their heads, but the recommendations were defended by Simon Jenkins, editor of *The Times*, who had served on the committee. He wrote in his own newspaper that the purpose of the commission was to offer swift redress through a voluntary correction, a right of reply, or agreed compensation. Publishers should ensure that editors made it work, although he had doubts on that score: 'Some [proprietors] may prefer a statutory to a voluntary system . . . Publishers could prefer the discipline of the law to keep their editors, and the editors of their rivals, in ethical check. They might welcome Calcutt's fallback of a legal tribunal funded by the state. It would get them off the hook of internal discipline.' But he concluded: 'The freedom to search out news is worth keeping outside the courts or the control of the state. A framework for such freedom is on offer. The press should seize it.'

The Home Secretary, David Waddington, accepted the report's recommendation, telling the Commons that the new commission would amount to 'positively the last chance' for self-regulation and emphasising: 'This is not an idle threat.' He said that the working of the commission would be reviewed after eighteen months to see whether it was necessary to make it a statutory body – if so it would be headed by a judge and would have powers to award compensation. It would need only one serious instance of a newspaper flouting a ruling by the commission to trigger this ultimate sanction.

Launched in the wake of so stern a threat, in reality the Press Complaints Commission proved something of an anti-climax. Its budget of £1.5 million, provided by the various representative bodies of the newspaper industry, was double that of the old Press Council, but in most other respects its functions and status were scarcely distinguishable from those of the body it replaced. Its chairman was Lord McGregor of Durris, the former chairman of the Advertising Standards Authority whom many press proprietors would have preferred to Louis Blom-Cooper when he was made chairman of the Press Council. In accordance with the Calcutt recommendations, the remainder of the commission consisted of seven representatives of the press and five of outside interests. McGregor insisted that the press representation should be at the highest level: editors only. He also added two retired journalists of his own choice: David Chipp, the former editor-in-chief of the Press Association, and Sir Edward Pickering, an executive of News International and a former editor of the *Daily Express*.

National newspaper editors on the panel were Max Hastings from the *Daily Telegraph* and two from the tabloids – Brian Hitchen of the *Daily Star* and Patsy Chapman of the *News of the World*. In the days before the commission formally came into existence on 1 January 1991, Lord McGregor gave several interviews explaining the thinking behind his appointments.

'The Press Council was a rather *de haut en bas* body, operating as an outfit external to the industry,' he told the *Independent*. 'This one is an integral part of the industry, set up by the industry to do a job. There must be a regular and unceasing dialogue between the commission and the press.'

He wanted tabloid editors on it because he didn't want it to be 'editors of posh papers sitting in judgment over the tabloids'. He explained: 'At the end of the day if we can't capture the tabloid editors we've failed and we can only capture them by getting them to work on the commission with us.'

The Press Council at first refused to accept its demise but eventually bowed to the inevitable, although Louis Blom-Cooper expressed misgivings about whether this new attempt at self-regulation would work any better than the old. Certainly the code drawn up by the commission, in consultation with editors and bodies representing the industry, scarcely differed from the codes established by the Press Council in 1990 or by the national newspaper editors in 1989. It called for accuracy and a right of reply, barred intrusions into privacy and subterfuge by reporters and their forcing their way into hospitals – this last proviso a response to the action of *Sunday Sport* in smuggling a photographer into the hospital where the television actor Gorden Kaye was recovering from a serious accident. Many of the rules were subject to the qualification that they could be breached 'in the public interest', for the purpose of detecting or exposing crime or anti-social conduct, protecting public health and safety or preventing people being misled by false statements.

That turned out to be an elastic loophole, and any hopes that a place on the commission would make editors more circumspect in their approach to intrusion were quickly scotched. In a radio interview Patsy Chapman, editor of the *News of the World* and a commission member, said she regarded the role of herself and her fellow tabloid editors as being that of 'turkeys trying to postpone Christmas'. Within weeks she was running a smear story against Clare Short, the Labour MP who had incurred the wrath of the Murdoch empire by her campaign against the *Sun*'s page three girls. The paper reported her friendship more than ten years earlier with a black man who had convictions for fraud, wounding, theft and living off the earnings of a prostitute, and who was eventually killed in a gangland murder.

Before the story appeared, Ms Short complained in the House of Commons that she and some of her acquaintances had been harassed by *News of the World* reporters and that £20,000 had been offered for pictures of her in a nightie. She asked the Press Complaints Commission to prevent publication of the report. Ms Chapman went ahead and published, explaining in an editorial why she had done so: 'We do believe a newspaper in a democracy is most certainly entitled to make inquiries about an elected Member of Parliament, whose wages you pay and whose character is likely to be coloured by his or her experiences in life, just as yours or ours might be.'

In a letter to *The Times*, Ms Chapman denied that she had sought the nightie picture and wrote:

These facts about an MP and former Labour front bench spokes-woman, who has made a public stance on many occasions concerning the police, I believe are proper matters for investigation by a free press . . . We have made it clear that we will give all co-operation to the investigation by the Press Complaints Commission and expect to abide by its adjudication.

The commission ruled in favour of Ms Short and the *News of the World* duly published the ruling. It did so with a better grace than its rival, the *People*, which disagreed with a commission ruling in August 1991 on its publication of a snatched picture showing a naked Princess Eugenie, the baby daughter of the Duke and Duchess of York. A few weeks earlier the *Sun* had published a picture, taken some years ago, of the Duke of York, when he was merely Prince Andrew, bathing in the nude. In that case the PCC had not issued a ruling because nobody complained. In the case of the *People* and Princess Eugenie, the Duke himself fired in a complaint and the PCC responded quickly, condemning the paper for its intrusion into the family's privacy and warning that this was just the kind of behaviour that could provoke the Government into legislating.

The *People* published the commission's ruling but indicated its disagreement with it. It carried a joint statement from Robert Maxwell, the proprietor, and Bill Hagerty, the editor, which argued: 'It is not the role of the Commission to anticipate what Parliament might do. If Parliament wants to pass even more restrictive laws upon the press, the Commission should be opposing it, not threatening in advance with what it believes Parliament might do.'

Whether a snatched picture of a naked baby was an incitement to perverted lust or just a charming family snapshot was a matter for debate. Hagerty instigated just such a debate in the *People*, asking readers what they thought. Nearly four-fifths of them could see nothing wrong with the picture. Lord McGregor, though, thought the paper's treatment of the commission's ruling provocative, saying it 'seems to continue the spirit of flagrant disregard for the rules which the industry has itself established'. He was particularly disappointed because only a month earlier he had told a conference of editors that self-regulation seemed to be working and 'there is a very good chance the day has been saved permanently'.

Hagerty struck back at McGregor's criticism in a letter to *The Times*, accusing him of waving the big stick of statutory enforcement so as to secure non-statutory enforcement – which he found illogical. The case did not in fact appear as grave as the commission implied: the royal family do not come into the category of private individuals that the rules are there primarily to protect. (While the row was going on, some equally intrusive holiday snaps of the Princess of Wales in a bikini appeared in all the tabloids and nobody complained.) The significance of the case was that Robert Maxwell, proprietor of the *People*, publicly supported his editor, seeming to confirm Simon Jenkins's theory that some proprietors might not regard statutory regulation as necessarily a bad thing.

At the end of its first year not many could detect a difference between the old PC and the new PCC. Louis Blom-Cooper, not worrying whether he would be accused of sour grapes, wrote an outspoken article in the *Observer* saying bluntly that the PCC represented no improvement: 'In the quality of its small output of adjudications, it does not enhance any public esteem it may have acquired. Its judgments have been cursory, short on facts and on the application of the Code of Practice to those facts.'

Lord McGregor, naturally enough, disagreed. He thought the commission's first year had resulted in a great improvement in the behaviour of the press and a consequent lessening of the danger of statutory regulation. But the occasional lapse still gave him the chance of renewing his strictures. After Paddy Ashdown's infidelity (see p. 198) was reported extensively in the papers, he warned in *The Times*: 'If some sections of the press now turn themselves into providers of little Kinsey reports on politicians and parliamentary candidates, then all the gains of the past 12 months will be lost.' (The Kinsey Report was an American survey of human sexual behaviour in the 1950s.)

*   *   *

The underlying dilemma may be incapable of resolution. A free press must be free to offend people. Any mechanism put in place to protect those unjustly pilloried will equally be used as protection by others who have something to hide – something it would be in the public interest to expose. A purely free press would rely on a market mechanism, in that a paper offending too many readers will find its circulation dwindling. That happened to the *Daily Star* during its brief link-up with the *Sunday Sport*, yet sales of the *Sun* and the *News of the World* began to sag only when their editors signed the self-restraining declaration and were persuaded by their proprietors to abide by it. The lowest common denominator remains a powerful marketing formula.

12
Hounding the Royals

What had stayed their hand was Fleet Street's long-standing reticence where the privacy of the royal family was concerned. There is nothing servile in this tradition ... It is founded on the premise that if the exalted position of the monarchy is to be preserved in the face of the encroaching cynicism of modern life, it must be held above carping and criticism.

Edward, Duke of Windsor, on British press
reporting of his affair with Wallis Simpson

When he retired as editor-in-chief of the *Daily Telegraph* and *Sunday Telegraph* in August 1987, Lord Hartwell wrote an article in the latter paper headlined 'How Newspapers Have Changed in My Lifetime'. Discussing the reporting of the royal family, he wrote:

When I was a gossip writer on the *Daily Sketch* ... in 1936 I well remember the shock we felt when our rival, the *Daily Mirror*, came out with a story (quite true) that Queen Mary had been wearing peep-toe shoes. Criticism of the royal family was extraordinary in those days. It was the first raindrop before the storm. In the three years remaining until the war, the *Mirror* increasingly bulldozed the boundaries of taste, so that it was attacked not only from the pulpit but also by sociologists.

If revealing Queen Mary's penchant for peep-toe shoes was seen as having 'bulldozed the boundaries of taste' – and that in the year of the abdication crisis – it is a measure of the change in royal reporting that half a century has brought. Stories about a member of the royal family taking up a daring or outrageous fashion trend nowadays appear in the tabloids possibly once a week, on average. Virtually anything a royal figure says or does, albeit of the utmost triviality in itself, makes headlines because of the obsession of nearly all sections of the press – not

The *Daily Mail* front page of 5 June 1992 pre-empted the revelations contained in the *Sunday Times* serialisation of Andrew Morton's *Diana: Her True Story* which began two days later.

just the tabloids – with royalty. And in no area of reporting is invention given a freer hand.

Take a single issue of *Today*, chosen at random, dated 18 March 1991. The main front-page story, headlined 'Baa Royal Appointment', told how the Prince of Wales was supplying the Tesco chain, 'his favourite supermarket', with 'stress-free lambs' reared on a vegetarian diet on his own farm. It added that the Prince was also giving architectural advice to Tesco in respect of a new store they were building on his land in Dorset. In a characteristic attempt to provoke controversy, the report noted that there was a special bond between the Prince and Tesco: 'It could be a friendship worth a fortune and the envy of other High Street giants. The publicity and product endorsement Tesco is getting from Charles would have cost millions of pounds.' A short editorial comment reinforced the point: 'The future king should not be seen to be too closely involved with any one firm. Next time he wants to sell any of his farm produce, perhaps he should do it through Sainsbury's or Safeway.'

If ever a story was overdone to destruction, this was it. A strap on the bottom of page three read 'Thought for Today: And with Prince Charles's Tesco lamb, of course, you have Royal Mint Sauce.' Just above this was a second royal story – Viscount Althorp, the Prince of Wales's brother-in-law, had been made redundant by the American television network NBC, for which he had worked in London.

The main feature page, opposite the editorial page, was wholly devoted to an article about the flirtatious ways of the Princess of Wales, headlined 'The Princess of Wiles'. One of the Sunday tabloids had the previous day revealed her friendship with a 'dashing Guards officer' who had split with his fiancée because of his passion for the Princess. *Today*'s article was written in the way that characterises such confections, with apparent authority and inside knowledge but no sources quoted except a 'Kensington Palace insider'. Former conquests were listed, and by stressing repeatedly that the Princess's flirtations were entirely chaste, that none of the men mentioned had gone 'where no-one save Charles has gone before', the author, Sandra Parsons, succeeded in raising suspicions that the opposite could be the case. In an article as coquettish as the behaviour it purported to describe, she wrote: 'The truth is that the Princess of Wales has become the Princess of Flirts, unable to resist notching up an impressive list of "conquests".'

Ms Parsons consulted a psychologist, who pronounced: 'She is in the unusual position of being unassailable, so her flirtatiousness harks back to the days when nice girls didn't.' (A few months later all the tabloid papers were reporting an apparent coolness between the Prince and Princess and questioning whether their marriage was in difficulty. And not long after that came the stories of the marriage in crisis that I describe on p. 238.)

The paper's main cartoon by Gaskill on page nine was on another royal theme: a poor joke related vaguely to the front page splash. It depicted the Duke and Duchess of York in their four-poster bed in their new home, which the Prince of Wales had redesigned as a supermarket.

The Chris Hutchins *Confidential* gossip column (now defunct) was seldom without a royal reference, however tenuous, and sure enough it included one on this particular morning: 'Currently occupying the bed that was Princess Diana's when she stayed on Richard Branson's Caribbean island Necker is Oprah Winfrey . . .'

There was nothing unusual about that day's issue of the paper. Sundays are often slow news days, with few domestic stories except what politicians say in TV interviews. Cobbling together some plausible royal yarns is one way of filling the main news and feature slots. Nobody takes them too seriously. *Today* followed up the Prince of Wales story next day with a consumer test on the stress-free lamb, but within a few days the subject was, like most other royal stories, forgotten. It is hard, from this distance, to imagine a time when a report about the Queen's peek-a-boo shoes could have caused so much shock.

The change in the newspapers' attitude to the royal family has occurred gradually over the years. The abdication crisis was the last occasion on which total discretion was demanded and, for an exceptionally long time, secured by Buckingham Palace, despite the obvious constitutional importance of the King's desire to marry the twice-divorced Mrs Simpson, and despite the fact that the matter was being freely reported in other countries, particularly the United States. On 3 December 1936 the *Daily Mirror* was the first paper to break the self-imposed embargo and Edward VIII became the first twentieth-century monarch to experience the press in full cry. In his memoirs, he described the ordeal of reading the *Mirror* that morning:

> Publicity was part of my heritage and I was never so naive as to suppose that my romance was a tender shoot to be protected from the prying curiosity of the press. But what stared at me from the newspapers that were brought to my room on Thursday morning really shocked me. Could this be the King or was I some common felon? The press creates; the press destroys. All my life I had been the passive clay which it had enthusiastically worked into the hackneyed image of a Prince Charming. Now it had whirled around, and was bent upon demolishing the natural man who had been there all the time.

Eight days later Edward abdicated. He would not be the last member of his family to harbour such thoughts about the press, but World War Two temporarily halted the trend towards intrusive royal reporting. King George VI and Queen Elizabeth served as a focus for national unity against the external threat, and the newspapers helped them sustain that function by stressing their adherence to solid family values.

In 1955, ten years after the war ended, another royal love affair was treated much less gingerly. Princess Margaret, the Queen's sister, wanted to marry Group Captain Peter Townsend, but he, like Mrs Simpson, had been through a divorce. This time the papers – the mass-circulation papers at any rate – covered the story in detail, despite the lack of any official pronouncements from Buckingham Palace. They were on the side of the Princess, especially the *Mirror*, which published a front-page editorial urging her to make up her mind, headlined 'Come On, Margaret!'

This was thought by some to be going too far. At a conference of the Institute of Journalists in Malvern in September 1955, Sir Linton Andrews, editor of the *Yorkshire Post*, chairman of the newly created Press Council and a leading figure in the newspaper proprietors' establishment, said: 'Surely a member of the royal family has a private life which all decent people ought to respect? It is purely a matter of human decency. And when she has not made up her mind whom she should marry, it is impertinent of a newspaper to tell her "Come on, Maggie" [Maggie was his abbreviation, not the *Mirror*'s], as if she had been wavering . . . A great disservice has been done by reckless speculation.'

The alternative view was expressed at the conference by John Gordon, editor-in-chief of the *Sunday Express*, who said: 'At present many people seem to regard the royal family as something so high that it should almost never be talked about except in reference to royal processions. This idea, that nothing inconvenient to the royal family should be published, is wrong.' That was the view that prevailed in Fleet Street. At the end of October the Princess ended the speculation by announcing that she would not marry Group Captain Townsend, 'mindful of the church's teaching that Christian marriage is indissoluble'.

In 1978, by which time the Princess had married Tony Armstrong-Jones (Lord Snowdon) and divorced him, the *Mirror* re-ran its controversial headline over an editorial urging her to decide whether she was going to marry her close friend Roddy Llewellyn. 'Come On Margaret (Again!)' was the front-page message this time. But by then this kind of familiar address to the royals was not in the least bit shocking. In the intervening twenty-three years the attitude of the press to the royal family had changed from one of subservience, spiced with below-stairs gossip, to that of a spectator with front seats at a perpetual real life melodrama – or a royal soap opera, as it came to be known, after the fictional domestic serials on television.

Instead of being treated as though on a pedestal, entitled to the utmost respect and privacy, the lives of the Queen and her relatives were investigated and analysed at a higher level of intensity than if they were film or television stars. A landmark was the cherry brandy incident in June 1963. The fourteen-year-old Prince Charles, in his second year at Gordonstoun School, went on a sailing trip to Stornoway, on the Isle of Lewis, with four companions. Waiting for his detective in a bar, he ordered a cherry brandy. He was well below the legal drinking age and, as luck would have it, a local journalist went into the bar and saw him.

The newspapers were uncontrollable. It was Charles's first real taste of their hostile attentions and, according to Anthony Holden in his book *Charles*, it permanently soured his attitude to journalists.

By the 1960s the intrusive photographers, the paparazzi, had come on the scene, notably Ray Bellisario, probably the first to build a career on making sure that, wherever the most newsworthy royals happened to be, he would be there with his camera. The Queen, Princess Margaret and the rest found this immensely irritating, but there was nothing they could do about it so long as Bellisario and his later imitators did not trespass.

The royal family themselves were not entirely free of blame for the eventual corruption of their relationship with the press. If one event crystallised what was happening it was the television documentary about the Queen and her family made for the BBC by Richard Cawston in 1968, with the full co-operation of the palace, and screened in 1969. By the mid-1960s the Queen and her advisers felt themselves in a dilemma. It was hard to defend the monarchy on practical grounds and with a Labour Government having been returned in 1964, for the first time in thirteen years, there was always the possibility that an opportunistic politician, seizing the chance to make a radical gesture, might seek to abolish the anachronistic institution. One Scottish MP, Willie Hamilton, made a name for himself as an anti-monarchist and, although the press treated him as a clown, there was no telling whether his views might ultimately catch on.

The problem that confronted the Queen and her advisers was that if the royal family were to insist on preserving their mystique and remaining aloof from publicity – as they could if they were sufficiently determined – they would fade from view and their survival would be brought into question. They could not in any case abandon all public appearances, since opening and visiting institutions of various kinds is the only visible job they do. The monarchy is nothing unless it is seen to exist. Yet the nature of the reporting of royalty since Princess Margaret's marital dilemma meant that its mystique was fading and in terms of popularity the Queen, after fifteen years on the throne, needed what in marketing terms is called a relaunch. The Cawston documentary seemed a suitable way to do it, since the BBC was a responsible organisation and the film was under the ultimate control of the palace.

Yet far from satisfying viewers' curiosity about life inside the palace walls, Cawston's film made people yearn for more. This could not be provided in the context of a regulated television system whose cameras could only cover the royal family's activities to the extent that they were invited to do so. The newspapers laboured under no such handicap. They could talk to people close to the royal family, inveterate gossips who would relay them stories, often third-hand and inaccurate. They could then use their imagination to embroider them and spice them up by injecting a note of controversy. Sometimes, as in the old party game Whispers, the story as published would bear hardly any relation to the original breathless tip-off.

The palace press office has a rule, broken only on the most exceptional occasions, that no story about the royal family is ever denied. The reason is plain enough: if they were to be in the habit of denying most stories, those rare ones that they did not deny would be effectively confirmed. Yet the result is the anarchic situation where truth and untruth are indistinguishable. As Anthony Holden wrote in the preface to his 1988 book: 'As long as reporters have to crawl through the undergrowth of royal residences, literally as well as metaphorically, snuffling for stories like pigs for truffles, the tidal wave of invention will continue.'

The art of being a royal reporter is to pretend a relationship of easy intimacy with the leading members of the soap-opera cast, even though you spend the greater part of your time in the bushes outside palaces or country estates, or on the pavement outside hospitals awaiting the latest addition to the family. Royal reporters do occasionally meet the subjects of their obsessive writing on overseas visits where, being polite, the Queen and her relatives will usually host a reception for media representatives at each place they visit. The protocol (not always observed) is that conversations at such events are off the record: in any case the royals do not go in for the gossipy tale-telling that is the staple of such reporting.

A typical example of the modern technique came from James Whitaker in the *Daily Mirror*, praising the Princess of Wales in a report written while accompanying her to Nigeria in March 1990:

In 1980 when she first became talked about as Prince Charles's wife, I would tell her that this marriage must happen. 'Why?' she would say. 'What's so special about me? Why would I be suitable?' I would tell her that there were a million reasons why she should become the Princess of Wales, not the least of which was that she was unutterably charming and that everybody loved her for her freshness and naiveté.

Such a conversation may well have taken place; but if it had not, the Princess would, under the palace rules, be prohibited from denying it publicly, even if she thought it worthwhile. Readers, having no means of knowing whether to believe such stuff, place it in a category of its own, midway between the romantic novels published by Mills and Boon and the outpourings of gossip columnists. In September 1986 Donald Trelford wrote in the *Observer*: 'The royal soap opera has now reached such a pitch of public interest that the boundary between fact and fiction has been lost sight of . . . it is not just that some papers don't check their facts or accept denials: they don't really care if the stories are true or not.'

The Prince of Wales's long search for a bride, ending with his engagement to Lady Diana Spencer in 1981, inspired reporting at a greater level of pretended intimacy than ever before. In the weeks leading up to the engagement, the tabloids were packed with speculation about the intentions of the couple, most of it ill-informed, much of it contradictory but all of it delivered with absolute certainty. Photographers stationed themselves permanently outside Lady Diana's London flat and the kindergarten school where she worked. Robert Edwards, editor of the *Sunday Mirror*, got into dreadful trouble with the palace by running a story that the couple had spent a night together before their wedding in the royal train, concealed in a railway siding. The allegation offended the Prince and his fiancée so mortally that the palace insisted on a formal retraction. Lady Diana's mother, Frances Shand-Kydd, wrote to *The Times* to complain:

> Fanciful speculation, if it is in good taste, is one thing, but this can be embarrassing. Lies are quite another matter, and by their very nature, hurtful and inexcusable . . . May I ask the editors of Fleet Street whether, in the execution of their jobs, they feel it necessary or fair to harass my daughter daily, from dawn until well after dusk? Is it fair to ask any human being, regardless of circumstances, to be treated in this way?

Despite that plea, the Queen's Sandringham estate was alive with reporters and photographers during her New Year house party, when Lady Diana was a guest. The couple's engagement was announced on 24 February 1981. It was to be expected that coverage in the weeks leading up to the July marriage would regularly cross the boundary between excitement and hysteria, but it did not subside afterwards. In December, a little more than four months after the wedding, Michael Shea, the Queen's press officer, invited all the national newspaper editors to meet him at Buckingham Palace to discuss the question – the first such gathering for a quarter of a century. They all turned up except

Kelvin MacKenzie, the recently appointed editor of the *Sun*, who had a prior engagement with his proprietor, Rupert Murdoch.

Other Murdoch editors did attend, though, including Harold Evans of *The Times* and Barry Askew of the *News of the World*. Evans gives a detailed account of the occasion in his book *Good Times, Bad Times*. Shea, a novelist and former diplomat who had been appointed press officer to the Queen in 1978, said that, after her first few months of marriage and now expecting her first baby, the Princess of Wales was feeling beleaguered: everything she did was given headline treatment. Simply stopping her official car and popping into a sweetshop for some wine gums was a trigger for her constantly attendant bevy of photographers to start snapping away. After the lecture the editors met the Queen, who accused Askew of pomposity for suggesting that the Princess might send a flunkey to buy sweets for her.

The editors reported the meeting in their papers, and some wrote leaders sympathising with the Princess's desire for privacy, but there was no discernible change in the volume or the tone of the press coverage of the royal family. Scores of photographers on ladders spent days outside the hospital where the Princess gave birth to her two children, photographing the comings and goings. She grew used to it after a while, and in October 1985 she was sufficiently confident to agree to be interviewed with the Prince by Sir Alastair Burnet on Independent Television.

In the interview, she complained that there were too many stories about her in the papers. In particular, reports that she dominated her husband upset her so much that she sometimes had to steel herself before launching out on a day's engagements. The Prince also complained about media myths: 'I do not play with an ouija board. I don't even know what an ouija board is. Nor do I try to get in touch with Lord Mountbatten [long dead] and I would not necessarily want to.'

The following year the pair subjected themselves to ordeal by television again, this time in a two-part documentary. This was when the Prince admitted to talking to his plants: 'I go round and I examine them very carefully and see how they're getting on and I occasionally talk to them – they do respond in a funny way. And if they die I feel deeply saddened.'

But his and his family's continuing doubts about this kind of coverage were reported in the tabloids the following day. According to James Whitaker in the *Daily Mirror*: 'Prince Charles will never again allow TV cameras to film candid and intimate shots of his family life. He believes the TV men who spent nine months filming him and Diana for last night's documentary were too intrusive.'

And in the *Sun* Harry Arnold even had what purported to be a direct quote from the Prince: 'Even when I become king I shall never allow anyone to intrude so deeply into my private life.'

In the *Daily Telegraph*, Hugh Montgomery-Massingberd was frank about many viewers' motives in watching the programme:

> It is sad to think that those who do not appreciate the remarkable qualities of the questing heir to the throne were scrutinising the screen for signs that he has indeed gone off his trolley. Inevitably it was the touching revelation that he occasionally engages his plants in conversation that made yesterday morning's headlines, doubtless causing the more historically-minded cynics to recall the occasion when poor George III shook an oak tree at Windsor by the branch and proceeded to discuss the Protestant religion.

*　　*　　*

Over-exposure was beginning to make the royals into figures of fun – an outcome foreseen by those who thought, along with Edward VIII, that the mystique of monarchy could be sustained only through inaccessibility. In the 1980s, every tabloid paper felt obliged to appoint a specialist correspondent to report on the royal family. That increased pressure on them to create stories out of impossibly thin material – about changes in the hairstyles and dressing habits of the young princesses and duchesses, about remarks they let slip, however trivial, which might be blown up into 'rows' or 'gaffes'. But at least by now the Prince and Princess of Wales had another and younger couple to share the burden of incessant press attention. Prince Andrew's romance with Sarah Ferguson went through the same phases as that of his elder brother – identification of a prospective bride, followed by a mixture of coy hints and blatant denials, neither deterring reporters and photographers from trailing the poor woman wherever she went.

The usual 'exclusive' accounts appeared of whether or when the Prince had proposed and some, by chance and the law of averages, had to be right. After the engagement early in 1986 the papers were free to return to their inventive ways on other aspects of the royal drama. One of the depressing characteristics of Eddy Shah's new paper *Today*, launched just before the Andrew/Sarah engagement was announced, was that, far from breaking new ground, it unthinkingly followed convention in assuming its readers to be obsessed with royal stories. In the first weeks of its life it was even less accurate than its rivals, running a front-page splash announcing that the Princess of Wales was pregnant. Almost as soon as her first child, William, was born in the first year of her marriage, the press had reported numerous false pregnancies until the second, Harry, arrived in September 1984. Once she was safely delivered of him, a third pregnancy – unfulfilled as I write – was freely anticipated.

Miss Ferguson, quickly dubbed 'Fergie', was, to begin with, a welcome new member of the soap opera's cast. Pert and cheerful, she seemed to enjoy exchanging badinage with the royal reporters, as though they belonged to her section of the upper class, where such teasing was common currency among the young. She was also on the plump side, which gave reporters material for the snide joshing they enjoyed. The *Daily Express*, a few months after the wedding, grabbed a picture of her ample thigh through 'a daringly split skirt' she wore on a visit to a bank. After describing the incident, the reporter added pointedly: 'How Fergie seems to be losing weight remains a mystery. Last week she popped into a bakery in Henley-on-Thames to buy three fattening biscuits and yesterday a tea-shop owner revealed that minutes earlier she had tried to buy a selection of cream cakes.'

Soon the Duchess was plump with a purpose – she was expecting her first child. The usual vigil outside the hospital was mounted, but the generally joyful reporting of the birth of her daughter Beatrice was followed by a swift change in the tabloids' attitude to the latest royal mother. There always has to be one member of the family to act as the chief target for criticism and ridicule, and she filled that role usefully. She was frowned upon for the number of holidays she took and for leaving Beatrice in the care of nannies soon after her birth so that she could fly off to see her husband, serving in the Royal Navy. There were questions about what she had done with the royalties of her children's book, *Budgie the Helicopter*. When the couple had a new house built, the papers made much of the alleged vulgarity of its furnishings and decorations.

In January 1992 rumours about the Duchess's relationship with Steve Wyatt, a wealthy Texan, were fuelled by a cleaner's discovery in his flat of some pictures, seemingly innocent, taken when they were on holiday. Over the next few weeks came a growing number of veiled hints that the Yorks' marriage was in difficulty until on Wednesday 18 March the *Daily Mail* scooped its rivals with the news that they were going to seek a divorce. By last edition time, nearly all the papers were running the story.

What happened next typified the difficulties the royal family have always had with their press relations. The day after the story appeared the Queen issued a statement confirming the separation. After giving this statement to the BBC's court correspondent, Paul Reynolds, the spokesman, Charles Anson, entered into a discussion in which he accused the Duchess of hiring a public relations firm to leak the story to the *Mail*, adding that she was highly unsuitable to be a member of the royal family. Reynolds reported this in scarcely veiled terms, saying he had never heard a palace spokesman talk so roughly about one of his flock.

That briefing then became the main story for the tabloids. They assumed that because Anson was the Queen's spokesman he was speaking on her authority. 'Queen Puts Knife into Fergie' was the *Sun*'s front-page headline, and the effect of Anson's outburst was to provoke a rare wave of sympathy for the Duchess. The *Mail*, naturally enough, was incensed at the suggestion that it took its stories from PR firms. 'There's not a word of truth in it,' stormed the editor, Sir David English. Next day Anson apologised publicly to the Duchess and said that the Queen had not authorised his fit of pique.

Before Fergie, the most unpopular family member had been Princess Anne, the Princess Royal. On one celebrated occasion, when taking part in an equestrian event, she told photographers to 'naff off'. Since then, she had partly redeemed herself through tireless work for the Save the Children Fund. The wedding of the Yorks, though, served to renew her clashes with the press. Some papers had asserted that she was grumpy and bad-tempered during the proceedings. A spirited woman, the Princess hit back at the newspapers at a dinner given later in 1986 by Associated Press, the American news agency, in which she articulated many objections to the way the affairs of the royal family were reported:

On a personal level this summer, I suffered severe aggravation from the amount of unadulterated trivia, rubbish and gratuitous trouble-making that appeared in all sections of the so-called media in response to a perfectly normal family occasion . . . I am tempted to suggest the re-introduction of the Norman law where a slanderer not only had to pay damages but was also liable to stand in the marketplace of the nearest town, hold his nose between two fingers and confess himself to be a liar.

Her argument against the excesses of royal press coverage was weakened by the actions of some of the members of the royal family themselves, especially the younger ones. Far from being overwhelmed by publicity, some seemed to court it. They appeared with growing frequency on Terry Wogan's BBC talk show. Michael Shea, for one, thought the level of attention they sought was in danger of getting out of hand, but his advice was not always heeded.

The Queen's youngest son, Edward, had already caught the public eye by resigning from the Royal Marines and attempting to start a career in the theatre, and now he sought to use some of his show-business skills to support charities in a royal fund-raising event. In the spring of 1987 he persuaded his mother to approve a royal version of *It's a Knockout*, a popular old BBC television show in which competing teams race each other in stunts that are often demeaning – crawling through mud, getting soaked to the skin, dressing in ridiculous outfits and similar indignities. Edward's idea was to organise a game with four teams captained by him, the Princess Royal and the Duke and Duchess of York. The four royals did not lower themselves to the extent of actually taking part in the games, but just cheered loudly from the sidelines.

The BBC filmed the event, which attracted a wide audience, if little critical acclaim. When it was over Prince Edward asked reporters whether they had enjoyed it. Indignant over being kept at a distance from the action, they grunted non-committally, at which the Prince retorted: 'Thanks for being so bloody enthusiastic . . . One of these days you lot are going to have to learn some manners.' That put paid to any favourable publicity that might have arisen from the charitable aspects of the event.

Shea had been against the venture because it played up the circus element of the monarchy, but he had left the palace by the time it took place. Reporters had found him likeable, reasonable and useful; but even so instinctive a mollifier was unable to be truly effective in what was in essence an impossible job. The experience left him with a jaundiced view of the tabloid press in all its aspects. In an article in the *Edinburgh University Journal* in June 1988 he wrote:

> There is now a yawning split in the media, a schism, between those who write for publications that seek to inform and those who produce matter so devoid of balance or scruple or truth that surely even they cannot believe it . . . It is newspapers like *The Sun*, publishing their invented interviews, breaking embargoes and intruding inexcusably into people's private lives that are the true enemies of press freedom . . . The old conventions that certain matters in the private lives of public figures were private have been swept away. Gone is any real pretence of objective reporting.

The royal family, he went on, suffered 'constant, unrelenting exposure to fantasy writing' with 'as much factual content as your average fairy tale'. Because the palace did not comment on private matters and therefore seldom issued denials, 'the proprietors know that they can get away with any amount of nonsense'.

Such criticisms did not deter the tabloids, whose tactics sometimes came close to being illegal, especially when it came to obtaining documents or pictures acquired in dubious circumstances. There was a history of such incidents – as long ago as 1968 the *Daily Express* got into trouble for publishing a picture of the Queen in bed after the birth of Prince Edward. In the spring of 1982 the *Sun*'s photographer Arthur Edwards snatched a picture of the Princess of Wales, pregnant with her first child, on a Caribbean beach. The *Sun* published it and the Queen complained of the intrusion, coming as it did only a few months after her plea to editors for restraint. Next day the *Sun*, far from contrite, published the picture again, along with an editorial that defended its use.

In October 1988 the *Sun* offended the Queen again by publishing a picture, taken privately at Balmoral, of her and her mother, with the Duchess of York and Princess Beatrice. It had been sold to the paper by an employee of the laboratory where it had been processed. The *Sun* paid the Queen £100,000 for the invasion of her privacy, and apologised. Two years later it had to make another royal apology when it published a long-lens picture of Prince Charles and an old friend, Lady Romsey, embracing by a pool in Majorca. The caption reeked of innuendo but it turned out that the Prince was comforting Lady Romsey, who had just heard some bad news about the health of one of her children.

The editor of the *People*, Wendy Henry (an alumnus of the *Sun*, and then editor of the *News of the World*), paid with her job in 1989 for the publication of intrusive pictures. The paper's proprietor, Robert Maxwell, supported the palace's objections to photographs of Prince Harry and Prince William, the sons of the Prince and Princess of Wales, taken with a long lens when they were on a school outing. One showed Prince William urinating.

When it comes to royal stories, the papers' appetite for scoops regularly outweighs any moral scruples and indeed any normal considerations of decent behaviour. Below-stairs gossip from members of the palace staff is actively sought. The Queen took legal action to curtail the *Sun* series based on the revelations of Kieran Kenny, a former member of the royal household. After one instalment ('Koo's Romps at Palace') the court ordered the series to be ended because Kenny had broken his terms of employment.

One of the most wounding instances of unethical behaviour came in April 1989 when the *Sun* ran a front-page story revealing that someone had stolen some private letters to Princess Anne. The paper knew about it because someone had tried to sell the letters to its news desk but, making a pretence of virtue, the paper handed them to Scotland Yard. The story gave no details of the letters but it was not long before the *People* did so, explaining that they were written to the princess by Timothy Laurence, a 'dashing Navy heart-throb' and an equerry to the Queen. The revelation sparked a spate of articles about the difficulties in the Princess's marriage, and before long she and Mark Phillips had separated. But that did not stop the papers from another bout of frenzy in March 1991, when a New Zealand horsewoman claimed that Phillips had sired her five-year-old daughter during a one-night stand in a hotel room.

The investigation into who leaked the Princess's letters to the *Sun* brought further accusations of misbehaviour by the tabloids. The police questioned Linda Joyce, the Princess's maid and dresser, who was about to leave the royal service, and when word of that got out, some papers wrote of her as though she was the undoubted culprit. 'Royal Maid Stole Letters' was the unambiguous headline in *Today*. No charges were brought against her. On the Channel 4 programme *Hard News* the following autumn, Linda Joyce announced that she was forming an organisation called Response, so that victims of press abuse could get together in self-defence.

By now, intrusive and/or asinine royal stories were no longer a prerogative of the tabloids. Increasingly the serious broadsheet papers had decided that their readers, too, were interested in this kind of thing. *The Times* and *Telegraph* had long carried pictures of the royals fulfilling their formal duties, but now they began to report on them in the obsessive manner pioneered by the tabloids. In the week of Prince Andrew's engagement in March 1986, *The Times* became as excited by the prospective event as any of its down-market rivals – certainly as excited as the *Daily Mail*, where many of *The Times*'s recently appointed senior executives, including the new editor, Charles Wilson, had learned their trade.

On 17 March, after a weekend of press speculation about the engagement, *The Times* ran a picture and 400 words from the reporter and photographer who had been sent to join the throng at a sports club where Prince Andrew was presenting a badminton cup. The reporter recorded the colour and make of the car the Prince arrived in and quoted dialogue from onlookers ('Oh, it's Prince Andrew').

The following day a page one story told us that Buckingham Palace was remaining silent on the engagement rumours, yet a thousand-word article on the back of the first section was devoted to discussing 'a match made in heaven', accompanied by a snatched picture of Miss Ferguson arriving at work. Next day, still with no announcement, there was another picture of Miss Ferguson surrounded by photographers. The story accompanying it solemnly informed readers that although the press pursuit of the presumed bride-to-be 'degenerated into slapstick comedy', she handled it all with 'charm and aplomb'.

The engagement was announced on 19 March. The next morning *The Times* devoted half its front page to it, with two photographs, including a close-up of the ring. The whole of page three was given over to the engagement, with four stories and four pictures. Two-thirds of page ten was covered with a profile of the Prince and three more pictures. Finally there was a leading article that declared: 'We wish them both every happiness.' Nor was the story allowed to fade. Next day we were treated to Princess Anne's comments on page two, with a story on page three about boom times for the makers of royal souvenirs. The day after that *The Times* rounded off its coverage with a picture of Miss Ferguson's mother and stepfather.

Reputedly more sceptical papers such as the *Guardian* and the *Observer* became equally insistent in telling their readers more about the royal family than they might wish to know. On 13 November 1988 the *Observer*'s main front-page story, backed up with an interview on page three, was devoted to a ludicrous concoction asserting that the Prince of Wales, celebrating his birthday, was irritated at how the press had used the occasion to peddle 'tittle-tattle, half-truths, guesswork and fiction about his private life'.

By now the broadcasting organisations, too, had their own royal specialists and one of them, the BBC's Michael Cole, had provided – to his cost – a vivid example of the hazards for serious journalists when they fraternise with colleagues from less scrupulous organs. Just before Christmas in 1987 the royal reporters, self-styled (for good reason) the Rat Pack, got together for a seasonal lunch. The Queen's annual Christmas message was a regular source of stories in an often quiet news period and the talk turned to what it might contain. Cole, because he worked for the BBC, had seen a video of the pre-recorded speech and could not resist boasting of the fact to the others. He gave them a few details, not believing them to be newsworthy and not thinking for one moment that the tabloid reporters would write a story based on what they had heard at a private lunch with a colleague.

He had been naive on both counts. Next day six papers published an account of what the Queen proposed to say. The gentlemanly Cole admitted straight away that he was the source and the BBC instantly shifted him to other duties: he left not long afterwards to become spokes-man for the House of Fraser department store group. The royal reporter of *The Times*, Alan Hamilton, who also attended the lunch, had been decent enough not to write the story originally, and told us so in a self-righteous account a day later. Cole's expensive mistake had been to assume that the ratlike instincts of the pack were for professional use only, and could be switched off for social intercourse with colleagues.

The broadsheets' interest in the royals is essentially as gossipy as that of the tabloids but occasionally they dress it up as though some vital constitutional issue were at stake. This was the case with the most serious error that Michael Shea made at the palace. In 1986 first *Today* and then the *Sunday Times* ran accounts of an argument between the Queen and Mrs Thatcher, about the drift of Government policy. The Queen, it was reported, had been dismayed by the hard-right line taken by her administration over the dispute with the miners, over its support for the American bombing of Libya and on relations with the Common-wealth, especially over South Africa. The Queen was reported to be siding with the majority of Commonwealth leaders in believing that sanctions against South Africa should be strengthened, but Mrs Thatcher disagreed.

Andrew Neil, editor of the *Sunday Times*, thought Shea had confirmed the story to him, and a serious political row ensued. The differences between the two women were genuine enough but the paper exaggerated their constitutional importance. The Queen wields no influence over Government policy on such matters and would not seek to do so, although she would not feel inhibited from expressing her opinion.

From time to time the *Sunday Times* was highly critical of the royal family. Harold Evans, in *Good Times, Bad Times*, reports conversations with Murdoch that suggest he sets little store by the monarchy. Soon after Murdoch bought the paper he complained to Evans that the Queen had been granted a 12 per cent increase in her allowance at a time when restraint was being urged on everyone else – and the next day the *Sun* editorialised in that vein.

Evans reports that Murdoch often displayed symptoms of virulent and deeply felt republicanism. In January 1989 *Today* pointed out that no member of the royal family was to attend the memorial service for those killed in the Lockerbie air crash, because they were all still enjoying their New Year break.

'The royals have holidays of a length the rest of us can only hope for when we retire,' the paper said. 'That not one of them can be bothered to tear themselves away to go to Lockerbie is a scandal of which the Queen as family head should be deeply ashamed.'

The *Sun* took up the cause: 'The role of royalty is not just visiting schools or attending garden parties. If it does not recognise its part in the most solemn and demanding moments in our national life, one day it may have no role at all.'

Two years later, during the Gulf War, Murdoch's *Sunday Times* made a surprise attack on the royal family, especially the Duchess of York, who had been spotted behaving rowdily in a London restaurant while British troops were limbering up to fight the Iraqis. The paper cited other incidents of royal merrymaking while the world was in crisis, and asked querulously: 'Don't they know there's a war on?' Subsequent opinion polls, including one taken among *Sun* readers, suggested that many people agreed that the royal family were not pulling their weight in the national emergency, and questioned their overall behaviour and attitudes. A decade of intrusive reporting had succeeded in stripping the monarchy of the veneer of dignity which, at root, was its only justification, its *raison d'être*. A further stage in this degrading process was reached in June 1992, again thanks to the *Sunday Times*, which serialised a book about the Princess of Wales, asserting that she had tried to take her life several times because she was unhappy in her marriage. The tabloids eagerly followed up and embroidered the tale, while the Press Complaints Commission railed ineffectually against 'journalists dabbling their fingers in the stuff of other people's souls'.

Only one paper did not share the general press obsession with royalty. The *Independent*, when it launched in the autumn of 1986, had made a firm decision to ignore the social and even the gynaecological doings of the Queen's family, both in words and pictures. Andreas Whittam Smith, its founder, had an aversion to such trivia and the new paper carried virtually nothing about the royals except in the daily Court Circular, a terse and factual account of their main engagements. The success of the paper suggested that readers of serious broadsheets did not necessarily want to follow slavishly the news agenda set by the tabloids, and that in this market gossip was perhaps more intriguing to editors and their staff than to their customers. The lesson went unheeded, though: royal coverage continued in full flood.

13

Sources

The press and politicians. A delicate relationship. Too close and danger ensues. Too far apart, and democracy itself cannot function. There must be an essential exchange of information. Creative leaks, a discreet lunch, interchange in the Lobby, the art of the unattributable telephone call, late at night.

> Howard Brenton and David Hare in *Pravda*, 1985

Journalists and broadcasters define the arena within which Britain's political battles are fought. How much they affect the outcome of those battles is a moot point. It was discussed with some fervour immediately after the general election of April 1992, in which Labour failed to win the victory forecast by the opinion polls. Some believed the party's failure was due to persistent attacks on it by the predominantly Conservative press – attacks that became increasingly virulent as polling day neared. Dave Hill, the Labour Party's Director of Communications, spoke of the 'drip drip drip' effect of the vilification of Neil Kinnock, which he thought greater than any other figure in political history had been made to endure.

Since the beginning of the year the *Daily Mail*, for instance, had run numerous front-page stories highlighting weak areas of Labour's policies ('Smith's Squeeze on Taxes') or boosting the Conservatives ('Major on Top of the World'). They were little more than editorials leavened with selective and often disputed facts, containing such phrases as 'the politics of envy' and 'a double dose of misery'. The *Sunday Times* made much of a long account of Neil Kinnock's perfectly innocent dealings with the Soviet Embassy in London, based on research in the files of the KGB, the former Soviet security agency. On 8 April, the eve of polling day, the *Sun* devoted nine pages to an attack on Labour under the heading 'Nightmare on Kinnock Street'.

After the election some commentators suggested that the volume and intensity of these attacks from a predominantly Conservative press posed a threat to the democratic system itself. They appeared to forget that the press has always been politically partisan – indeed that was the main reason for the establishment of most of the eighteenth and nineteenth century newspapers. The belief that political reporting should be balanced and impartial has grown up only since the advent of broadcasting, especially television. Broadcasting is partly funded and wholly regulated by the state, which properly imposes a requirement of political impartiality. Broadcasters must stand above the battle, like umpires in a cricket match. The press, on the other hand, has always been amongst the players, an intrinsic part of the political process, rather than merely an onlooker. Any attempt to impose a requirement of impartiality would be a dangerous and unacceptable interference with press freedom.

As for the effect of such propaganda on voting behaviour, the evidence is inconclusive. More than half of *Sun* readers vote Labour but a survey by Market and Opinion Research International (MORI) after the 1992 election suggested that 4 per cent of the paper's readers switched to the Conservatives during the last week of the campaign – the week of 'Nightmare on Kinnock Street'. But that statistic is less impressive when set beside the finding that 2.5 per cent of readers of the *Daily Mirror* also switched to the Conservatives that week – and the *Mirror* support for Labour had been scarcely less frenetic than that of the *Sun* for the Conservatives. Moreover fewer readers of the arch-Tory *Daily Mail* – only 2 per cent – switched than did readers of the *Mirror*. That suggests that the influence of the newspapers is less pronounced than both they and the politicians believe.

The resignation of Margaret Thatcher as Prime Minister in November 1990 provided a cameo of how the press prepared the ground for a climactic political event, then failed to exert a decisive influence on its outcome. Theoretically, with an electorate of only 373 Conservative MPs, it should have been easy for the national papers to ensure the outcome they desired. Yet although the strident tabloids ran an enthusiastic campaign to boost the Prime Minister from March, when it was clear that discontent at her rule was growing, until November, when the challenge finally came, they failed to prevent her defeat.

The press, then, certainly did not create the dissatisfaction with the Prime Minister's increasingly autocratic style, but they could not decline to report the events that contributed to it – the poll tax, her attitude towards Europe, opinion polls recording disenchantment with the leadership, Sir Geoffrey Howe's resignation speech. Even tabloid readers, although interested in politics only spasmodically, required that such matters be covered. It was inevitable, though, that by reporting the fact of dissatisfaction they helped its spread, even though most of them disapproved of the treachery.

The efforts by 'loyalist' editors to contain the damage with fervent pro-Thatcher editorials bore no fruit, because they were cancelled out by ever more extensive coverage of the growing leadership crisis, as well as editorials in more thoughtful Conservative papers urging Mrs Thatcher to quit to give her party a better chance of winning the approaching general election. *The Times* leader on 5 November, calling on Michael Heseltine to oppose Mrs Thatcher in the leadership ballot, was credited by some as being the trigger for the drama of the ensuing two and a half weeks.

In general, though, news stories have a lot more political impact than editorials. Politicians like to influence both, but day-to-day they make more effort to cultivate the political correspondents, who write the news, than editors, who decide the paper's policy line. That is why they set such store by the lobby briefing system, through which the Prime Minister and other members of the Government and opposition parties supply correspondents with a regular stream of partisan information and guidance.

The Parliamentary Lobby came into being as a formal institution in 1885. Before that, as Colin Seymour-Ure records in *The Press, Politics and the Public*, members of the public as well as journalists were admitted to the Members' Lobby in the Houses of Parliament. When the public were excluded for security reasons, journalists were allowed in if they first had their names entered on the lobby list by the Serjeant-at-Arms, who controls the administration of such matters. At that time, says Seymour-Ure, the political correspondent was quite a new breed of journalist, for previously editors themselves had been the main conduit between politicians and their newspapers. This state of affairs persisted longest at *The Times*, which did not appoint a lobby correspondent until 1892. By then both the volume of political news and the demands on editors' time were increasing.

Some time between World Wars One and Two the regular lobby briefings by ministers and opposition spokesmen were instituted. This was an important development, for the first time introducing collective briefing, where before each correspondent had made his individual contacts.

Politicians soon learned to make good use of this chance to influence the editorial line of the press on contentious issues, and this was especially true of Neville Chamberlain in the months leading to World War Two. In his book *The Abuse of Power*, James Margach, a former political correspondent of the *Sunday Times*, records how Chamberlain used to react to questions that cast doubt on Adolf Hitler's good intentions: 'He was surprised that such an experienced journalist was susceptible to Jewish-Communist propaganda.'

The politicians usually conducted their own lobby briefings until World War Two, because Whitehall press officers were then a rare breed, compared with the hundreds employed today to handle the Government's media relations. The first Government press officer was George Steward, appointed by Ramsay Macdonald after he became Prime Minister in 1924, chiefly to counter the influence of the predominantly Conservative proprietors of the national press by cultivating their lobby correspondents. James Margach in another book, *The Anatomy of Power*, recalls that when he first became a political correspondent in the early 1930s Steward was still the only Government press officer.

The lobby system became further institutionalised during and after the 1940s, until there are now two briefings a day by the Prime Minister's spokesman, usually held in the mornings at Downing Street and in the afternoons in the lobby briefing room in the Commons, where most other lobby meetings are held. These twice-daily sessions were to become controversial in the 1980s, when they began to be seen as unacceptable attempts at news management.

It is still a matter for the Serjeant-at-Arms, acting on behalf of the Speaker, to decide which journalists should be given access to the lobby. Over the years the numbers have inevitably increased and alternates have been authorised, where previously only one named person from each publication was allowed to share the lobby's privileges. Operating with official permission (very seldom denied), these journalists are in effect licensed by the authorities in this particular part of their work. To counterbalance that, they are, at least in theory, masters of their own procedures. No politician or spokesman has the automatic right to summon a meeting of the lobby for a briefing: the rule is that they ask the lobby chairman to convene one. The chairman may refuse, but seldom does.

The rules of lobby journalism have been the same since the system began: that information obtained within its confines is unattributable except by agreement with the politician or spokesman in question. It is also forbidden for members to disclose the circumstances in which the information was obtained – from which grew the convention that lobby briefings, as far as the record is concerned, do not in fact take place. The phrase 'on lobby terms' has now entered the language to mean any information given to journalists unattributably, by politicians or anyone else.

This subterfuge over sourcing gives rise to the most serious objections to the lobby system. In theory at least, it allows politicians deniability: if something they let slip proves embarrassing they can pretend innocence. Critics say that it allows journalists to be manipulated by being fed false or slanted information or sometimes plain propaganda which, unless they ignore it altogether, they have to report on their own authority because they are not allowed to attribute it to its actual source. Bernard Ingham, Mrs Thatcher's press secretary during her eleven years as Prime Minister, aroused particular hostility by occasionally using his lobby briefings to pour scorn on a Cabinet Minister who had fallen from Mrs Thatcher's favour. He encouraged the reporters in their character-isation of Cabinet ministers on the left of the party, the opposite wing to Mrs Thatcher, as 'wets', vacillators without the backbone to pursue her policies of pure Conservatism to their logical conclusion.

Nigel Lawson, the former Chancellor of the Exchequer, a victim of this technique after his resignation in 1989, called it 'black propaganda'. A useful account of how Ingham applied it, and against whom, is given in Robert Harris's 1990 book, *Good and Faithful Servant*. Norman St John Stevas, Leader of the House of Commons, scored a double first – the first Cabinet minister dismissed by Mrs Thatcher and the first to suffer from the Ingham Effect. Asked why St John Stevas had fallen from favour, Ingham hinted that he had been responsible for leaks from the Cabinet. After the ex-minister complained, Mrs Thatcher gave a grudging apology, claiming that Ingham's briefing had been misunder-stood; but the damage had been done.

The following year Francis Pym, who had succeeded St John Stevas as Leader of the House, found himself the target of a subtle variation of the technique, being denounced by Ingham even before he left the Govern-ment. His offence was to have made a speech early in 1982 in which he expressed his opinion that the economy would get worse before it got better. Discussing this with the lobby, Ingham likened Pym to Mona Lott, a lugubrious character in the wartime radio programme *ITMA* whose catchphrase was: 'It's being so cheerful keeps me going.' Predictably, the papers took this up with glee. Surprisingly, Pym was made Foreign Secre-tary a few months later, but duly left the Government the following year.

Yet another Leader of the House, John Biffen, was a further spectacu-lar victim of Ingham's colourful phrase-making. In May 1986 he was interviewed on television and said the Conservative Party should present a more balanced image, and that Mrs Thatcher would not be Prime

Minister throughout the whole term of the next Parliament (an accurate prediction, as it turned out). Ingham told the lobby that Biffen was 'semi-detached' from the Government, so not to be taken seriously. After *his* departure Biffen said that he recognised that Ingham was only an instrument of the Prime Ministerial will, 'the sewer not the sewage'.

Ingham's final, furthest-reaching – and ultimately suicidal – attack was on Sir Geoffrey Howe, when Mrs Thatcher removed him against his will from the post of Foreign Secretary in July 1989. As a price for staying on, and thus avoiding a Cabinet crisis, Sir Geoffrey insisted on being made Deputy Prime Minister. The day after the new appointment was announced, Ingham told the lobby that the title was of no significance, merely one of courtesy, a meaningless sop. Sir Geoffrey, though, had his revenge just over a year later, when he resigned because of his disapproval of Mrs Thatcher's autocratic style and her position *vis-à-vis* Europe. His action set off the chain of events that resulted in Mrs Thatcher's (and Ingham's) removal from office in November 1990.

There was a difference between the way Ingham's poisoned jibes were reported by the political correspondents of the tabloids and the more responsible broadsheets. The Tory tabloids would usually present them as the unarguable truth, often without attribution, and sometimes use them as the basis for editorials that loyally reflected the Prime Ministerial view. The *Sun*, for instance, dubbed the Leader of the House 'Mr Misery Pym' following the Ingham assault on him. When the semi-detached Biffen was the target the *Daily Mail* reported unequivocally that he was 'in the doghouse'. The broadsheets, often using Ingham's most colourful phrases as direct quotes, made it clear, within the rules of the code, where the criticisms had come from. The effect, though, was scarcely different. The message was duly delivered and understood, as the Prime Minister and her amanuensis had calculated.

The tabloids' generally uncritical acceptance of Ingham's personal attacks on Mrs Thatcher's enemies was the chief reason why, quite early in his long period at Downing Street, he became an enthusiast for the tabloids and defended them stoutly against those critics who thought that by their disagreeable excesses they were bringing the trade of journalism into disrepute. He would tell such critics forcefully that not all the vices of journalism reposed in the popular press. He cultivated the support of the tabloids as a counterweight to the broadsheet papers, which increasingly irritated him with their lofty critiques of Mrs Thatcher's vigorous populism, what he called their 'effortless moral superiority', and even more so with their occasional attacks on his own methods of persuasion. It was relevant that Rupert Murdoch, one of

Mrs Thatcher's staunchest supporters, owned the two best-selling (and most criticised) tabloids, the *Sun* and *News of the World*.

What irritated Ingham about reporters on the serious papers was their fondness for investigation, for seeking scandals in government, for fanning the flames of the fire behind the smoke. He articulated this criticism in a number of speeches during his tenure at Downing Street. Addressing the Guild of British Newspaper Editors in May 1983, he said:

> Too often these days the assumption seems to be that Government is either automatically wrong, naturally perverse, chronically up to no good or just plain inept ... I can understand and sympathise with the suspicion with which the media regards Government and all its works. It must never cease to be vigilant. But it should not assume, as it so often seems to do, that Government is by definition up to no good; the fact that it is being secretive is not conclusive proof that there is something rotten in the State of Denmark.

He reinforced the theme in a speech to the International Press Institute in March 1985:

> Some journalists, at least, believe passionately that another Watergate is lying around just waiting to be uncovered ... I believe that the Watergate syndrome, combined with the broadcasters' 'confrontation' approach to interviews and the determination to take the mickey out of authority ... seems to require that any self-respecting reporter should knock seven bells out of symbols of authority, and especially Government. This goes beyond the normal and expected tension between Government and press. Its effect on our democracy is, in my view, corrosive.

For a time, Ingham's penchant towards the tabloids served him well – spectacularly well in the case of the Falklands War, where the tabloids played a vital role in whipping up support for the military effort against the Argentinians who were, on the face of it, unlikely enemies. In the end, though, his tabloid friends were powerless to save his patron as she struggled for her survival in November 1990. The strictures of the serious broadsheets, which owed Ingham no favours, proved more influential among Conservative MPs than the loyalism of the tabloids.

*   *   *

Journalists are seldom totally at ease with the formalised political 'guidance' that the lobby system embodies. Trained to seek all conflicting views on issues they write about, they feel guilty about relying too heavily on a single, highly partisan source. They do, of course, solicit opposing opinions on the issues of the day, but the two daily briefings from Downing Street generally set the tone and the agenda for their papers' political coverage. For the more questing and spirited political writers, it is all a great deal too cosy: it downgrades their role to that of messengers bringing down the word from on high.

The fact that they are mass briefings is at the root of some of the objections, although for other lobby members it is an important part of the attraction. The advantage is that each journalist knows what the others are being told, so nobody can be scooped. Yet those with a more rigorous view of their responsibilities like to feel that, in one-on-one conversations with their source, they can better exercise their skills of interpretation and come up with a fresh, perceptive analysis.

The first serious attempt to modify the lobby system had come in 1973, not from a journalist but from Donald Maitland, a career diplomat seconded from the Foreign Office to be press officer to Edward Heath when he became Prime Minister in 1970. Maitland thought the convention absurd whereby all regular communication between Downing Street and the political press was unattributable, so he took to making on-the-record announcements, although sticking to the lobby rules for a large part of his briefings. Many traditionalist members of the lobby were uneasy about this. After all, it compromised their special status, their carefully acquired mystique, if they spent too much of their time just writing down official on-the-record statements. Any cub reporter could do that.

Maitland's tenure – like Heath's – was short and a much more serious attempt to change the rules was made in 1975 by Joe Haines, Harold Wilson's press secretary, towards the end of Wilson's second term as Prime Minister. Haines, a prickly man, was, like Ingham, a former journalist (later to become one again) and in some other respects resembled him, although their views differed on how best to exploit the lobby. Both were convinced of the virtues of hard work. In Ingham's case he applied the philosophy to himself, ensuring that he was fully briefed on every controversial aspect of Government policy before he met the lobby every morning. The churlish Haines shifted the obligation of hard work on to the lobby journalists themselves. He did not see why he should spend the first half of every morning telephoning each government department for an update on their policies, just to save the journalists the phone calls that he felt it was *their* obligation to make. So he declined to answer questions about the activity of any department except Downing Street. He also stopped journalists from travelling on the Prime Minister's plane on overseas visits, because he thought it corrupted what should, in his view, be an arm's length relationship between government and press.

All this irritated the lobby journalists, who became increasingly at odds with Haines. 'I'm not there to help Fleet Street,' he would explain. 'I'm there to help the Prime Minister.' He was the first Downing Street press officer to see his role as primarily political. His predecessors had at least paid lip service to being objective and neutral, rather than partisan. He complained when some lobby journalists went to report to members of the Conservative shadow cabinet about the content of his briefings: trading with the enemy. In this respect, if in no other, Ingham followed Haines's example. There was never any doubt that he was reflecting the Conservative views of Mrs Thatcher.

Haines was also frustrated by not being able, under lobby rules, to make an on-the-record denial of something he had said unattributably which had, in his view, been distorted in the reporting. In June 1975 Haines wrote to the chairman of the lobby and, going further than Maitland, said that he would no longer give unattributable briefings at all. Statements made on behalf of the Prime Minister would henceforth all be on the record. While this deprived the journalists of two fixed points in their day, it is impossible to say whether it increased the level of hostility to the Prime Minister that was always to be expected from the predominantly Conservative papers, regularly briefed or not. One man, at least, clearly saw the move as counter-productive. When Wilson resigned the following year to be succeeded by James Callaghan, Tom McCaffrey, the senior civil servant Callaghan chose as his press secretary, immediately resumed lobby briefings on the traditional terms.

The first rebellion against the system from within the press itself took another ten years to materialise, with the launch of the *Independent* in the autumn of 1986. Its political editor Anthony Bevins, formerly of *The Times* and the *Daily Mail*, agreed with Andreas Whittam Smith, editor of the new paper, that it was time someone stood up to challenge the lobby system, and that the *Independent* was ideally placed to do it. Bevins told Ingham that he and his colleagues on the new paper were no longer prepared to abide by the old lobby rules. If they attended his regular briefings they would insist on attributing to him everything that he said.

Bevins invited the *Guardian* and the *Observer* to join him in this stand. The *Observer* decided not to but Peter Preston, editor of the *Guardian*, wrote to Ingham in September 1989 telling him that in future his paper's representatives at Ingham's briefings 'shall refer openly to "a Downing Street spokesman" or "Mrs Thatcher's spokesman" and, as relevant, quote what that spokesman says – whether it is a description of Mr Pym as "Mona Lott" or Mr John Biffen as "a semi-detached member of the Government".' Ingham replied, quite correctly, that to change lobby terms would be a matter for the lobby, not for him. But he indicated that if the briefings did become attributable he would no longer be able to provide them, or if he did they would not be on the same level of frankness.

At the end of October 1986, members of the lobby decided by sixty-seven votes to fifty-five that the system should stay as it was. The *Independent* and the *Guardian* representatives henceforth excluded themselves from the daily briefings, to be followed in January 1989 by the *Scotsman*. It was not hard for the correspondents of these papers to discover what had been said at the briefings – much of it, after all, appeared on the Press Association wire, and the rest they could get from friends who still attended. When the rebel papers reported what they had thus gleaned, they attributed it directly to Ingham or a Downing Street spokesman.

Ingham, although relieved that most of the lobby stayed intact, was angry with those who had broken ranks and, to deter others who might be considering a similar gesture, withdrew from as much contact with the renegades as he could, while maintaining the obligation of the press office to provide them with minimal factual information. He stressed that there would be no question of discreet lunches where he would reveal to them individually all he disclosed to the lobby and more. When Mrs Thatcher travelled overseas and seats for the press were available on her plane, the three non-conformist papers were not allowed on it.

The three papers' coverage of politics was not seriously damaged by their withdrawal from the lobby. Indeed, because Ingham's 'steers' were, in the rebel papers, directly attributed to him, their readers were clearer about their source. Yet by his uncompromising response he held the line against other waverers.

When he left Downing Street along with Mrs Thatcher in November 1990, the schism in the lobby was quickly healed. John Major, the new Prime Minister, brought a spokesman of his own with him – Gus O'Donnell, who had worked for him at the Treasury. O'Donnell, a less combative man, said he did not much mind how journalists attributed his statements, as long as they stuck to the rules in other respects. This concession tipped the balance in favour of the convenient option and the three erstwhile rebels came to heel. Neil Kinnock, the Labour Party leader, had long held all his briefings on the record and said he would continue that practice had he been elected Prime Minister in 1992. But he lost, and the lobby survived.

*   *   *

Although Ingham co-ordinated Government information, a position for-malised in 1988 when he took overall charge of Whitehall press relations, he was never the only person briefing journalists on lobby terms. Special-ist correspondents covering education, labour matters, defence and the like have established their own groups that are briefed under the same rules by the relevant ministers and officials, either regularly or on an ad hoc basis. There are, for instance, daily briefings of diplomatic corre-spondents by a member of the Foreign Office News Department.

Cabinet ministers can choose between briefing the lobby or their own specialist group of journalists or both, and they were never obliged to ask Ingham's permission. Occasionally such initiatives lead to grief. Misunderstandings deriving from unattributable briefings are no new phenomenon. One of the most infamous occurred in 1967 when Lord Chalfont, a junior Foreign Office Minister in the Labour Government, recklessly told British diplomatic correspondents covering a conference in Lausanne that, if President de Gaulle of France exercised his veto on British membership of the European Community, Britain would rethink its entire relationship with Europe and might even pull its troops out of NATO. What Chalfont saw as a legitimate – if none too subtle – exercise in the art of persuasion was, when transformed into large black headlines, exposed as a crude attempt at blackmail. It did not work. De Gaulle deployed his veto anyway and British troops stayed in Europe. After the 'leak', Chalfont offered Wilson his resignation, but it was declined.

This was an early example of one of the chief fallacies of unattribu-table briefing – its vaunted deniability. If anything goes seriously wrong, as it did on this occasion, it is theoretically possible for the minister to maintain that he never said anything of the kind, and under the rules of the game the journalists will not directly contradict him. Yet if all the papers come out with a similar interpretation of what was said, such a denial defies reason. The very informality of the briefings, the false bonhomie – and, when they take place during an overseas visit, as Chalfont's did, the glasses of whisky being sipped – lead ministers to be less cautious than they would be at a formal press conference.

Briefings that backfire are often the sign of a government in difficulty and there were two notable instances during Mrs Thatcher's troubled third administration. In November 1989 Nigel Lawson, the Chancellor of the Exchequer, held one of his six-monthly chats with the political correspondents of the Sunday papers. One of his themes was that he would like to target social security payments more accurately towards those most in need of them. On the strength of the briefing, quoting senior Cabinet sources, the journalists wrote that the Government were considering means-testing some benefits, including the Christmas bonus to old-age pensioners. Next day Lawson denounced the reports as a 'farrago of invention' and explained that, far from cutting some benefits, the Government were going to introduce an extra payment for pensioners. The credibility of his denial was compromised, however, when it emerged that the Treasury tape recorder, on which the briefing was supposed to have been recorded, had not been working, and there was thus no official account of the exchange.

The following March the Transport Minister, Paul Channon, got into trouble after lunching with four political correspondents at the Garrick Club. They were talking about the terrorist bomb that had destroyed a Pan American passenger jet over Lockerbie, Scotland, in December 1989. Channon's department had been subject to criticism over lax airport security and the minister was anxious to convince the journalists that investigations into the bombing had been thorough and were about to bear fruit. As a result of the lunch, reports duly appeared in the four papers on the lines of this one, in *The Times*: 'It was clear last night at Westminster that the authorities are poised to name the culprits and the country – presumably in the Middle East – where they are hiding.' The story went on to say that tracing them had been 'one of the most remarkable feats of criminal detection ever known'. The other papers used similar phrases, and *Today* claimed that a man was actually under arrest for the bombings.

Other journalists had seen Channon lunching with the four reporters, so it was foolish of him to deny – as he did to the *Glasgow Herald* – that he was the source of the story. When journalists' credibility is directly challenged in this way there is a strong temptation to bend the rules of non-attribution to breaking point. The Glasgow *Daily Record* – whose sister paper, the *Daily Mirror*, had been represented at the lunch – called Channon 'a liar'. Forced to explain himself in the Commons, he denied he had misled the quartet, although he did admit to having told them that investigators of the bombing were making 'brilliant progress'.

Discussing the case in *The Times* a few days later Hugh Stephenson, professor of journalism at City University, said that Channon 'fell foul not of the lobby system but of the lunching system'. Four months later he was dropped from the Government. It was not until the end of 1991 that two Libyans were formally accused of the bombing and attempts made to extradite them from Libya.

*   *   *

Attempts to manipulate the press for flying political kites, gaining support for a controversial policy or settling political scores, are part of a long tradition. While their victims are confined to the political arena, such initiatives are relatively harmless. More sinister are official attempts to manipulate information with wider implications. One of the most blatant concerned the shooting in Gibraltar on 6 March 1988 of three IRA terrorists by the SAS, where disinformation and contradictory information, much of it put out by the Ministry of Defence, stirred up a controversy that took years to die down.

The first piece of false information came in the Ministry's initial account of the shooting. This said that a bomb had been found in a car parked by one of the IRA team in the centre of the town, and that the three were shot because the SAS feared that they might be armed, or have the means to detonate the bomb by remote control. Next morning's papers all reported that the bomb had been defused by the military, and most of them revealed its size (500 lbs was the most common figure). Next day Sir Geoffrey Howe, the Foreign Secretary, told the Commons that there had been no bomb and the terrorists – who were certainly planning to plant one – were unarmed. This swift change of story led to questions whether the three had been deliberately executed by the SAS as part of a shoot-to-kill policy.

The *Daily Telegraph*, which could usually be relied upon to support the official line in such matters, published a surprisingly critical editorial:

> The Government must tell why it gave a succession of contradictory accounts to the world about Sunday's events. Unless it wishes Britain's enemies to enjoy a propaganda bonanza it should explain why it was necessary to shoot dead all three terrorists on the street rather than apprehend them with the considerable force of police and SAS which appears to have been deployed in the locality.

There was, however, little press investigation into the exact circumstances of the shooting. Roger Bolton, the editor of Thames Television's current affairs programme *This Week*, observed this gap and sent two reporters to Gibraltar to investigate. In April Thames announced it would be screening an hour-long programme on the shooting, called *Death on the Rock*. Thames and the Independent Broadcasting Authority decided to go ahead with the programme even after Sir Geoffrey Howe called for its postponement until after the inquest.

The programme made two main points: that it ought to have been clear to the authorities that the car parked in Gibraltar did not contain a bomb; and that the SAS gunmen had not shouted a warning to their three victims, who were putting their hands above their heads as a gesture of surrender when they were shot. The main witness on the second point was Mrs Carmen Proetta, who lived just opposite the garage where the shootings had taken place. Nobody enquiring into the incident had approached Mrs Proetta until the Thames reporters did.

Next morning the newspapers, keen to support the Government's version of events, were almost unanimous in denouncing the programme – and so did Mrs Thatcher, who called it 'trial by television'. Many papers spiced their fury with a vicious smear campaign against Mrs Proetta, based on false information apparently disseminated in Gibraltar. Among their allegations – all untrue – were that she had been a prostitute and was a director of an escort agency for rich Arabs. The *Sun*'s headline dubbed her 'The Tart of Gib'. In fact, when she worked for a law firm three years earlier, she had briefly lent her name as a director of an agency called Eve International which needed a Gibraltar national on the board. The company never traded. She won substantial libel settlements from the newspapers involved.

Because of the fuss about the programme, Thames Television initiated a formal enquiry into it by Lord Windlesham, a former junior minister in the Conservative Government who had in the 1970s been chairman and managing director of Associated Television. His report, published on 26 January 1989, vindicated Thames and the programme-makers on all but a few minor points. He said that although the programme could be said to have been one-sided, it had not prejudged the case or broken the IBA's impartiality guidelines; it had not tried to pressurise witnesses or misused their evidence; it was not sympathetic to the IRA; it had not prejudiced the inquest and did not amount to trial by television. The programme's critics, led by the Prime Minister, now denounced the Windlesham report itself. A statement from Downing Street said that Mrs Thatcher still thought the programme partial and inaccurate.

Less than six months later the *Sunday Times*, which had made the fiercest and most sustained attack on the programme, had direct experience, on an entirely different matter, of how information from the Ministry of Defence has to be treated with extreme caution. In its issue of 2 July 1989, the paper reported that the Ministry had removed secret documents from Birkbeck College, part of the University of London, and that some defence research contracts might be moved elsewhere. The story said there were fears over security springing from the suspect political affiliations of some of the staff. The story had originally come from a source at the college but had been checked with the Ministry press office which, after initially denying it, later rang the paper back to confirm that the salient 'facts' were true.

However, after the story had appeared in both the *Sunday Times* and the *Mail on Sunday*, George Younger, the Secretary of State for Defence, wrote to Lady Blackstone, master of Birkbeck, saying the reports were false. The Ministry press office issued a statement saying that the allegations were 'entirely misconceived'. The exact truth is impossible to ascertain but it seems likely that there were discussions at the MoD about the political activities of a few members of the Birkbeck faculty and that the possibility of moving papers and defence contracts was raised. Somebody in Whitehall must have decided that to confirm the story would give a favourable impression of a Government alert to threats to security and, at the same time, cracking down on the leftist sympathies of some academics engaged in official research. Only when the negative aspects of the story became clear, after publication, was the line reversed.

Just as Joe Haines said he was not there for the benefit of the press but of the Prime Minister, so does the Defence Ministry, to a much greater extent, believe it is there to protect the national interest, and that exploiting and misleading the press by distorting the news is a legitimate means to this end. The press and its readers accept this in wartime, when the armed forces impose formal censorship on dispatches from reporters with the troops, and even require them to wear uniform. There were controversies over the way this power was exercised in both the Falklands War of 1982 and the Gulf War of 1991, but there were few who maintained that the military had no right to exert it.

The Defence Ministry, however, believes that the country is to some extent permanently at war against implacable if not always obvious enemies. There are therefore few circumstances in which it could not justify manipulating information: the Gibraltar shootings certainly constituted, in the Ministry's view, a clear instance of the national interest demanding reticence in questioning the actions and motives of the SAS squad. Most of the press, though, believes that in nearly all cases, sometimes even in wartime, the public interest is best served by the publication of the whole truth, rather than a sanitised or distorted version of it. The contradiction between these philosophies is incapable of any mutually satisfactory resolution.

When the press clashes with governments on political grounds, rather than on those of security, the arguments are less clear-cut and if anything harder to resolve. Every action of an elected government can be interpreted in two ways: as partisan, in that it is invariably criticised by the opposition parties; or as patriotic, in that the government is doing what it was elected to do in the public interest. That is why it is a fiction to suppose that the two kinds of activity can be separated. Downing Street press officers, when they explain and put a gloss on government policies, are inevitably attempting to drum up support for those policies among the electorate. Ingham and Haines, by being more blatantly partisan than others in that job, were at the same time being less hypocritical.

Newspapers that object to such heavy-handed steering can and did boycott the lobby and other places where they might be exposed to it. But to some extent – and this was certainly Ingham's view – there is hypocrisy here too. No newspaper is politically innocent: they all have their own agendas and a truly impartial newspaper would be a strange beast. (Some thought that the *Independent* was going to try to be such, but a paper that does not identify itself with a political party or vested interest does not have to be without opinions, just without bias.) The selection of news is as much a political act as commenting on it.

There is nothing undemocratic or sinister about a government seeking to ensure exposure for its views or favourable publicity for its actions, so long as the papers are free to reject its pressures if they wish. It is more worrying when governments, not content merely with trying to exert influence, seek the means to enforce control over what goes into the press. Mrs Thatcher and her administration gave a number of signs of coveting such powers, as I shall discuss in the next chapter.

14

The Truth, the Half Truth and Nothing But...

It is unacceptable in our democratic society that there should be a
restraint on the publication of information relating to government
when the only vice of that information is that it enables the public
to discuss, review and criticise government action.

Australian judge Mr Justice Mason

If ministers were clumsy in getting journalists to write what they wanted
them to – or thought they wanted them to – their efforts in the 1980s
to suppress what they did *not* want to see published were even more
ham-fisted. The most elaborate fiasco was the long-running case of
Spycatcher, the memoirs of Peter Wright, who worked for MI5, Britain's
counter-espionage service, between 1955 and 1976. On learning in 1985
of plans for the book to be published in Australia, the Government took
legal action to prevent it, on the grounds that members of the security
services have a lifelong duty not to reveal details of their work.

There was nothing in *Spycatcher* that could be said to bear directly on
Britain's security interests in the 1980s. It contained material of a historical nature that would certainly have been known to the security services
of potential enemies. There were, for sure, one or two revelations likely
to *embarrass* the British security services by revealing first the broad scale
and non-accountability of their activities – Wright wrote of a plot to
discredit Harold Wilson during his second term as Prime Minister from
1974 to 1976 – and then the incompetence with which many operations
were carried out, which caused dismay at the United States Central
Intelligence Agency. There was also evidence of personal rivalry within
the service, including speculation whether some senior MI5 men were
in fact working for the Russians.

The Government would clearly not have gone out of its way to publish
such facts: the issue was whether it was necessary or legitimate in a

TREACHEROUS ESTATE

democracy to strive so hard to keep them secret. Even Dr David Owen, leader of the Social Democratic Party, who usually supported the Government's hard line on restricting the rights of the press in sensitive areas, said when the case had nearly run its course: 'It was perverse to drag the whole thing on and on through the courts, boosting the book sales and making the Government a laughing stock.'

Publication of the book was first proposed in Australia, where Wright lived, so the Government's initial attempt to stop it was made in the Australian courts. To show how seriously the Cabinet – particularly Mrs Thatcher – took the issue, Sir Robert Armstrong, the Cabinet Secretary, was dispatched to spend several weeks in Australia as the chief Government witness. (During his appearance in the witness box Sir Robert coined a phrase that instantly entered the language when he confessed under cross-examination that he had been 'economical with the truth' when answering a question about the Government's attitude to previous books about the security services.)

The Australian courts ruled in favour of the book's publication and the decision was confirmed at all the appeal stages through which the Government insisted on pursuing it, regardless of the cost to the exchequer. In Britain, meanwhile, legal action was taken against newspapers that proposed to publish extracts from the book and reports based upon it. Here again the Government was prepared to commit as much as it took in legal fees to explore every judicial avenue, and it says much for the equal persistence of newspaper editors and proprietors, fighting as they saw it for an essential libertarian principle, that they too fought their way through the courts. The *Guardian* and the *Observer* were, in 1986, the first papers to be prevented from publishing the material but gradually most of the broadsheet press was brought into the net of litigation that dragged on until 1991.

By that time, though, the Government had already lost the substantive case against the book. In July 1987 it was published in the United States, where the constitution forbids prior restraint. The *Sunday Times* managed to print quite long extracts to coincide with the publication, before being enjoined in turn. Once the US edition was on sale it was impossible to prevent its being brought to Britain. Technically it was against the law to sell it – although some bookshops defied the ban – but visitors to the United States could bring back as many copies as they wanted in their luggage and, partly on the strength of that, the book quickly became an American best-seller.

For some time afterwards, though, the Government persisted with the attempt to prevent publication in the press of Wright's main assertions. When the High Court lifted the injunctions after the book's publication the Government appealed, losing in the Appeal Court but winning by a margin of three to two in the House of Lords, where one of the minority, Lord Bridge, said: 'Freedom of speech is always the first casualty under a totalitarian regime . . . The present attempt to insulate the public in this country from information which is freely available elsewhere is a significant step down that very dangerous road.'

In December 1987 the Government sought a permanent injunction forbidding the press from ever publishing anything relating to the contents of *Spycatcher* except for the bare outlines of Wright's allegations that were already widely known. Refusing the request Mr Justice Scott said that press freedom was 'one of the bulwarks of our democratic society' and that the absolute protection sought by the Government for the security services 'could not be achieved this side of the Iron Curtain'. The Appeal Court confirmed this ruling and finally, in October 1988, so did the House of Lords. Lord Goff, one of the law lords, said that if the government wanted the courts to prevent the disclosure of information, the case had to be made not only that the information was confidential but that it was in the public interest to keep it so. He said: 'In a free society there is continuing public interest that the workings of government should be open to scrutiny and criticism. It follows, therefore, that in such cases there must be demonstrated some other public interest requiring that publication be restrained.'

The newspapers were now free to publish what extracts they liked, although aspects of the case drifted through the legal system for several more months. It was not until April 1991 that the last *Spycatcher* judgment was made by the House of Lords, and this went against the press. The Lords decided that the *Sunday Times* in July 1987 had been in contempt of court in publishing extracts from *Spycatcher* because, although there was no injunction against the paper itself, it knew of the injunctions against others.

Mrs Thatcher and her supporters pursued the case so doggedly because they were convinced, like Bernard Ingham, that the national interest was best served by a press that saw itself as a cheer-leader for democratic governments rather than an inquisitor of them. The notion that independent information media could act as a check on an over-mighty executive – the mainspring, after all, of the argument for a free press – did not enter her calculations. How could this non-elected bunch of irresponsible scribblers, of notoriously uneven quality, have a legitimate constitutional role to play? There was a genuine philosophical difference here. Ingham best expressed Mrs Thatcher's view on this matter, as he did on so many, in a speech to a conference of editors in Cardiff in 1983: 'When people talk about a right of access to information, I am not clear from what that right derives. The right is not written into the constitution. It does not arise from law . . . I was taught that the newspaper I represented had no rights in the community beyond those of the ordinary citizen.'

Most editors would agree with the last sentence but would add that, in their view, the ordinary citizen in a democracy *does* have the right of access to information relating to the way in which elected representatives and government employees are conducting the affairs of the nation. It is certainly important to know that, as Wright revealed, one set of people, paid by the state, is engaged in trying to 'de-stabilise' the leader of a recently elected government. While opponents of free disclosure often cite national security as a ground for suppressing information, in this case national security demanded disclosure for the protection of the elected Prime Minister.

Many argued that the information passed to the *Guardian* in 1983 by Sarah Tisdall, a clerk in the Ministry of Defence, was something the public had a right to know: the arrival of the first American Cruise missiles in Britain. Yet Tisdall was sentenced to six months in prison after the *Guardian* had obeyed a court order to hand over the document that she had passed to them, thus enabling the Ministry to identify her as its source.

Implicit in the Ingham/Thatcher doctrine is the notion that there are some kinds of information – such as that which Tisdall passed on – with which 'ordinary citizens' may not be trusted and indeed with which they do not want to be burdened. In a television interview in January 1988 Mrs Thatcher asserted that 'ordinary folk are much more in touch with security matters than people in the media' – meaning that, outside the excitable echelons of the press, there is understanding and sympathy for the view that intelligence secrets should be safeguarded. Many people, even some in the press, accepted her cynical view of the public's attitude to freedom of information. At a seminar organised by the International Press Institute in April 1989 Max Hastings, editor of the *Daily Telegraph*, said: 'We have seen the Government putting great pressures on the press without it costing them a single vote. It is because the British public sees talk of press freedom as cant and is so entirely disenchanted by the press in general and the tabloids in particular.'

That was certainly the assumption behind the Official Secrets Act passed in 1989, in the wake of the *Spycatcher* row. It was the second attempt by the Thatcher administration to strengthen laws against leaks from the Government and official bodies. The first, soon after she became Prime Minister in 1979, had to be abandoned because it was too extreme for many on the Conservative left. The new attempt was inspired in part by *Spycatcher* but even more by the case of Clive Ponting, the Ministry of Defence official acquitted under the old Act of leaking secrets about the sinking of the Argentinian battleship *Belgrano* in the Falklands War. The new Act's passage through the Commons was preceded by an edict from the Home Secretary, Douglas Hurd, in October 1988, barring direct interviews on television and radio with members of extremist groups in Northern Ireland – including Sinn Fein which, although a supporter of IRA terrorism, also had representatives on elected local councils. (The Home Secretary enjoys absolute authority over broadcasting, but not over the press.)

The new Official Secrets Act was in some respects less restrictive than its predecessor, which dated from 1911. Under the old Act, disclosure of any government secret, however trivial, was technically an offence. Not many cases under the Act reached the courts, but one that did in 1970 underlined its indiscriminate nature and provoked the judge, Mr Justice Caulfield, to call in open court for its reform.

The case concerned the Nigerian Civil War, which began in 1968 when Eastern Nigeria, led by Colonel Ojukwu, broke away from the rest of the country and declared itself an independent state called Biafra. Britain supported the federal Government in Lagos and supplied arms to help defeat the insurrection but the true extent of the British involvement was not revealed until the beginning of 1970, just before the rebels conceded defeat. That was when the *Sunday Telegraph* published almost the whole text of a report written by Colonel Scott, defence adviser to the British High Commissioner in Lagos. They had received the report from Jonathan Aitken, a Conservative parliamentary candidate (later an MP) as well as a journalist. Aitken had been given it at fourth hand – Colonel Scott gave a copy to Colonel Cairns, a member of an international team of military observers, who in turn gave it to a former member of the team, who showed it to Aitken.

Aitken, Cairns and Brian Roberts, editor of the *Sunday Telegraph*, were prosecuted under the Act, which in effect made it an offence to communicate any official information to an unauthorised person. Section 2 also made it an offence to *receive* any such information. The three men were acquitted after a sympathetic summing-up by Mr Justice Caulfield, who called for the Act's reform. It took a long time coming.

In 1975 there was another seminal controversy about what government secrets should and should not be secret, when the *Sunday Times* announced its plans to publish extracts from the diaries of Richard Crossman, who had died the previous year and who had been a member of the Labour Cabinet from 1964 to 1970. There was enormous pressure from Whitehall on Harold Evans, the paper's editor, not to publish the diaries, which contained details of discussions around the Cabinet table – details that are supposed to remain secret for thirty years at least.

In his book *Good Times, Bad Times*, Evans gives an engrossing account of the minuet he danced with Sir John Hunt, the Cabinet Secretary, over publishing the diaries, resulting, after nine instalments had already been published, in an injunction against further episodes, as well as against publication of the diaries in book form. The Government did not invoke the Official Secrets Act but the law of confidence, which bars the disclosure of anything learned under conditions of confidentiality. The Chief Justice, Lord Widgery, decided that it would not be against the public interest for the diaries to be published.

These small defeats did not, as we have seen in the *Spycatcher* affair, deter governments from continuing to enforce secrecy where they could. The new Official Secrets Act in 1989 covered secrets under only four heads: defence, intelligence, international relations and security. However, in these areas it was tougher than the old law. The defence by which Ponting had been acquitted, that disclosure was in the public interest, was now ruled out, as was the defence that the information had already been disclosed overseas, the argument that swayed some of the most important of the *Spycatcher* judgments. The Act also laid down a lifelong duty on members of the security services, and people associated with them, never to disclose details of their work, and strengthened the rules against leaks by government employees or contractors.

The absence of a public interest defence went to the heart of the administration's attitude to the press. Why should journalists or anyone else have the power to decide independently what was for the public good, when the Government had been elected to do just that? An offence was an offence whatever the motive for carrying it out. What, then, about someone in the security service who had found evidence of serious wrong-doing by one of his superiors? Could he not legitimately expose it? John Patten, Minister of State at the Home Office, said that to allow a public interest defence for such 'whistle-blowing' would be 'like arguing that only a small murder had been committed to rid the globe of a scoundrel'.

Mr Hurd, in articles in the *Daily Telegraph* and *UK Press Gazette*, argued that there was no need for a public interest defence because under the legislation the prosecution had in most cases to convince a jury that any leak of information had harmed the national interest. 'The first duty of government remains to protect the nation from potential adversaries abroad and from terrorists and other criminals at home,' he wrote. 'If these tasks are to be done effectively, the information about them must often remain secret.'

These and other articles by Mr Hurd were part of a counter-offensive against the virtually unanimous condemnation of the new measure in the serious press. Hundreds of thousands of solemn words, seeking to alert readers to the potential threat to everyone's freedoms, were penned by editorial writers and liberal columnists. 'The entire debate,' wrote Peter Jenkins in the *Independent*, 'is premised not on the idea of freedom but the need for secrecy.' In the *Guardian*, Hugo Young declared that 'no other measure so closely touches the quality of our democracy, the very lifeblood of the relationship between the citizen and the state.' The *Observer* called the Bill 'stubborn, wrong-headed dangerous nonsense . . . simply unworkable in a peacetime democracy'.

The critics had some friends in Parliament, but too few. In the event, only four Conservatives voted against the Bill, which was passed by a convincing majority of 125. The Labour Party promised that, if returned to power at the next election, it would introduce a new Bill greatly increasing the press and the public's access to official information.

* * *

A product of the ambivalent relationship between the press and government is the D-notice system, described by Colin Seymour-Ure in *The Political Impact of the Mass Media* as 'the practice of voluntary censorship'. The arrangement had its origins in World War Two, when a Defence Press and Broadcasting Committee was established, including representatives of the press as well as officials from the Defence Ministry and Foreign Office. If it seems possible that a piece of information with implications for national security is about to be made public, the committee will issue a D (for Defence) notice, asking for the item to be suppressed in the national interest. Newspapers are not obliged to comply: failure to do so is not in itself an offence, although in some cases offences under the Official Secrets Act may be committed. Editors habitually do obey D-notices, however – and on a rare occasion when one was accused of not doing so, a famous row ensued.

In February 1967 the *Daily Express* printed a front-page exclusive by its defence correspondent Chapman Pincher, known for his close contacts within the security services. The report said that thousands of private cables and telegrams were regularly vetted by security officials.

The Prime Minister, Harold Wilson, who was more sensitive to press criticism than most, angrily told Parliament that the publication of this information was 'in clear breach of two D-notices' and that the *Express* had been so informed before publication. He added:

> Unfortunately, the confidence and trust which are the basis of the whole system have been called into question by the action of one newspaper in initiating this morning a sensationalised and inaccurate story purporting to describe a situation in which, in fact, the powers and practice have not changed for well over 40 years.

There was in truth a dispute over whether the *Express* had or had not been warned that the story breached a D-notice. Pincher said he had been told over lunch by Colonel Sammy Lohan, the secretary of the D-Notice Committee, that it did *not* amount to a breach, although Lohan tried to dissuade him from publishing it in any case. Wilson then set up a committee under Lord Radcliffe to look into the facts and to make recommendations for reforming the D-notice system. When the committee accepted Pincher's version of events, Wilson published a White Paper which, while accepting the committee's modest proposals for updating the D-notice system, also insisted that in the *Express* case his version of events was the right one.

The press, as it invariably does when its relations with government are the issue, took the side of the *Express*. The result of the fuss was to highlight the ambiguous nature of the relationship, and Wilson was later to admit that he had been wrong to make such an issue of it. In his book, *The Labour Government, 1964–70*, he wrote that it was 'in personal terms one of my costliest mistakes of our near six years in office', and added: 'It was a very long time before my relations with the press were repaired.' He also offered, as an aside, the unsurprising but none the less significant revelation that, according to the public opinion polls, 'the electorate had not the slightest interest in the subject', confirming that clashes between the press and the administration are seen as of critical importance by few except politicians and journalists.

In wartime the relationship takes on a different aspect. The peacetime principle that all facts are there to be discovered and reported has to be modified for the duration of the hostilities; which was why journalists originally agreed to serve on the Defence Press and Broadcasting Committee. Few dispute the necessity for some form of military control – including censorship – over information that could be of help to the enemy and put the lives of British troops in danger. The degree of such control, and to what kinds of reporting it should be extended, are invariably topics of contention.

In the Falklands War the issues presented themselves starkly. In April 1982 Argentine troops occupied the Falkland Islands, a small British colony in the South Atlantic. Although most British people supported the Government in sending a Task Force with the aim of making the Argentinians withdraw, some did not – and many newspapers and broadcasters reported their contrary views. Similar objections had been raised twenty-six years earlier at the time of the Suez invasion, when supporters of the action felt, as they felt over the Falklands, that it was disloyal and damaging to the war effort to allow such doubts to be expressed in print.

In the early days of the Falklands War the BBC was fiercely criticised, and its chairman hauled over the coals by a committee of MPs, because on *Newsnight* Peter Snow had said: 'Until the British are demonstrated either to be deceiving us or to be concealing losses from us, we can only tend to give a lot more credence to the British version of events.'

What riled the MPs was the suggestion that the British spokesmen might be as capable of making misleading statements about the progress of the war as the Argentines. This is a perfectly balanced contention but balance, dispassion, objectivity and to some extent accuracy are qualities little admired when a nation is at war. In his foreword to Valerie Adams's *The Media and the Falklands Campaign*, Professor Lawrence Freedman wrote:

> A military commander has an interest in accurate information being withheld and, on occasion, inaccurate information being disseminated. The media have another interest. They live off information, and scavenge for it wherever it might be found. Their reputation depends, in part, on the accuracy of the information they can obtain. This inevitably leads to a degree of tension between the commanders and the media, especially at times of armed conflict.

Professor Freedman points out, however, that no newspaper or broadcaster would want to be accused of helping lose a war or endangering the lives of citizens by being too free with information. At the same time, commanders know that they cannot expect to fight wars in secret. Both sides are therefore prepared to see at least something of the other side's point of view, and indeed anyone looking back over the newspapers of the period would be hard put to find much evidence of conflict between them. The mass-market tabloids, in particular, vied with each other to be the most assertively supportive of the British troops in action

– an attitude economically summed up in the famous front-page headline over the *Sun*'s account of the sinking of the Argentinian battleship *Belgrano*: 'Gotcha'.

Yet even such unquestioningly patriotic coverage does not give unqualified satisfaction to the military authorities. The attitudes encapsulated in that headline can so easily turn – as they did in the early days of World War Two – into criticism of the leadership of the fighting forces if things go wrong.

No such crisis of confidence, however, surfaced during the Falklands campaign, when nearly all the disputes over press coverage occurred on the margins, where the choice between disclosure and suppression was not clear-cut. There was particular indignation about the number of military experts who speculated, mainly on television, about British tactics for prosecuting the war. These 'armchair generals', as they were dubbed, were attacked in the tabloid press for helping the Argentinians read the minds of the British military, although there was no evidence that this had any effect on the way Argentina conducted the war.

Even the most criticised incident, where the BBC reported the position of British troops about to attack Goose Green, did not prevent a convincing victory there. And the Ministry of Defence cleverly exploited the media's liking for strategic speculation by giving a blatantly false steer, just before the troops landed at San Carlos, that no such landing was imminent.

When it came to what the press could report about the actual fighting, the military held the whip hand because of the geographical circumstances. No reporters could get to the Falklands unless they travelled with the Task Force, and they could transmit their reports back to Britain only through the military communications system. Thus the military not only insisted on applying censorship to material which, in their view, could damage their cause, but also had the means of absolute enforcement. Even if the censors could find no formal grounds for amending a reporter's dispatch, they could, if they felt its overall attitude to be less than helpful, push it to the back of the transmission queue, ensuring that it would arrive too late to be used in full or at all.

The reporting of battlefield setbacks proved the most difficult area. On purely military criteria there is seldom a good reason to conceal news of a defeat, because the opposing army will certainly know about it already. This is where Home Front anxieties come into play. If readers and viewers are told that the fighting is going badly and that many British troops have been killed, will that weaken popular support for the war?

It has become part of the received wisdom that the withdrawal of United States troops from Vietnam, in circumstances amounting to a defeat, was a result of a build-up of public opposition to the war fuelled by constant pessimistic reports and vividly horrifying pictures of the fighting on US television. The British armed forces saw it as their job to avoid any such public disillusion over the Falklands and were therefore looking at the impact of adverse reports on people's morale, not just their effect on their prosecution of the military campaign. Setbacks such as the sinking of ships were never suppressed, but they were not always reported in full as soon as they happened, and there was seldom a hint that they may have been the result of any failure in planning on the British side.

The Gulf War of 1991 was more complicated in terms of media relations because of the international composition of the Task Force. Allied nations sent troops to the Middle East to drive President Saddam Hussein of Iraq from his small neighbour Kuwait, which he had annexed. The Americans were by far the largest element of the force and it was their view that prevailed in the matter of dealing with the press.

Pools of accredited correspondents were attached to individual units and were subject to military discipline, in some cases wearing uniform. They were not allowed to go anywhere without military authorisation, and their dispatches had to be officially approved. The British pools were called 'media response teams' and the American 'combat correspondent pools'. American correspondents, with their native aversion to prior restraint on publication, initially resisted the restrictions imposed on them more stoutly than the British did. They then complied until the last days of the war, when in response to competition they ducked out of the controls and were able to operate effectively and with little risk, because by then the Iraqis had virtually stopped fighting. Some British correspondents, mainly those who knew their way round the Middle East, stayed out of the pool system altogether.

The Ministry of Defence, after consulting some senior journalists, drew up a set of ground rules for the coverage. These required first that reporters stayed with their military escorts and followed instructions, then that they refrained from reporting the following details: specific troop locations, numbers of personnel and volume of equipment, names of military units, future operations, current operations, security preparations, rules of engagement and special forces and their techniques. The BBC brought out guidelines for everyone involved in the coverage which, although aimed at broadcasters, addressed issues that face all media in modern war reporting. The document began with a clear statement of the inherent contradictions of the form:

> When the country is at war we do not want to add to the dangers facing the armed forces. Our audiences in Britain are understandably most sensitive to the war suffering inflicted on the troops and their families. We also have to be very sensitive to those concerns.
>
> It is equally important that the need for trustworthy news is at its greatest during times of crisis. People should have confidence that they are being told the truth, that whatever information is withheld from them is justified and is withheld for no longer than necessary.
>
> We must be prepared to withhold information for a while at the request of the military authorities in the field and of the Ministry of Defence, so long as they give satisfactory reasons for our doing so ... We should seek to give significant information withheld as soon as the reason for holding back has gone.

On whether and how to report opposition to the war, the guidelines were firm: 'In spite of sensitivities we must reflect any significant opposition in the UK (and elsewhere) to the military conflict. Those who speak and perhaps demonstrate against war are part of the national scene to be reported.'

As in the Falklands War the newspapers, especially the raucous tabloids, felt less of an obligation to be even-handed. At the height of the Gulf War the *Guardian* published a telling table of the language employed by the press in a single week, contrasting phrases used to describe the Allied troops with those about the Iraqis:

> We have Army, Navy and Air Force; they have a war machine ... We dig in; they cower in their foxholes ... We launch [missiles] pre-emptively; they launch without provocation ... Our missiles cause collateral damage; theirs cause civilian casualties ... Our men are lads; their men are hordes ... Our boys are professional; theirs are brainwashed ... Ours resolute; theirs ruthless ... Our boys fly into the jaws of hell; theirs cower in concrete bunkers ... We have reporting guidelines; they have censorship ... We have press briefings; they have propaganda.

Because the Gulf War was over quickly and with relatively few Allied casualties, the difficult issues relating to covering such a conflict in the last decade of the twentieth century were never fully explored. If the war had been longer and had gone less well for Britain, pressures on the media to identify themselves totally with the national effort would have increased. A commitment equivalent to that given in World War Two would have been sought; but, if granted at all, it would have been granted less readily.

*　　*　　*

Restrictions on what journalists regard as the proper practice of their profession are not confined to handling official or military information. The question whether reporters should be required to disclose confidential sources has from time to time been brought before the courts, when the verdict invariably goes against the press. In 1963 two *Daily Sketch* reporters, Reginald Foster and Brendan Mulholland, were sentenced to three months in jail for refusing to disclose sources of personal information about William Vassall, a convicted spy.

In 1980 Granada Television made a programme revealing mismanagement in British Steel, a nationalised concern: a matter clearly of great importance to the people. Some of the programme's most important disclosures were based on leaked documents, and the House of Lords ordered Granada to disclose the source, arguing that the press had no protection in law when it relied on unauthorised information.

Ostensibly to remedy this legal vacuum, the Contempt of Court Act was introduced in 1981. Like the Official Secrets Act eight years later, this was trumpeted by the Government as enhancing press freedom, whereas in practice its effect was to restrict it. Section 10 of the Contempt of Court Act lays down that a court may not require journalists to reveal their sources except 'in the interests of justice or national security or for the prevention of disorder or crime'. It did not save Sarah Tisdall from being shopped by the *Guardian*, or the *Independent*'s business correspondent, Jeremy Warner, from being fined £20,000, with £100,000 costs, for declining to disclose sources for a series of revelations about insider dealing connected with takeover bids.

In 1990 William Goodwin, a 23-year-old journalist on the trade publication the *Engineer*, was fined £5,000 in a case that arose from a tip-off he had received about the financial position of a company, based on a confidential document prepared by the company to support its application for a bank loan. The company was determined to discover the source of the leak and went to law in an attempt to make Goodwin reveal it. In the High Court, Mr Justice Hoffmann ruled that Goodwin was not protected from having to do so by the 1981 Act and ordered Goodwin to deliver his notes, containing the name of the source, to the court. The Appeal Court reinforced the order and, when he refused to comply with it, Goodwin was in contempt.

The House of Lords confirmed the verdict of the other two courts but did not send Goodwin to prison, as was within their power. Instead, he was fined a modest £5,000, and he maintained his silence, despite Lord Bridge's judgment, which stated:

> No one has a right of conscientious objection which entitles him to set himself above the law if he does not agree with a court's decision. That would undermine the rule of law and is wholly unacceptable in a democratic society. Freedom of speech is itself a right which is dependent on the rule of law for its protection and it is paradoxical that a serious challenge to the rule of law should be mounted by responsible journalists.

Critics of the press maintain, like Lord Bridge, that journalists too often claim privileges which the law does not grant them and which they do not deserve, given their deplorable record on the invasion of privacy and similar matters. Journalists respond that because they have no constitutional protection, such as the press enjoys in the United States, they are obliged to act high-handedly and defy the law on occasions, in the greater interest of fulfilling their historic role as defenders of the people against overweening governments or large vested interests. Often the only way of uncovering such abuses is through unauthorised disclosure, and if informants think there is a danger of being identified they will be deterred from speaking out.

Because the two sides begin with conflicting presumptions about the proper relationship between the press and the law, the dispute will not be resolved unless Britain should one day get a constitution which defines that relationship clearly.

15
Let's Make a Deal

Beware of enterprise: beware of public spirit: beware of conscience
and visions of the future . . . And when you find journalists glorify-
ing the Capitalist system as a splendid stimulus to all these qualities
. . . restrain the unladylike impulse to imitate the Sacristan in the
Ingoldsby Legends, who said no word to indicate a doubt, but put
a thumb unto his nose, and spread his fingers out.

George Bernard Shaw, *An Intelligent Woman's*
Guide to Socialism and Capitalism, 1928

No editor, however nationally independent, can afford to alienate his
paymaster. Thus in countries where the press is owned by the government, its reporting of politics cannot be other than tainted. The British
press is owned for the most part by large businesses and this is why, of
all its functions, its reporting of business matters is in some respects the
least satisfactorily carried out.

It is not simply a matter of a newspaper avoiding negative comment
on its proprietor's other business interests – even actively promoting
them – but in a wider context it will be reluctant to discredit the capitalist
system in which it operates by suggesting that its rules and practices
are inherently suspect. It is an unspoken constraint but one of which
journalists are from time to time made aware. A business correspondent
who sought to question the profit motive and the other values of the
business community would invite the hostility both of his proprietor and
of potentially useful sources in the City, as well as of the advertisers
who provide the bulk of the papers' revenue.

That helps explain why the few major stories critical of big business
in the mainstream press in recent years – the *Sunday Times* investigations
into the thalidomide scandal and Pergamon Press come to mind – have
mainly been researched by teams of journalists who do not report business affairs full time. Even the *Guardian*, whose overall philosophy is
more opposed to big business than that of any other national paper, has

not devoted many resources to seeking out scandal and corruption in the City, although it eagerly follows up any such stories after they have come to light elsewhere.

All specialist reporters rely to some extent on personal contacts: that was how Chapman Pincher achieved many of his scoops, including the one on the D-notice affair. Although such contacts often produce important stories there is a danger that the relationship will be exploited by informants to ensure that their own version of events is the one that gains currency.

Financial public relations was invented in the early 1960s, when City journalism began to develop from being a largely technical service for insiders, catering to perhaps 10 per cent of readers or fewer, into a full-fledged part of a paper's news coverage, with an emphasis on personalities. The process began in the takeover boom of the 1950s, when astute businessmen such as Charles Clore, Isaac Wolfson and later Jim Slater recognised that shares for most companies were under-priced given the value of their assets, and took advantage of low interest rates to borrow the money they needed to become powerful forces in the market.

Until then company chairmen and directors had been private, shadowy figures who shunned the limelight. Now they were persuaded by image-makers that the more they could get their names and pictures on to the papers' City pages – and even sometimes into the gossip columns – the higher their share price was likely to rise. The concept of the fashionable share and the fashionable entrepreneur began to take hold as a new class of individual investors came to the market, choosing their shares on different criteria from the hard-nosed professionals who had hitherto dominated the City.

The newspapers soon began to see opportunities in this trend. Frederick Ellis of the *Daily Express* was the first City editor to develop personality-oriented financial information in the mid-market press and he was quickly followed by Patrick Sergeant, who became City editor of the *Daily Mail* in 1960. Sergeant had joined the *Mail* seven years earlier as deputy City editor, at a time when financial coverage was limited to a tiny space at the bottom of an inside page and consisted almost entirely of a stock market report compiled by three elderly assistants. When he was made City editor he was given a whole broadsheet page – at first page two and then further back in the paper – to develop a hard news approach. The share boom and the new style of City reporting fed on each other: the more people could be persuaded to take an interest in the stock market, the higher the prices climbed, and this in turn fuelled greater interest in what Ellis and Sergeant were writing.

In 1966 Sergeant began *Money Mail*, the first of the weekly family finance supplements that later proliferated in the mid-market and up-market papers. He recognised that middle-class readers, new to the world of finance, needed a stream of up-to-date advice on what to do with their money, and that in supplying this he was also creating an attractive market for financial advertisers, especially the recently created unit trusts: Save and Prosper used to take a page in *Money Mail* every week. When the *Daily Mail* was turned into a tabloid in 1971, two or three pages a day would be devoted to the City, with *Money Mail* running at some sixteen pages weekly.

Even the mass-market tabloids were beginning to take an interest in the goings-on in the City. Their technique has always been to render complex issues more comprehensible by reporting them in terms of personalities. Mirrorscope, the *Daily Mirror*'s 1960s reader-friendly format for covering serious issues, accommodated business stories by highlighting the people involved.

Something comparable was happening in the financial pages of the quality broadsheets. Nigel Lawson, just before he turned to politics and an eventual seat in the Cabinet, was an innovative City editor of the *Sunday Telegraph*, from its launch in 1961 to 1963, when he was succeeded by Kenneth Fleet. Lawson can claim to have introduced to the quality press the concept, borrowed from the mid-market papers, of reporting City matters primarily through personalities, and was one of the originators of the business profile. His successors developed the style and it was soon imitated in all the quality Sundays.

*　　*　　*

John Bloom, who made a fortune in the 1960s selling cheap washing machines, was one of the earliest of those forced (though not unwillingly) by the media into the role of an entrepreneurial whizz-kid; and equally quickly forced into bankruptcy and the criminal courts when his fragile empire collapsed. Another star of that seminal decade, Jim Slater, was a specialist in takeovers and asset-stripping and a favourite with the press until the early 1970s, when things began to go wrong and adulation was transformed into criticism. He withdrew from the City in 1975.

Some business pages have come to resemble the sports or entertainment pages. Winners and high fliers are sought, stars of the future tipped. Captains of industry, finance and commerce are interviewed and profiled as though they were film or television personalities. They are lauded for their boldness and vision: the point is seldom made that, as in Bloom's case, it is not always easy to distinguish boldness from sharp practice.

It was the same a decade later when both the British and the American press created a superman image for John DeLorean. The former General Motors executive with an eye for a stylish suit, an ear for a telling phrase and a convincingly earnest manner charmed the British Government into handing him £84 million in grants to build a factory in Belfast for a sports car that proved a comprehensive disaster. The press, notably the *Sunday Telegraph*, did play something of a revelatory role here when, acting on information from employees, it reported serious shortcomings in the company's operations. DeLorean's business collapsed and he was eventually arrested on charges of drugs dealing, though never convicted. He still owes the British Government $8 million.

For both DeLorean and Bloom, the distorted image created by the press when they first came on the scene contributed to the messy outcome of their stories. The tone of reporting in their early boom days implied that their magic touch could overcome normal rules of business behaviour, deceiving those with whom they dealt as well as the two men themselves.

Soon after Roy Thomson bought *The Times* in 1966 the paper's business coverage was greatly increased and placed in a separate section, in the hope of attracting those readers who previously relied exclusively on the *Financial Times*. The *Sunday Times* had begun a separate business news section some years earlier and had found it a lucrative magnet for advertisers.

It might have worked better at *The Times* had the *Financial Times* not responded so quickly and effectively to the challenge by broadening its coverage of both City and general news. Some businessmen found *The Times*'s financial coverage too academic – especially the writings of the economics editor Peter Jay – and too little concerned with the day-to-day practicalities of the City, especially when compared to the lively coverage of the Sundays. The big financial advertisers, with their multi-page ads for new share issues and the like, remained loyal to the *FT*. The *Times* Business News, although still a separate section, has never been the money-maker that Lord Thomson, Denis Hamilton and William Rees-Mogg hoped when they started it in the 1960s.

*   *   *

In 1986 a glossy magazine called *Business*, modelled on *Fortune* in the United States, was launched jointly by the *Financial Times* and the American-owned magazine house Condé Nast. The whole magazine was devoted to the now familiar technique of discussing business primarily in terms of personalities rather than issues. Making effective use of modern colour photography, the illustrations usually portrayed the 1980s breed of executive draped round or behind their desks, as carefully posed as fashion models. A product of the relatively short-lived Thatcher boom, *Business* closed in 1991 in the depths of the subsequent recession.

In November 1986, *Business* published its honour roll of the 'Top 40 Under 40 – a compendium of those likely to go on to even greater success'. The magazine explained how it had arrived at its list of up-and-coming go-getters: 'Confidential soundings have been taken during the past months from Britain's business leaders of today. All have been asked the question: "Who are the big winners of tomorrow?"'

This was one of the 'big winners' who emerged from these confidential soundings: 'Olivier Roux, 36, has shot to the top of one of the country's major public companies, Guinness. As director of financial strategy and development, he has played a major role in forming the group's policy and style in approaching mergers and acquisitions.'

Just two months later, that citation was to prove deeply ironic, not to say embarrassing. For Guinness's policy and style in its acquisition of the Distillers Group in the spring of 1986 were the subject of a Board of Trade enquiry, followed by criminal proceedings. And exactly who was responsible for forming that policy and style – Roux or the chairman Ernest Saunders – remained a matter of contention. Part of the takeover bid was in Guinness shares and to bolster its value the company paid £25 million to a 'concert party' of investors who bought shares and thus kept the market price high – a ruse with a long history but not allowed under the City's increasingly stringent rules for takeovers.

As a consequence of this support operation, the Guinness share price rose in March and April 1986, when the bid was progressing, at a far greater rate than the share price of a rival bidder, James Gulliver's Argyll Group. Yet there was no suggestion in the City pages then that something illicit might be going on. Saunders was friendly with several leading financial journalists and received a largely sympathetic press.

Saunders was a persuasive man. If he thought he detected something less than enthusiasm for his company in a section of the press, he had no compunction about protesting to newspaper executives. In their book *The Guinness Affair*, Nick Kochan and Hugh Pym disclose how Saunders complained to Andrew Knight, then chief executive of the *Daily*

Telegraph group, about coverage of the Distillers bid in the group's two papers: he disapproved particularly of the sceptical stance of Ian Watson, then City editor of the *Sunday Telegraph*. Saunders made a similar approach to Lord Stevens, chairman of the *Express* group.

In his book *Takeovers*, written with James Srodes, Ivan Fallon of the *Sunday Times*, who had also known Saunders for a long time, wrote of the same trait:

> Long-term relationships seemed to mean less to Saunders than to most senior businessmen. Journalists who had known him for years but who dared to oppose him in his bid battles suddenly found themselves regarded as enemies. He several times complained to proprietors, and he also spread around legal threats, even to leading City editors who regarded themselves as his friends.

It was Kenneth Fleet who had broken the story of Guinness's interest in Distillers in *The Times* of Saturday 18 January 1986. Four and a half months later, after Saunders had won, Ivan Fallon wrote enthusiastically in the *Sunday Times*: 'In the past month, Ernest Saunders has joined a unique club of British managers which probably numbers no more than three. The chief executive of Guinness can now stand beside the modern legends of British commercial success.'

By July came the first public sign that all was not as it should have been with the Distillers victory. To gain the support of Scottish investors in the whisky company, Saunders had promised to appoint as chairman of the merged group Sir Thomas Risk, governor of the Bank of Scotland. When it came to the point where he had to deliver on this pledge Saunders drew back, signalling this change of heart through an inspired story written by Fallon.

'Ernest Saunders, as the world now knows, has performed one of the great wonders of the modern commercial world,' he reminded any readers who had not been paying attention, but he went on to suggest that in order to reap the benefits of the merger Guinness needed tough and undivided leadership. 'The company is in a mess and tougher action is urgent. Lord Iveagh's willingness to step aside [as chairman] should permit Saunders to assume the role of executive chairman: no "rent-a-chairman" would be needed.'

Next morning Fleet echoed the plea, reporting on a meeting on 14 July between Saunders and Robin Leigh-Pemberton, Governor of the Bank of England, who was naturally anxious that Guinness should keep its promise by appointing Risk. Fleet wrote in those delicate tones that imply impeccable sources which the writer is constrained from revealing:

> Though no direct account is available of their conversation, Mr Leigh-Pemberton is unlikely to demur from the central truth that the duty of the Guinness board is to serve the best interests of their shareholders as they conceive it. That duty must take precedence over previously outlined plans for board structures and appointments, which, though they were embodied in legal documents and may, in some senses, be legally binding, are nevertheless subsequently judged to be inadequate for dealing with the company's problems.

In other words, it was a good idea to ditch Risk, and it was duly done. In the event, Sir Thomas must have been relieved to have been bumped from the ticket. He did not have to get involved in the fracas the following January, when Roux, *Business* magazine's 'big winner of tomorrow' and Saunders himself were among those forced to resign, as well as some executives from Morgan Grenfell, the bankers who had advised Guinness on the takeover. Saunders was convicted and imprisoned.

Even after it was clear that the former chief executive would take his place not beside the modern legends of commercial success but of idols with feet of clay, Fallon and his co-author James Srodes could ask in their book *Takeovers*: 'Who knows whether, a decade from now, under new management and with a splendid record behind it, analysts will not regard Guinness-cum-Distillers as one of the great companies of the world? Saunders' legacy may, in the long term, be seen as not all bad, at least so far as one major company is concerned.'

Five years later Fallon could justify that prediction: by 1991 the Guinness share price stood at nearly £10, compared with £3 when Saunders was forced to quit and only 40p when he was appointed to rescue the company from the brink of bankruptcy. All the same, it does no service to readers if the bonds of friendship between businessmen and City journalists, lubricated by the craft of public relations, inhibit the inquisitive function of the press, which should, with hindsight, have asked more questions about the buoyant Guinness share price while the bid was in progress, rather than after the event.

*   *   *

The question whether financial journalists have the will or the ability to alert readers to potential scandal was raised most acutely in the case of the Bank of Credit and Commerce International (BCCI), forced by the

Bank of England to cease trading in July 1991 after an audit by the accountants Price Waterhouse had found evidence of substantial fraud and malpractice. Founded in 1972 by Agha Hassan Abedi, a persuasive Pakistani who professed high ideals, BCCI had become the fifth largest bank in the world with more than 400 branches in sixty-nine countries, many of them in the Third World. Several central banks of small African and Asian countries had close links with BCCI and substantial deposits in it. In Britain, because it offered marginally better interest rates than the main High Street banks, it attracted the funds of numerous small entrepreneurs – especially Asian shopkeepers – and of local authorities seeking a haven for short-term deposits.

Many of these deposits, it now emerged, were used to offset BCCI's bad debts, including some incurred through unwise loans to friends and associates of its senior executives. Moreover, the bank served as a conduit for laundered money from drugs deals and for the transfer of funds by wealthy Third World figures in breach of their countries' strict exchange control regulations.

One of the main puzzles of the BCCI affair, and the aspect that highlights the role of the financial press, was why depositors – in particular responsible public authorities – continued to pour money into the bank right until the end, well after the first questions had been raised about its probity. As long ago as 1979 the Bank of England had refused to grant it a full banking licence, partly because even at that early stage it had come under the critical scrutiny of the United States regulatory authorities, who were concerned at its reluctance to disclose information about its affairs. To cater for slightly unorthodox institutions such as BCCI, the bank created a new category of 'licensed deposit takers'.

Ten years later, investigations by US Customs into Colombian drugs deals revealed that BCCI, whose chief shareholder by then was the Sheikh of Abu Dhabi, was a conduit for laundering the proceeds of such deals. It was also said to be involved in financing arms sales. In January 1990 the bank pleaded guilty to charges of handling $32 million of drugs money and was fined $15 million, with five of its former executives jailed for between three and twelve years. The bank soon became known in financial circles as the Bank of Cocaine and Colombia International.

These court cases were reported extensively in the press, and most prudent City professionals steered clear of BCCI. After its collapse, nearly everyone claimed to have known that something was amiss. Christopher Fildes wrote in the *Spectator* just after the bank's suspension: 'Hands up, anyone who thought there wasn't a fraud at the Bank of

Credit and Commerce International.' Yet although insiders may have known something was wrong, many of the victims of the collapse had scarcely an inkling. Fildes continued: 'The Bank [of England] has powers of discipline which stop short of an outright busting, but they are all of them exercised behind closed doors. No names, no pack-drill, and, for the depositor who has not heard the gossip, no warning.'

No national newspaper mounted a full-scale investigation into the bank before its suspension, asking explicitly whether it was a safe haven for funds. One reason for this was the fate of the sole attempt at such an exposé, in the left-wing weekly *New Statesman* in 1981. A series of three articles by the Pakistan-born journalist Tariq Ali cast doubt on the bank's probity, but they attracted a libel action which the journal was forced to settle out of court. The fortnightly *Private Eye* from time to time ran items that cast the bank in a poor light, but these were not followed up in the mainstream press.

Newspapers accused of failure to probe thoroughly – and thus failure to protect their readers – replied in their defence that the libel laws made it virtually impossible to do so. Just after BCCI's suspension, the *Mail on Sunday* wrote in an editorial:

> Not this newspaper, not any newspaper, alerted its readers to the true state of affairs. Yet every newspaper had someone on the staff who had a fair idea of what BCCI was all about. We ourselves had information that there was nasty work afoot. So why did we not publish? Why did other newspapers not publish? The answer is straightforward. The law of libel in this country.
>
> Some businessmen issue writs almost whenever their name is mentioned, hoping to cower newspapers, wearied by the time and expense of fighting them off, into simply leaving them alone. Journalists wanting to subpoena senior civil servants to give evidence on their behalf cannot do so when the civil servants claim, and are almost invariably granted, crown immunity. Because there is no right of public information in this country, because newspapers are unable to argue, as the American press is able to do, the public interest, they have no defence in law other than the absolute proof of their allegations. As absolute proof is very rarely available to anybody about anything, and as the press in this country has such formidable hurdles to jump to acquire such proof, it is to all intents and purposes muzzled.

That was a powerful reason why Robert Maxwell's manipulations of pension funds and the like went undetected until after his death, although he had been publicly denounced by an official inquiry as untrustworthy some years earlier. He was a more frequent and determined litigant than anyone – and again it was only *Private Eye* that regularly suggested he was dishonest.

Every day financial journalists, like those in other specialist areas, receive calls from people who claim inside information on some alleged commercial skulduggery. Often the sources are disgruntled former employees or associates of the person they are trying to discredit and in nearly all cases the allegations, although not necessarily false, are unprovable. City journalists resent suggestions that they are less aggress- ive than other kinds of reporter in the pursuit of scandal, pointing out that it is not the job of, say, a crime reporter to prevent crime, or a defence correspondent to stop wars. Why should people expect financial reporters to be policemen? They see their task as analysing those facts about a firm that are in the public domain, deducing from them whether it is being competently run and thus represents a safe investment. The great majority of the companies they write about are not, after all, run fraudulently: when fraud does occur it is generally in small companies and the number of victims is small. Scandals on the scale of BCCI, Guinness and Maxwell are rare – and even in the Guinness case the shareholders did not suffer.

This may be an unglamorous and unheroic view of a City journalist's role, but those who hold it believe that by operating in this low-key fashion they provide a more useful service to the public than if they dissipated their energies in attempts to blow the whistle on swindlers. The *Financial Times* itself has occasionally been criticised, by impatient members of its staff among others, for what they see as its reluctance to pry too closely behind the balance sheet. The *Financial Times* provided the most revelatory coverage of the Maxwell scandal, but again it was after the event.

As for the comparison with the United States made in the *Mail on Sunday* editorial, defenders of the City press corps point out that the incidence of commercial fraud in the United States is at least as high as in Britain and probably higher. The American press is allowed to be bolder in its investigations but it does not appear any more successful.

While all that is true, another factor, never mentioned by editors when they seek to defend themselves against charges of pusillanimity, is that newspaper proprietors take a much greater interest in their papers' financial coverage than in any other area of the news. When Esmond Harmsworth, the second Viscount Rothermere, ran Associated News- papers, he would have regular weekly lunches with Patrick Sergeant, the *Daily Mail*'s City editor, to catch up with business gossip. The first Lord Beaverbrook took a comparable interest in his papers' financial writers.

Supporters and beneficiaries of the free market capitalist system are unlikely to want to see in their newspapers the kind of inquisitive reporting that calls capitalist values and practices into question. They prefer their City writers to operate from within the establishment rather than outside it. That is why critical coverage is likely to remain, for the most part, the preserve of smaller publications such as *Private Eye* and the *New Statesman and Society*: but these, lacking wealthy proprietors, are far more vulnerable to threats of legal action and have limited resources to devote to combating them. The system ensures that, when the City does have murky secrets to hide, it will not be the mainstream press that reveals them.

16

The Twenty-first Century

> The mass tabloid market is huge but has only three players. With
> lower costs per unit we can fragment that market and then there's
> no reason why others can't come into it, serving smaller markets.
>
> Eddy Shah, before launching the *Post*, 1988

The press is more sensitive than other industries to changes in the
economic climate. Advertising, its main source of revenue, is among the
first items of expenditure to be cut when business is bad. Unemployment
increases so there are fewer job vacancies to announce. Company cars
are cut back, so the big advertisers in the motor industry draw in their
horns. As property sales stagnate, so do prices, and people defer selling
and thus advertising their houses.

All this helps explain the sudden decline in the newspaper industry's
confidence at the start of the 1990s. As the old decade was ending it
seemed that, freed at last from the dispiriting limitations on its development imposed by outdated technology – and by the powerful print unions
who would not allow it to be modernised – the press had entered the
sunlit uplands. Costs were markedly lower and, at the height of the
Thatcher boom, revenues were increasing to the extent that new papers
could be launched with realistic hopes of quite rapid success, without
seriously damaging the prospects of the existing ones. Optimistic fore-
casters spoke sagely of 'gaps in the market' waiting to be filled, and
optimistic entrepreneurs such as Eddy Shah believed them.

Yet by the end of 1991, within five years of the Wapping breakthrough
and the launch of *Today* and the *Independent*, the industry was nervously
eyeing the balance sheets again, for all the world as if 1986 had never
happened. In the euphoria, it had been all too easy to overlook the reality
of the market place: the reduction of the industry's cost base could only
be advantageous in the long term if you assumed no drop in revenue.

Selling advertising is a highly competitive business and, especially during a recession, essentially a buyer's market. Advertisers with

reduced budgets bargained mercilessly for discounts, until the papers' profit margins sank to something like the level they were at before the cost reductions took effect. With five daily broadsheets and six tabloids competing for revenue, and a comparable number on Sundays, advertisers had plenty of scope for striking favourable bargains. The plumpest papers were not necessarily the ones earning most from their advertising sales but those discounting their rates most heavily.

The *Daily Telegraph* group provides an example. Following the move to Docklands and the introduction of modern production techniques the group, which had maintained its highly desirable circulation and readership profile throughout its years of difficulty, recorded a pre-tax profit for 1989 of £41.5 million compared with £29.2 million for 1988, virtual break-even in 1987 and losses for the two years before that. In 1990, though, the upward curve flattened out and the profits were down to £38.5 million, with only a slight increase in 1991.

The *Telegraph* papers were positively blooming with fiscal health compared with News International, Rupert Murdoch's British operation, which in August 1991 announced a loss for the previous financial year of £336 million, due to the necessity for high interest payments on loans and the continued losses on British Sky Broadcasting, the satellite TV operation in which News International is the largest shareholder.

The younger and more fragile *Independent* was even more seriously affected. Its 1989 profit of £3.25 million was transformed in 1990 into a loss of £7.85 million. Included in this loss was the cost of launching the *Independent on Sunday* but that accounted for less than half of it. In the year ended September 1991 it lost £10.3 million, including a £1.9 million provision for redundancy payments incurred when the Sunday paper was more closely integrated with the daily and was forced to raise a further £16.5 million, mainly from the Spanish and Italian newspaper groups that were becoming the company's most important shareholders. The future of the *Independent*, however, still looked secure, with a circulation not far below that of *The Times*. In the six months ended March 1992 it registered a small profit of £465,000.

The other paper launched in 1986, *Today*, hung on, but was performing the worst of all the tabloids and there was continual speculation over how long News International would be prepared to bankroll it. Eddy Shah, its founder, has quit the newspaper business. None of the other new papers launched post-Wapping have survived – except the *Sunday Sport*, which does not really qualify as a newspaper – and there have been no fresh attempts since Robert Maxwell's *European*, still struggling to find an identity and a viable circulation base.

As recently as 1989 Charles Wintour could write, in his book *The Rise and Fall of Fleet Street*: 'It is no longer a rarity for new national newspapers to be launched.' That turned out to be true for only a short period, and it is impossible to predict when or whether it will become true again. It is more likely that the next decade will see a reduction in the number of titles, not an increase.

Circulation is less directly affected than advertising revenue by the economic climate: one theory has it that people read more in hard times, especially magazines. But when advertising revenue goes down, newspapers are tempted to raise cover prices to make up the shortfall. This depresses circulation and in time cuts the revenue from advertising still further. Circulation of all daily papers went down by more than 1,330,000 between May 1990 and May 1992, with the tabloids suffering most (9.5 per cent lower compared with a 6.5 per cent drop in sales of the qualities).

The tabloids, as a group, have been in decline for some years. Between 1986 and 1991 their sales dropped by 8 per cent, while those of the quality broadsheets went up by more than 10 per cent. The decline accelerated in the early 1990s. Coinciding as it did with the willingness of juries to award heavy libel damages against the most scurrilous papers, this was interpreted by some media writers as evidence of the public's disapproval of the tabloids' increasingly sleazy sensationalism.

While it is impossible to be certain about the reasons for such shifts of attitude, I suspect that popular disillusion with the tabloids stems from what they fail to provide rather than from high-minded disapproval of what they do print. Readers, whose main source of news is now television, increasingly want more serious coverage than that offered in the *Sun*, *Mirror* and *Daily Star*. The fact that sales of the main mid-market tabloids – the *Mail* and *Express* – held up better than the rest between May 1990 and May 1992 indicated that a body of readers were trading up to those more authoritative papers.

Circulation patterns during the Gulf War, at the beginning of 1991, seemed to confirm that: tabloid sales for February 1991 were 3.5 per cent down year on year, despite the great public interest in the war evidenced by the increase in viewing figures for TV news. Broadsheet sales also fell in that time, but only by 1.1 per cent in a period just following a spate of price increases that would normally have been expected to cut into sales by a lot more than that. The circulation of the Sunday broadsheets increased during the war, but fell away again severely soon afterwards. That all suggests that a growing number of readers wanted more responsible coverage of an important story than the mass-market tabloids were providing.

Expensive promotions do not increase sales of the tabloids as a group: TV campaigns and prize competitions appear to succeed only in temporarily switching readers' allegiance from one title to another. All the same, with tabloid sales standing at nearly 12 million a day (and more on Sundays) it would be absurd to forecast that the market will continue to decline so remorselessly that it eventually peters out. More likely, the tabloid proprietors will adjust their product to win some of the lost readers back, and there is evidence of this happening.

The outcry by politicians, echoed by writers in broadsheet newspapers, over the tabloids' intrusiveness and vulgarity seemed to result in a moderation of their tone of voice at the beginning of the 1990s. On television, Channel 4's *Hard News* campaigned remorselessly against the worst excesses of the press and, while watched by few tabloid readers, it reinforced the emerging middle-class consensus that something needed to be done. Threats of legislative curbs, coupled with the creation of the new Press Complaints Commission to replace the Press Council, were all part of the same process.

It is unlikely, though, that the tabloids would have responded at all to this moral pressure had their sales figures not shown them to be failing, despite repeated loud claims to the contrary, to give their readers what they wanted. The lowest common denominator – that holy grail sought by the editors of all mass-market tabloids – had shifted perhaps one notch up from the bottom of the barrel, away from the salacious extreme. Confirming that trend, sales of the raunchy *Sunday Sport* dropped by nearly a quarter between May 1990 and May 1992.

The threat of legislation to prevent gross intrusion into privacy was dangled over the press by politicians, by the Calcutt Committee and by Lord McGregor, head of the new Press Complaints Commission, but it may never have had the chilling effect on tabloid editors that these harbingers of doom (as well as broadsheet leader-writers) imagined. As Simon Jenkins had perceptively observed in his *Times* article on the subject (see Chapter 11), some newspaper executives appeared to take the view that, if legislation did come, that was something they would have to deal with when it happened: in the meantime they were not going to engage in high-stakes combat with their rivals with one hand voluntarily tied behind their backs. The *News of the World*'s attitude over Clare Short, and the *People*'s over the commission's ruling on the naked picture of Princess Eugenie, are examples.

Whatever the government felt about the efficacy of the new regulatory regime – and there was scant evidence to suggest that, since the ousting of Mrs Thatcher the previous November, they had given it much thought at all – McGregor's dire threats of imminent legislation were scarcely credible seeing that within months there was going to be a general election. There would certainly be no time to legislate before the poll. The Labour Party continued to maintain that, regardless of whether the PCC was perceived to be working or not, it would bring in a bill to protect privacy early in its administration if elected to power. The Conservatives were not going to do anything to alienate the predominantly friendly press before the election, and having won it they could well be too overwhelmed by gratitude to savage the hand that had helped them stay in office.

In the PCC's first year of operation, there did seem to be fewer cases of intrusion into purely private lives (as distinct from the lives of the royals), although it would have been too much to expect a total change in the nature of the beast overnight. While it was convenient for editors to assert that they were restraining themselves in response to the general show of concern, a more powerful motive was their perception that the public's taste for lurid scandal was beginning to abate.

*   *   *

The last decade of the twentieth century is likely to see fewer changes in the national press than seemed probable a few years earlier. Although the industry will regain its profitability when the recession ends, it will never provide a quick route to unimagined success and prosperity, as Eddy Shah hoped *Today* and later the *Post* would. Shah's vision of numerous small papers serving discrete sections of the market, as explained to me in the quotation that prefaces this chapter, is a false one. The launch of new titles will surely be as rare a phenomenon in the years to come as it was before 1986.

The existing small group of proprietors and their immediate successors, or industrialists of like motivation, will continue to dominate the industry and will, as now, have no compunction about using their papers to promote their other commercial interests when it seems desirable. They will appoint editors who have learned the craft at the side of the present incumbents and who share their background and attitudes.

The tabloids will clean up their act only to the extent that they think it necessary to slow the decline in their circulation. Relations between the press and government are likely to remain largely unaltered. Even if formal lobby briefings were to be abolished it would be only a cosmetic change. Confidential chats between politicians and trusted political writers will remain an integral part of the way we run our public affairs. The only result of weakening the lobby as an institution would be to allow ministers to be more selective in choosing which journalists will be favoured to receive their leaks – a reason why the opponents of any change tend to be those who work for the less influential papers, who could find themselves bypassed in favour of colleagues with clout.

In their essentials, the workings and the structure of the British press are still much as they were thirty years ago and are likely to remain so. The most obvious differences are physical; in the locations and conditions in which journalists operate and the consequent change in their relationship with one another. The newsrooms of popular papers used to be noisy, raucous, sometimes near-riotous places when a big story was breaking. Typewriters clattered, phones rang, news editors screamed for more copy and the printing presses rumbled underneath. Even if there was never quite the same excitement in the offices of the quality broadsheets, the sense of urgency was there.

Now it is hard to distinguish the one kind of newsroom from the other. Walk into a large open-plan office in Wapping, where young men and women stare earnestly into computer screens, tapping keyboards with cool efficiency, and it is hard to tell right away whether you are in the newsroom of the *Sun* or the *Sunday Times*. You may have to wait to see whether the editor walking on to the floor to goad the workers into activity is the Cockney Kelvin MacKenzie or the Scot Andrew Neil.

The old Fleet Street ethic and its attendant bonhomie have been weakened by the diaspora but have not entirely vanished. The long lunch hour is rarer but not yet extinct – in some cases it can be longer, given the time it takes to get from Docklands to the Garrick Club and other West End haunts. It is certainly easier to stay in the compound at Wapping, Canary Wharf or Kensington, nibbling a sandwich at your desk and sipping coffee from a machine, than to venture into the pubs nearby, which are anyway too far from any other newspaper office to allow for the camaraderie between rivals that used to be one of Fleet Street's most engaging features.

Journalists' memoirs still lionise the hard-drinking hacks whose colleagues rallied round to write and file their copy for them if they were insensible in the afternoon, but there is now nowhere to swap such anecdotes, nowhere you can drop in and hear the likes of René McColl and Donald Wise telling tall tales of their exploits in foreign parts, the ruses they had to employ to get their messages to the head of the cable office queue. Even if the *Daily Express* and *Daily Mirror* could nowadays afford to spend so lavishly on sending them overseas, foreign reporting is no longer like that. Portable word processors and satellite telephones have reduced reliance on local communications – and in any case the days are gone when the visiting fireman could treat the natives in a high-handed, proconsular manner. Journalists have, too, become better educated in the last three decades, and bring qualities other than initiative and effrontery to the craft. The resulting journalism is less glamorous but probably superior in most other respects.

The increasing size and sophistication of the international press corps, dominated by television, is another reason why it is harder to garner stories simply through the exercise of bare-faced cheek. Often print journalists can do no better than tag along with a friendly TV crew, knowing they are certain to be scooped by the pictures that appear on home screens before their stories get into print.

So even if the Press Club and the Fleet Street pubs were still there, playing their old role as theatres for reciting tales of derring-do, sharp practice and eccentricity, the tales themselves would be rarer and less exciting. That is why journalists mourn the end of the Street. They have lost an irreplaceable way of life. Readers, though, have suffered no such detectable hardship. The changes of the late 1980s have brought them more papers to choose from, for the most part better written and better printed, and many of them in colour. For those to whom Fleet Street was no more than a name, or a place where the bus would get stuck in formidable traffic jams, the changes since the 1960s, the decade in which Denis Hamilton revolutionised the posh Sundays and Rupert Murdoch did the same for the tatty tabloids, have all been for the good. We have more and better writers producing more and better newspapers – and doing their livers a favour into the bargain.

Appendix:
The National Newspapers,
Their Owners and
Their Politics

Paper	Frequency[1]	Circulation[2]	Politics[3]
News International (Rupert Murdoch)			
Sun	D	3,665,006	R
The Times	D	387,386	R
Today	D	459,621	CR
News of the World	S	4,815,894	R
Sunday Times	S	1,147,667	R
Mirror Group Newspapers			
Daily Mirror	D	3,641,269*	L
Sunday Mirror	S	2,816,935	L
People	S	2,215,465	L
Associated Newspapers (Lord Harmsworth)			
Daily Mail	D	1,683,768	R
Mail on Sunday	S	1,958,660	CR
United Newspapers (Lord Stevens)			
Daily Express	D	1,518,764	R
Sunday Express	S	1,652,659	R
The Daily Telegraph plc (Conrad Black)			
Daily Telegraph	D	1,058,082	R
Sunday Telegraph	S	567,497	R
Newspaper Publishing plc (Andreas Whittam Smith)			
Independent	D	372,240	CR
Independent on Sunday	S	374,084	CR

Paper	Frequency[1]	Circulation[2]	Politics[3]
Manchester Guardian and Evening News			
Guardian	D	409,660	CL
Lonrho ('Tiny' Rowland)			
Observer	S	548,305	CL
Pearsons			
Financial Times	D	287,120	CR

[1] Frequency: D = Daily, S = Sunday.
[2] Circulations are the ABC figures for the six months ended 31 December 1991.
[3] Politics: L = left, R = right, CL = centre left, CR = centre right.
[*] Includes Glasgow *Daily Record*.

Bibliography

Adams, Valerie. *The Media and the Falklands Campaign* (Macmillan, 1986)

Baistow, Tom. *Fourth-rate Estate: An Anatomy of Fleet Street* (Comedia, 1985)

Barson, Susie and Saint, Andrew. *A Farewell to Fleet Street* (Historic Buildings and Monuments Commission, 1988)

Belfield, Richard, Hird, Christopher and Kelly, Sharon. *Murdoch, the Decline of an Empire* (Macdonald, 1991)

Bolton, Roger. *Death on the Rock and Other Stories* (W. H. Allen, 1990)

Bower, Tom. *Maxwell the Outsider* (Aurum, 1988)

Brendon, Piers. *The Life and Death of the Press Barons* (Secker and Warburg, 1982)

Brenton, Howard and Hare, David. *Pravda* (Methuen, 1985)

Brodzky, V. (ed.). *Fleet Street: The Inside Story of Journalism* (Macdonald, 1966)

Chester, Lewis and Fenby, Jonathan. *The Fall of the House of Beaverbrook* (Deutsch, 1979)

Chippindale, Peter and Horrie, Chris. *Disaster! The Rise and Fall of the News on Sunday* (Sphere Books, 1988)

Chippindale, Peter and Horrie, Chris. *Stick it up your Punter: The Rise and Fall of The Sun* (Heinemann, 1990)

Churchill, Randolph. *What I Said About the Press* (Weidenfeld and Nicolson, 1957)

Cleverley, Graham. *The Fleet Street Disaster* (Constable, 1986)

Cleverley, Graham. *The Kettering Standoff: A Study of a Strike* (Areopagus, 1978)

Cockett, Richard. *Twilight of Truth: Chamberlain, Appeasement and the Manipulation of the Press* (Weidenfeld and Nicolson, 1989)

Cowen, Sir Zelman. *The Press and the People: 33rd Annual Report of the Press Council* (1986)

Crozier, Michael. *The Making of The Independent* (Gordon Fraser, 1988)

Cudlipp, Hugh. *At Your Peril* (Weidenfeld and Nicolson, 1962)

Cudlipp, Hugh. *Walking on the Water* (Bodley Head, 1976)

Edwards, Robert. *Goodbye Fleet Street* (Jonathan Cape, 1988)

Evans, Harold. *Good Times, Bad Times* (Weidenfeld and Nicolson, 1983)

Fallon, Ivan and Srodes, James. *DeLorean: The Rise and Fall of a Dream Maker* (Hamish Hamilton, 1983)

Fallon, Ivan and Srodes, James. *Takeovers* (Hamish Hamilton, 1987)

Garland, Nicholas. *Not Many Dead: Journal of a Year in Fleet Street* (Hutchinson, 1990)

Glasgow University Media Group. *War and Peace News* (Open University Press, 1985)

Grose, Roslyn. *The Sun-sation.* (Angus and Robertson, 1989)

Haines, Joe. *Maxwell* (Macdonald, 1988)

Hall, Richard. *My Life with Tiny* (Faber, 1987)

Hamilton, Denis. *Editor-in-Chief: Fleet Street Memoirs* (Hamish Hamilton, 1989)

Harris, Robert. *A Good and Faithful Servant* (Faber, 1990)

Harris, Robert. *GOTCHA! The Media, the Government and the Falklands Crisis* (Faber, 1983)

Harris, Robert. *Selling Hitler* (Faber, 1986)

Hart-Davis, Duff. *The House the Berrys Built* (Hodder & Stoughton, 1990)

Hobson, Harold, Knightley, Phillip and Russell, Leonard. *The Pearl of Days: An Intimate Memoir of the Sunday Times, 1822–1972* (Hamish Hamilton, 1972)

Holden, Anthony. *Charles, a Biography* (Weidenfeld and Nicolson, 1988)

Ingham, Bernard. *Kill the Messenger* (HarperCollins, 1991)

Jameson, Derek. *Last of the Hot Metal Men* (Ebury Press, 1990)

Jenkins, Simon. *The Market for Glory: Fleet Street Ownership in the 20th Century* (Faber and Faber, 1986)

Kemsley, Viscount. *The Kemsley Manual of Journalism.* (Cassell, 1950)

Kiernan, Thomas. *Citizen Murdoch* (Dodd, Mead, New York, 1986)

King, Cecil. *Strictly Personal* (Weidenfeld and Nicolson, 1969)

King, Cecil. *The Cecil King Diary, 1965–70* (Jonathan Cape, 1972)

King, Cecil. *The Future of the Press* (MacGibbon and Kee, 1967)

Kochan, Nick and Pym, Hugh. *The Guinness Affair* (Christopher Helm, 1987)

Koss, Stephen. *The Rise and Fall of the Political Press in Britain* (Hamish Hamilton, 1981 and 1984, and Fontana, 1990)

Lamb, Larry. *Sunrise* (Macmillan, 1989)

Leapman, Michael. *Barefaced Cheek: the Apotheosis of Rupert Murdoch* (Hodder & Stoughton, 1983)

Levin, Bernard. *The Pendulum Years: Britain and the Sixties* (Jonathan Cape, 1970)

MacArthur, Brian. *Eddy Shah, Today and the Newspaper Revolution* (David and Charles, 1988)

Margach, James. *The Abuse of Power* (W. H. Allen, 1978)

Margach, James. *The Anatomy of Power* (W. H. Allen, 1979)

Melvern, Linda. *The End of the Street* (Methuen, 1986)

Munster, George. *Rupert Murdoch, a Paper Prince* (Viking, 1985)

Negrine, Ralph. *Politics and the Mass Media in Britain* (Routledge, 1989)

Porter, Henry. *Lies, Damned Lies and Some Exclusives* (Chatto and Windus, 1984)

Private Eye. *Rock Bottom: The Gibraltar Killings – Government and Press Cover-up* (Pressdram Ltd, 1989)

Royal Commission on the Press, Report of the (HMSO, 1976)

Russell, Leonard (ed.). *Encore, Second Year: The Sunday Times Book* (Michael Joseph, 1963)

Sampson, Anthony. *The Changing Anatomy of Britain* (Hodder & Stoughton, 1982)

Seymour-Ure, Colin. *The Political Impact of the Mass Media* (Constable, 1974)

Seymour-Ure, Colin. *The Press, Politics and the Public* (Methuen, 1968)

Stoppard, Tom. *Night and Day* (Faber and Faber, 1978)

Taylor, S. J. *Shock! Horror! The Tabloids in Action* (Bantam, 1991)

Thomson, Roy (Lord Thomson of Fleet). *After I Was Sixty* (Hamish Hamilton, 1975)

Tomalin, Nicholas. *Nicholas Tomalin Reporting* (Deutsch, 1975)

Tunstall, Jeremy. *The Media in Britain* (Constable, 1983)

Wesker, Arnold. *The Journalists: A Triptych* (Jonathan Cape, 1979)

Wesker, Arnold. *Journey into Journalism* (Writers and Readers Co-operative, 1977)

Williams, Francis. *Dangerous Estate* (Longmans, 1957)

Wilson, Harold. *The Labour Government, 1964–70* (Weidenfeld and Nicolson and Michael Joseph, 1971)

Wintour, Charles. *Pressures on the Press* (Deutsch, 1972)

Wintour, Charles. *The Rise and Fall of Fleet Street* (Hutchinson, 1989)

Wright, Peter. *Spycatcher* (Viking, 1987)

Index